WIZARDS
A HISTORY

P.G. MAXWELL-STUART is Lecturer in History at the University of St Andrews and is an acknowledged expert on the occult. His other books include *Witchcraft: A History* (Tempus 2004), *Witch Hunters: Professional Prickers, Unwitchers & Witch-Finders of the Renaissance* (Tempus 2003), *The Occult in Early Modern Europe: A Documentary History*, and *Satan's Conspiracy: Magic & Witchcraft in Sixteenth-Century Scotland*. He is currently writing *An Abundance of Witches: The Great Scottish Witch-Hunt 1658-1662*, also for Tempus. He lives in St Andrews.

Praise for *Witchcraft: A History*

'Combines scholarly rigour with literary flair'
The Independent on Sunday

Praise for *Witch Hunters: Professional Prickers, Unwitchers & Witch-Finders of the Renaissance*

'The lurid tales of orgies and other debauchery told by these individuals still make for shocking reading today'
The Daily Mail

'A grim story of Renaissance witch-finders'
BBC History Magazine

'P. G. Maxwell-Stuart has firmly established himself among the new wave of British witchcraft historians through his mastery of demonological and related works, and through his ability to link 'witchcraft' with the much wider early modern belief in magic... A learned, informative, at times very subtle book, yet one which is eminently readable'
Professor James Sharpe, The Times Literary Supplement

WIZARDS
A HISTORY

P.G. MAXWELL-STUART

TEMPUS

First published 2004

Tempus Publishing Limited
The Mill, Brimscombe Port,
Stroud, Gloucestershire, GL5 2QG

British Library Cataloguing in Publication Data.
A catalogue record for this book is available from the British Library.

ISBN 0 7524 2840 3

Typesetting and origination by Tempus Publishing Limited
Printed in Great Britain

Contents

A Note on Translation

All translations are my own with the exception of Llorente's *History of the Spanish Inquisition* where I have used a nineteenth-century version, and the *Comte de Gabalis* for which I have used the published translation of 1913.

Introduction

The ritual magician is not a person to be treated lightly. What he or she does is often fraught with danger, and far from being an attractive, rather amusing cartoon figure who waves a wand and causes immediate suspension of the laws of nature, the real magician runs risks every time he works his craft. Frederick Hockley (1808-85) recorded an unnerving experience he had as a result of trying to comply with instructions given to him by a spirit.

> I had been looking in the crystal one evening for a long time without having a vision. Before I left off, I asked the spirit of the crystal, very earnestly, when I could have a vision, for it was so very wearisome to look and to anticipate, and then be disappointed. This message immediately came.

> 'Procure a glass vessel a foot deep, flat inside, and six inches square; fill it with water from a fish-pond; let the neck of the vessel be sufficiently large to admit your three fingers. Cut the middle finger of your left hand, and having put a strip of paper round the outside of the middle of the bottle, write with the blood of the finger you have cut, this one name... Paste this strip of paper round the bottle, and then insert the

finger you have cut and two other fingers into the neck, and from it into the water let a drop of blood flow. If you do this, you will see and hear of that which will instruct you in spiritual knowledge, and aid you in all that you desire appertaining to the world.'

Although I thought it could not be good, I did not desire anything evil, and I thought, foolishly, that I could hear, and see, and know what they said, without allowing them to influence me, or without for one moment surrendering myself to their possession. I would not do it again. It was not the power, but the knowledge that I sought. I was at the time in a house with a good many people in it, and, fearing that someone might interrupt me, I locked the door. Before I began I had been obliged to have the glass bottle made to the exact size, and I wrote the name on a vellum band and sealed it on. This I placed on the table, and very soon without any call – I used nothing more than the name on the bottle – the water began to change to a thick, dirty-red liquid, and from this there formed, as the water again became clearer, a spirit more like an animal than even a distorted human figure; it had a tail as long in proportion to its size as is the tail of a mouse to the rest of the animal, and it had peculiarly shaped horns. It increased in size so as to fill the entire bottle, the tips of the horns rising above the water in the neck of the bottle. When I saw its head coming above the water, I thought I should be able to prevent its getting larger by putting a stopper on the top. I could not find anything to place over it at the moment but a book from the mantelpiece. The instance that I had stepped across for the book, the horns of the spirit were visible to me above the bottle. Very quickly you may imagine I was back with the book. I am very strong – as strong, I believe, as most men – I can lift a couple of hundredweight, and now I had occasion to put my strength forth. I tried to press the book on the neck of the bottle with all my might, but I could not move it one inch. My hands and the book in them went up as easily as I could have lifted a baby's hands. I grew desperate. I tore the band off the bottle; I used exorcism. There was no fire in the room, and no light, or I would have immediately burned the band. I could not tear it, and I had no means of destroying it. The spirit all this time was gradually getting out of the bottle.

I could not think what to do. I took the bottle up, threw it down and broke it; the water of course ran all over the carpet, and I thought for a moment that I had got rid of the spirit, but I was mistaken, for from the water, as it lay on the floor, it rose again much larger than before.

I went to the door, but I was afraid to open it; then in an instant I thought he might be only visible to me and not to others, and that if I were with other people he would disappear from me, and I tried the door, but could not open it. I forgot that I had locked it. Again I used the form of dismissal and exorcism, but it was of no use. Having done this, I asked him what he wanted. He asked me to test his power by naming anything I desired, and said that if I found that he gave it me and if I would promise him obedience, he would do the same in all other things.

I resolutely told him that I would not – that had I known he was evil and could escape from the bottle I would not have called him; still he did not leave, and I then felt the place to be insufferable, so oppressive as to be almost suffocating. My eyes seemed to burn, I was getting giddy, and appeared to see instead of the one figure a thousand of all shapes and sizes. I still remained with my hand on the lock; the room became confused and dark for one instant only, then all was light. The evil spirit was gone, and I noticed that every drop of water was gone from the surface of the carpet, and that on the white ground which surrounded the pattern was a single red spot. Although unnerved whilst the spirit was present, I was not the least so the moment it was gone, and, on stooping to pick up the small pieces of bottle, I observed round the red spot a circle containing words. Even then, by an impulse I could not control, I was all on fire to know what those words were, down on my knees I deciphered with much difficulty, '….Returns blood which is too white for sacrifice'. The red spot rose above the carpet, the words disappeared, and there only remained a little piece of cold congealed blood: this I removed. In an adjoining room I burnt the band which had been round the bottle, threw away the pieces of bottle, and determined to be more cautious in future.

(*The Spiritualist*, 2 July, 1880)

In an age which takes for granted the certainties of science, the notion that these can be breached at will by individuals asserting themselves against both the personal imprisonment and the deadness of the cosmos which these 'certainties' imply is very attractive. There is, moreover, a child-like desire for wonders and instant gratification which magic may be called on to satisfy and which therefore suits the strain of infantilism observable in modern western society. 'Magic', however, is actually not an easy word to define, and neither is its spelling consistent. Aleister Crowley preferred 'magick', (as, indeed, did Daniel Defoe, though for somewhat different reasons), in order to distance his lofty conception of it from the popular association with conjuring-tricks and illusions; and at various times and in various places, people have offered views or interpretations of the subject – does one call it an art or a science? – according to their personal predilections and the prevailing intellectual, social, and religious climate of their own community.

Thus, the fourteenth-century Arab sceptic Ibn Khaldun maintained that magicians have a natural ability to affect people through exercise of their mental powers, with the aid of astrological and mathematical influences, and by the creation of images and illusions in the minds of their clients or audience, (*Muqaddimah*, chapter 6, section 27). Christianity, however, tended to introduce sinister, non-human entities into the process. Adso, a monk of the tenth century, for example, wrote,

> Antichrist will have magicians (*magi*), workers of harmful magic (*mal-efici*), diviners (*divini*), and enchanters (*incantatores*) who, under inspira-tion from the Devil, will nourish him and instruct him in every iniquity, deceit, and forbidden art. Evil spirits will be his guides, his constant companions, and friends who never leave his side. (*De Antichristo*)

But it took several centuries before the character of the magician and his powers was set out in detail which covers every eventuality except one, the missing aspect being perhaps the most important and most noble. In a short treatise on magic, Giordano Bruno makes ten points. People turn to a magician for his wisdom. (This is the *magus* as 'wizard', a word formed from the Middle English *wys* – wise – and the suffix *ard* which, again in Middle English, has the sense 'someone who does something to excess, or who does what is discreditable'. In its earliest usage, therefore, 'wizard' sounds a negative, critical note.) Magic itself, continues Bruno, involves working wonders and producing illusions. It uses the natural sympathy and antipathy which exist between every created thing to achieve its ends, and these are assisted by words, incantations, numbers, images, sigils, characters, and so forth. Magic invokes spirit-beings and ghosts by means of ceremonies strongly religious in tone and content. It employs objects taken from or associated with individuals to loose and bind and weaken; and it foretells the future in many different ways. But finally, and most significantly, magic depends on a pact between the magician and an evil spirit, made with a view either to causing harm or rendering assistance. (This is the magician as witch as well as sage, and we shall find that he – in later centuries he and she – slips in and out of various categories in disconcerting fashion, making it difficult to pin down exactly what makes him different from any other kind of magical practitioner.)

What is missing from Bruno's list is the magician as ritualist, a priest-like figure making use of elaborate ceremony to contact God or angels in their own, non-material territories, more closely allied to the mystic than to the witch or fairground huckster. It is hardly surprising that Bruno made no mention of this aspect of magic. He himself was burned for heresy in 1600, and there were many others whose activities were regarded askance by both Church and State, since they seemed to ape the behaviour of the former, while exhibiting eccentricities of thought and conduct which could be considered inimical to the latter. The twentieth century, of course, saw things in its own, distinctive way. 'Magic', wrote one of its most important magicians,

> is a scientific method. It is a valid technique. Its approach to the universe and the secret of life's meaning is a legitimate one. If it assists us to become more familiar with what we really are, it is a Science – and a most important one'.
>
> (Israel Regardie: *The Art and Meaning of Magic,* 26)

From servant of Antichrist to co-worker with demons to self-psychoanalyst, the magician has travelled a long way over the last two millennia. But just in case the West should imagine that magic has now transformed itself entirely into the subject-matter of films or children's novels, or become an excuse for middle-class eccentrics to indulge themselves in a relatively harmless way, let us remind ourselves that much of the rest of the world takes magic as seriously as Europe once did, and that in cyberspace the Harry Potter novels have evoked as much condemnation as praise, on the grounds that magic is much too momentous a subject for trifling. What follows is a brief account of the wizard as ritual magician, and the difficulties people have always had in properly understanding his aims and intentions.

I

The Ritual Magician
and his Work

One day in 1530, Benvenuto Cellini fell into conversation with a
Sicilian priest and discovered that the man was a practitioner of magic
– a 'necromancer', as he calls him in his autobiography. Together they
decided to carry out a magical operation and, not long after, Cellini,
the priest, and two others, (a friend of Cellini's and one of *his* friends,
also, as it happened, a magician), entered the Colosseum in Rome at
night and there began a ritual of conjuration.

> The priest, in accordance with the practice of necromancers, started to
> trace circles on the ground with the finest ceremonies you can possi-
> bly imagine. He also brought along expensive ingredients which would
> give off sweet-smelling smoke, and fire, and also stuff which would
> make an unpleasant smell. As soon as he was ready, he made an open-
> ing in the circle, took us by the hand, and placed us one by one within
> the circle. Next, he gave each person something to do. He told the
> other necromancer, who was acting as his assistant, to hold the penta-
> cle; the others he instructed to make sure the fire was ready for the
> fumigants. Then he began his conjurations.
>
> (*Vita* 1.64)

These preliminaries and invocations lasted for more than an hour and a half, but then suddenly the Colosseum was filled with a great number of demons. Cellini was preoccupied with casting sweet substances on the coals and did not notice, but when the priest urged him to ask the demons to grant a request, he said they should enable him to be with his Sicilian lover, Angelica, a girl who had been prevented by her suspicious mother from joining him in Rome. The demons, however, gave no reply; so the priest urged Cellini to repeat the ritual on another occasion, this time in company with a pre-pubertal boy. To this Cellini agreed, and when they all re-assembled, he brought with him a twelve-year-old lad whom he employed to run errands for him. The ceremonies were repeated as before, with perhaps even greater elaboration, and the magician started his invocations, calling upon the demons by name, 'commanding them by the goodness and power of God Uncreated, Living, and Eternal, using Hebrew, Greek, and Latin'. At once the Colosseum was filled with a huge number of spirits, and this time Cellini received an answer to his request, the answer being relayed to him by the presiding magician: 'Within one month you will be with her'.

The number of demons, however, continued to multiply and the magician started to become very nervous. His evident fright began to infect everyone, especially the boy, who was sheltering beneath the protection of the pentacle. Cellini says he tried to conceal his own fear for the boy's sake and whispered what he hoped would be soothing words. But the lad was terrified and said he could see an enormous number of men threatening to destroy them: that four armed giants were trying to break into the circle: and that the whole amphitheatre was burning, with fire about to fall on top of them. In an effort to drive the spirits away, the magicians then burned foul-smelling asafoetida. One man, Agnolino Gaddi, had to be roused from a stupor of fear and so frightened was he that the moment he moved he farted, which made Cellini laugh. His laugh roused the boy, who had covered his eyes so as to see no more, and thereupon began to take courage because the demons 'were beginning to go away in a great frenzy'. Exhausted by their ordeal, the magicians remained where they were, within the circle, until the time of morning prayer and then gingerly made their way out of the Colosseum and so homewards, preceded, the boy said, by two of the night's demons leaping about or running over the rooftops or on the ground.

Modern readers may be tempted to treat these episodes as moments of Gothic diversion in the otherwise sober, if braggadocio, account of an artistic life full of incident. To do so, however, would misunderstand them entirely and therefore miss the point, for the episodes, (which I have curtailed and reduced to their principal elements), illustrate many of the characteristics which are to be found in a complex rite of magic.

The circle, for example, is a notable feature of this kind of performance. Such circles may be concentrative or protective or, of course, both at once. The concentrative circle acts as a focus for the power or entity being invoked or summoned. In simple form it may consist of a physical ring or a repeated circular movement. Thus, in Moray a common magical cure used to be effected by passing a wreath of woodbine three times up and down round the body of a sick child or consumptive adult, while in January 1662, three women from Penicuik were accused of being witches because they had been seen going round a fire in an open field at two o'clock in the morning, 'every one of them have a napkin [*handkerchief*] in her hand', (*CH2/297/1*), and the man who had seen them felt ill when he reached home, and the horse he rode on died. A more elaborate circle, however, seems to have been used in rites of evocation. Florimond de Rémond (*c*.1540-1602) tells us that a young girl, Jeanne Bosdeau, who was appealing against a capital sentence passed on her for being a witch, admitted 'without pain or torture... that when she was young, an Italian had debauched her and, on St John's Eve, had brought her at midnight into a field where, with a rod made from holly-wood, he made a large circle, murmuring certain words which he read from a black book. Thereupon there appeared a big horned goat, all black, accompanied by two women: and immediately after them, a man dressed as a priest', (*L'Antichrist*, 1597, chapter 7). Here the circle does not act as a protective device for the magician, since neither he nor the girl stays inside it. Similarly, in Marlowe's play, *Dr Faustus*, neither Faustus himself nor Mephistophilis whom he conjures is bound by the circle at all, and indeed Marlowe makes it clear what the circle is actually for.

> Within this circle is Jehovah's name,
> Forward and backward anagrammatiz'd,
> The breviated names of holy saints,
> Figures of every adjunct to the heavens,
> And characters of signs and erring [*wandering*] stars
> By which the spirits are enforc'd to rise.
>
> (Act 1, scene 3)

The general, (though not undisputed) view of creation in earlier times was that it consisted of perfect circles. Each of the seven planets described a circular orbit and commanded its own sphere; beyond and above them were further 'heavens' whose exact nature and number was a constant topic of speculation, but which were envisioned as perfect spheres enclosing those of the planets; and below all these came the four elementary spheres of fire, air, water, and the earth, the last of which was the dwelling-place of humanity.[1] All these spheres fitted neatly inside one another, like onion-layers, to form the globe of creation. The magician's circle, or circles, thus mirrored the upper heavens, regions wherein incorporeal beings were naturally to be found; and by placing names of power within his magical construct, the magician therefore sought to persuade those non-human entities he wished to evoke that he had created for them in miniature a universe similar to that they already knew and already inhabited, and one into which they would feel compelled to move by the superior potency inherent in those names. This can be seen clearly in detailed instructions contained in the *Heptameron*, a manual for magicians attributed to Pietro d'Abano (1230-*c*.1315):

> The manner of constructing circles is not always one and the same. It
> is customary to change it according to the kind of spirits which are to

be evoked, and the places, seasons, days, and hours; because in setting up a circle it is necessary to take into consideration at what time of year, on which day, and in which hour you are making it: which spirits you want to summon, the star and region over which they preside: and which particular tasks they carry out. So you should make three circles nine feet wide and a hand's breadth apart from each other. In the middle circle, first wrote the name of the hour in which you are doing the work; secondly, the name of the angel of the hour; thirdly, draw the sigil [*seal or signature*] of the angel of the hour; fourthly, the name of the angel who presides over the day on which you are doing the work, along with the names of his subordinates; fifthly, the name of the current season; sixthly, the name of the spirits ruling in that period of the season, and the name of their governors; seventhly, the name of the head of the ruling sign of that period of the season in which you are doing the work; eighthly, the name of the land according to that period of the season in which you are doing the work; and ninthly, to complete the middle circle, write the names of the sun and moon according to the foresaid scheme of the season, because when the season changes, so do the names. In the outer circle, in four angles, you should draw the names of the presiding angels of air for the day on which you are doing the work – namely, the King and his three subordinates. Outwith the circle, in four angles, draw pentagrams. In the outermost circle, you should write four divine names with crosses between each. In the middle circle, write Alpha towards the east and Omega to the west, and divide the centre of the circle with a cross.

This multiplicity of circles, however, not only has the power to focus the attention of non-human entities and provide a sacred space within which they can manifest themselves; it also erects a protective barrier which, should the magician confine himself inside it, will defend him from possible assault by the spirits he has summoned, spirits which, by their nature, are more powerful and more knowledgeable than he, and thus potentially very dangerous. The fragility of this bastion, and the real danger awaiting anyone inside the circle, can be illustrated by an example from modern times. In early December 1909, Aleister

Crowley and Victor Neuberg went into the Algerian desert beyond the small town of Bou Saada and then, in the fine sand, traced a circle within which Neuberg was to sit for protection and note whatever Crowley did and anything resulting therefrom. Outwith this circle, they drew a triangle and it was herein that Crowley performed a magical ceremony intended to invoke Choronzon, an especially potent and malign spirit. Crowley was successful. The demon appeared and kept trying to break into the circle, and did so after obliterating part of the circle with sand. Taking the form of a naked man, it leaped upon Neuberg, trying to tear out his throat with its teeth. Neuberg repeatedly stabbed it with a magical dagger he had with him as part of his own magical apparatus, and finally managed to drive the demon out of the circle, which he then quickly reconstituted. Back within the triangle, it continued to menace Neuberg and threaten him, but at last it disappeared and Crowley and Neuberg, exhausted from their ordeal, were able to purify the area with fire and then destroy both triangle and circle.

The sweet and foul-smelling fumigations used by Cellini and the others were also standard practice. Cornelius Agrippa explained why and gave detailed recipes in his *De Occulta Philosophia*, (written 1509-10). Certain suffumigations peculiar to the planets, he said, have the effect of allowing human beings to receive celestial gifts via the air they breathe, since the air, which is tinged with the special qualities of those planets, enters our inward parts and thus opens us up to those same qualities. Suffumigations may also cause wonderful effects such as thunderstorms and lightnings, and produce or dismiss the likenesses of demons (*daemonum idola*) – an interesting phrase, since it implies that the demons themselves do not actually appear, but only images of them, like holograms. Agrippa, however, seems to modify this almost at once by saying that burning certain herbs 'makes demons *and* shapes outwith the human mind (*figurae extraneae*) appear: whereas if small-age is added to them, [the resulting smoke] puts to flight the demons and their likenesses', (Book 1, chapter 43, my italics).

The careful distinction between apparition and hallucination was caused by earlier periods' acute awareness that the eyes and brain can easily be deceived. 'It is a simple fact', said the Portuguese inquisitor Manuel do Valle de Moura, 'that inward manifestations and revelations are sometimes granted by God or by a good angel... But it is also a simple fact that inward visions and external apparitions may have their origin in a demon', (*De incantationibus*, 1620, pp. 142-3). Visions of any kind might be corporeal, which meant that they were seen by the eyes, or spiritual, which meant that they presented themselves to the intellect alone. *Discretio spirituum*, 'discernment of spirits', was a constant theological and intellectual preoccupation, for the Devil was immensely ingenious in his cunning, and found it easy to deceive people into taking illusion for reality. Devout individuals who saw the Blessed Virgin, witches who averred they flew to a Sabbat and took part in its rituals, people who received visitations from the dead – all such reports needed the most rigorous investigation to find out whether the experiences they claimed were genuine or delusory.

This uncertainty accounts for the use of the boy during the second ceremony. He was there to see what the others either did not, or might not be able to see. Indeed, it is quite clear that Cellini himself was unable to see the hordes of demons conjured by the priest, and although modern cynicism is likely to reach for a child's vivid imagination as the explanation most acceptable to its rationalist bent, this fails to take into account the possibility that the boy could have been telling the truth, or that he was truthfully reporting sights which he genuinely believed he was witnessing. Certainly contemporary readers of Cellini's *Vita* would have had little difficulty in accepting these latter versions. Using a boy as a seer had been common magical practice since ancient times,[2] and Cellini's inability to see the spirits reminds one of the sixteenth-century English mage, John Dee, who was obliged to employ a series of scryers to look into his crystal ball or disk of polished obsidian and recount to him details of the multitude of spirits they saw therein, because he himself did not possess the gift.

Hebrew, Greek and Latin were the languages used by Western practitioners of magic because they represented the instruments of three components which went to make up Western ritual practice – power, learning, and liturgical apostrophe. Hebrew was both the original language of the earth before the confusion of tongues introduced by Babel, the language understood by angels, and also the medium in which God had chosen to lock up certain secrets of His creation. It contained the Tetragrammaton, the ineffable name of God which must not be pronounced, and the letters of its alphabet could be combined and re-combined to produce other names of God and names of both angels and demons, as described in the twelfth-century Kabbalistic text, the *Bahir* (107). This pointed out that the Tetragrammaton alone could go through twenty-four permutations three times over, thereby producing seventy-two names of God, while Johannes Reuchlin explained, 'When Kabbalists could not pronounce in a meaningful way the name of any angel, they were accustomed to seek aid in one of the names of God which they added to it and so produced a name which was complete', an example being the addition of the divine name *El* to the roots Mich-, Gabr-, and Raph-, to form the names of three of the principal archangels, (*De arte cabalistica*, 1517, Book 3, page 58);[3] while Giovanni Pico della Mirandola made the famous observation that the addition of the letter *Shin* to the Tetragrammaton provided proof of the divinity of Jesus, (*LXXI Conclusiones*, 1486, nos. 14 and 15). Moreover, because individual Hebrew letters expressed numbers as well as sounds, one meaningful word whose letters added up to the same numerical value as those of another meaningful word could thereby reveal the occult (i.e. hidden) sympathy which existed between them – a technique of literal manipulation known as *gematria*. Other techniques, such as *notarikon, temurah*, and *ziruf* treated individual letters in various ways so as to produce new words which were regarded as having a similar sympathetic significance. Hence it is not surprising that there developed a strong tradition, beginning in the Hellenistic period and thence transmitted to later times, that because Hebrew was a most powerful language of magic, Jews were likely to be magicians.

Greek, by contrast, was the language of learned mysticism. Pythagoras, Plato, Porphyry, Plotinus, Iamblichus, Proclus and Psellus were constantly quoted as authorities when scholarly discussion turned to the relationship between the physical, preternatural, and supernatural worlds and their respective inhabitants, and it was through such works that magical practitioners became acquainted with the Greek names of *daimones*, (spirit-intermediaries between divinities and human beings), and thus were enabled to give evidence in their incantations of extensive and detailed learning. This was important because the goal of their magical work was to enter into conversation with the spirits they evoked, and they needed to demonstrate to those spirits not only a mastery of every technique whereby the spirits could be held in check and, for a while at least, dominated by the much weaker and less knowledgeable humans, but also the fact that the humans could name the individual spirits and so enhance their temporary power over them. Names in Jewish and thence in later Christian tradition were believed to contain or express an individual's essence. To know someone's name was to know him or her, and this was true even in respect of God. A ninth-century Jewish account of Jesus, the *Toledoth Yeshu*, hostile to Christian tradition, for example, tells us that Jesus sneaked into the Temple in Jerusalem where he learned the name of God, and it was this knowledge which enabled him to perform his various miracles. Then Judas Iscariot learned the divine name and entered into a kind of magical rivalry with Jesus, the two of them flying through the air engaged in combat. Thus, naming was one of the most important components in both ritual magic and licit exorcism – naming God by his various, almost infinite names, opened paths to the source of ultimate, irresistible power; and naming the spirits by theirs exposed them to the fact that they were unable to deceive the operator and so were vulnerable to his commands which were issued on the authority of God. 'I adjure you', says one exorcism recorded by Girolamo Menghi,

> by Him who discharged the four principal rivers of Paradise – Gehon, Phison, Tigris and Euphrates – that you may have no authority or power of keeping your name silent, but that you tell me at once who you are, or who is your master: for I am the servant and minister of Christ.
>
> (*Flagellum daemonum,* 1586)

Latin, on the other hand, in spite of its being the lingua franca of intellectual discourse in the West, was here used principally because it was the language of Church ritual. One may note that Cellini's Sicilian magician was a priest, and that one of Satan's attendants in Florimond de Rémond's anecdote was 'dressed as a priest'. Indeed, the involvement of priests in magic – particularly that type of magic we are discussing here – during the Middle Ages especially was so widespread that it formed a kind of clerical sub-culture, and grimoires frequently contain instructions that Mass be said as part of a consecrating rite. A fifteenth-century manuscript says:

> Thy syrcle muste be made on suche howers & dayes as be connevoyent
> for the sprytes of the earthe... & 3 dayes before that consecrate 3 Masses,
> 1° of Saynt Sypriane, 2° De Trinitate, 3° De Assumptione Beate Marie.
> (*Cambridge University,* Add. 3544)

This does not mean, of course, that ritual magicians were always priests or even clerics. Some kind of familiarity with Latin and ritual behaviour was undoubtedly more widely spread among the laity than is sometimes supposed or acknowledged. But priests were peculiarly endowed at their ordination with extraordinary powers, and if a layman could not work the miracle of transubstantiation, he could certainly assume the guise, the language, and the behaviour of a priest for lesser, but still more-than-human ends.

In consequence, he tended to follow a long-standing tradition which almost required the practitioner of ritual magic either to wear priest-like garments while performing the rites, or to use Latin if not for the whole then at least for key moments of the proceedings, or to do both. A late-Byzantine magical treatise, *Apotelesmatike Pragmateia*, for example, specifies that the magician shall wear garments of clean, white linen, which have not been worn before, with divine names and signs embroidered on the neck of the tunic, the stockings and undergarments, a parchment headband, and thin, white, leather gloves, (412-13, 416, 425). The gloves are unusual, but were probably meant to be symbols of superior rank, since gloves formed part of the formal clothing worn by bishops and those of higher ecclesiastical status, or perhaps they were associated with sacerdotal power. Samuel Harsnett, a seventeenth-century clergyman eager to show that Catholic exorcisms were little better than juggling tricks, commented sarcastically on the use of a priest's glove in one of these.

> Maho, Sarah's chief devil, with much ado was compelled to tell his name, and the first word he spake was out of Sarah's hand. Then was one of the priest's gloves taken and put upon her hand. Maho durst not abide it, but went his way straight, and he was so scared as we do not find that ever he came there after. It seems he had stepped thither only to grace the priest's gloves; for you have observed that her hand was none of his ordinary haunt, or else, if he could not endure the glove by reason of some scenting quality the priest's hand had left behind him, we may imagine the priest had been using his hand holily and well when it savoured so strongly that the Devil could not abide it.
>
> (*A Declaration of Egregious Popish Impostures*, 1603, chapter 15)

Clothing which comes even nearer the long, spangled robe worn by many modern film or cartoon magicians than that described in the Byzantine treatise appears in the *Songe du Vieil Pelerin* by Philippe de Mézières (1327-1405), who describes superstition as follows:

> This old woman[4] was dressed in a garment quite unlike any other, for it was covered in figures, triangles, and squares which are not easy to describe. It was tailored and embroidered at a time chosen astrologically. The garment was white and scattered all over with black figures known as 'darts' (*guivres*), a word which refers to the cunning tricks of birds, wild animals, lines, rules, squares, and Greek, Hebrew, and Chaldaean letters.
>
> (2.141)

One is therefore not surprised to find the figure of the sacerdotal magician firmly embedded in modern occult fiction, as in Dion Fortune's Dr Taverner who, in preparation for a ceremony, opened his suitcase and took out the most wonderful robes I have ever seen in my life. Stiff with embroidery and heavy with bullion, the great cope looked like the mines of Ophir in the shaded light of that sombre room. Taverner put it on over an emerald soutane, and I fastened the jewelled clasp upon his breast... It seemed as if a priest-king of lost Atlantis had come, in response to an invocation.

(*The Secrets of Dr Taverner*, 1926, 226)

As for the use of Latin, even after the Protestant reformation, which encouraged the use of the vernacular in church, Latin retained a role in magical practices, especially perhaps those intended to cure illness or disability, even if it were only *in nomine Patris et Filii et Spiritus Sancti*, as in the otherwise Gaelic-language charm of Sandy Skipper's wife in nineteenth-century Caithness, an area of Scotland long Calvinised, which did not prevent the cure-wife from calling upon the Virgin Mary and St Brigid, too, for assistance. In Shakespeare's *Second Part of Henry VI*, the 'conjuror' Richard Bolingbroke performs the necessary ceremonies for raising a spirit, makes his magic circle, and summons the demon Asmath with a long Latin invocation, (Act 1, scene 4); while in Robert Greene's *Friar Bacon and Friar Bungay*, the German magician Johann Vandermast evokes Hercules with the much simpler command *Prodi, prodi*, ('Show yourself, show yourself') which could have been delivered in English, except that Latin is the lingua franca of humans and spirits, as is shown by Hercules' first words, *Quis me vult*? ('Who wants me?'). In his treatise on witchcraft, *A Candle in the Dark* (1656), Thomas Ady records that during the reign of James VI and I there was an itinerant 'conjuror' (in the modern sense of the word) who used to perform pseudo-magical tricks for people and

at the playing of every Trick, he used to say, *Hocus pocus, tontus talontus, vade celeriter, iubeo,* a dark composure of words, to bind the eyes of the beholders, to make his Trick pass the more currantly without discovery.

(p.29)

24

The last three words mean 'Come quickly, I order [you]'; the first four mean nothing. They are bogusly Latinate, intended to sound grand and portentous, and are thus forerunners of the cod-Latin exclamations – 'petrificus totalus!' – of J.K. Rowling's Hermione in the *Harry Potter* series, which represent a final remnant of this liturgically inspired system of ritual magic.

Now, if we consider the closing stages of the two rituals in which Cellini played a part, we may be struck by two things, for Cellini's responses to the two rituals are very different. In the first, he is more preoccupied than nervous and when the demons appear, he is almost taken by surprise when the priest-magician invites him to ask them for a favour and can think only of the relatively trivial one of being reunited with his Sicilian lover, Angelica. Now, there is a superficial reminiscence here of Marlowe's Dr Faustus who, placed in a similar situation, with an immensely powerful demon apparently at his call, asks for a vision of Helen of Troy. But Marlowe was writing a play and, regardless of whatever subtleties of character he might incorporate in his portrait of Faustus, was also obliged to provide theatricalities for his audience. Hence the other trivial exhibitions of Faustus' newly-acquired power, such as the knockabout farce in the Papal Court. The context of Cellini's request, however, is entirely different. The man is purporting to record two genuine experiences of his participation in ritual magic, and there is no reason to disbelieve the sincerity of is account, since we know perfectly well that magicians of every type and kind abounded in European society at the time. So Cellini's triviality is of a different kind from that of Faustus. Faustus' wish to see Helen springs from intellectual curiosity; Cellini's desire to be reunited with Angelica comes from being taken off guard. Surrounded by demon forces he himself cannot see, his mind seizes up and is unable to consider or weigh rationally the awesome possibilities now open to him; so he produces, as his request, the subject which has been occupying him emotionally for some time past. It is just the reaction one might expect under these circumstances.

The second ceremony, however, is not at all the same. Cellini's experience is altogether different. At first all seems to be going well and, having once asked to see Angelica again, Cellini naturally repeats his request. But at this point the presiding magician appears to lose control of the situation, and his growing fear infects the rest of the company, especially the boy who can see the demonic entities. In the midst of this common terror, Agnolino Gaddi farts and Cellini laughs. How are we to interpret this fart and laughter? Again, an apparent literary parallel will prove to be misleading. The first-century BC poet Horace, who is regularly quoted by early modern demonologists as a source for Roman 'witches', wrote a poem about two female necromancers, Canidia and Sagana, who sacrifice a black lamb in a graveyard in order to summon up the dead so that they can be questioned anent the future. Put into the mouth of a wooden statue of the god Priapus, the poem describes both the women and their activities, and then says that as their ritual was coming to an end, Priapus farted and the women ran away 'to the sound of loud laughter and derision', (*Satires* 1.8). Horace's purpose here is to mock. Cellini, on the other hand, is clearly not intending to be funny. Indeed, the context is one of extreme terror. Everyone has been overtaken by it, even though Cellini presents himself as trying to put on a brave face for the boy's sake. Gaddi's fart is thus the same kind of physiological reaction to fear as the involuntary evacuation of a hanged person – as Maria Sidoli has said anent a severely traumatised child: 'like a skunk, he both protected himself and attacked his enemies with a barrier of poisonous smell'[5] – and Cellini's laugh is not produced by humour but by that same crisis of nerves which causes someone to laugh during a funeral service.

Cellini's account of both episodes, then, is true to life in detail and also rings true psychologically. We should therefore take his anecdote seriously and learn from it not only that well-educated men were ready to undertake or participate in the performance of ritual magic, but also how deeply such performances informed their distinctive relationship with the incorporeal worlds which bordered upon their own and could be caused to invade or be invited to enter it.

The term 'ritual magic' needs definition, of course. The jurist Johann von Fröcke said that:

magic is called 'ritual' because it is produced and achieves its ends by means of certain ceremonies… Consequently, it can be defined either as the art of rendering one's acts propitious by the use of certain ceremonies, or of evoking good or evil spirits.

(*De crimine coniurationis spirituum*, 1721, chapter 6, section 1)

This is the kind of operation described in modern times by Stanley Tambiah as a performative act, or a series of performative acts, which is intended to effect the transference of a desideratum from one party (let us say a divine or demonic being or some source of power superior to human) to another (let us say a human, or a material object such as an amulet or a herbal concoction), with 'ritual' here referring to a combination of words, spoken silently or aloud, and stylised behaviour which is inherently different from that of everyday life and akin, in some fashion, to the words and behaviour commonly associated with religious activity.[6] (Hence the frequent requirement of the magician that he fast and abstain from sexual activity for a certain time before the performance, and wear garments reminiscent of those belonging to priests.)

Now, all magic involves ritual of some kind, it is true, but my intention hereafter is to survey those forms of magical operation which (a) are very elaborate in themselves and so require a notable degree of learning and persistence of will on the part of the magician ('the person who undertakes this kind of thing must be of a resolute and steady disposition', says the priest to Cellini); (b) have a goal which transcends the immediate practical aims of curers, cursers and manipulators of human emotion – such as seeking to penetrate the mind of God by divining His future intentions through direct interrogation of those angels or demons better placed to know what the future is meant to be; and (c) demonstrate the magician's mastery of preternatural power by producing some marvel well beyond the known and usual abilities of ordinary human beings. In other words, ritual magicians set out to discover how to suspend or manipulate the laws of nature, and they do so most frequently by trying to create the necessary conditions which will allow different modes of existence to overlap, thereby providing a space and opportunity for non-human entities to manifest themselves and either furnish the human operator with the required information, or temporarily alter natural law on his behalf.

Why did people think this was possible? Theology told them of the existence of such beings, of course, and visitations of angels, demons, ghosts, fairies, trolls and so forth in visible and often audible form confirmed the truth of the theory. But science, or 'natural philosophy' as it was called, also encouraged belief in multiple worlds unseen by the majority, but glimpsed by a privileged few. Not only had Earth itself revealed a continent and peoples unknown to the West before the fifteenth century, but in 1655 Pierre Borel's *Centuria observationum microscopicarum* and Robert Hooke's *Microscopia* both told their readers (and illustrated for them) details about the minutiae of creation quite unknown to the doyen of natural philosophers, Aristotle. Also, Giordano Bruno's theory, which proclaimed the possibility of countless suns and an infinity of worlds, (*De l'infinito universo e mondi* 1584, dialogue 5) seemed to be supported in 1609 by Galileo's telescope, which provided views of heavenly bodies unaccounted for in the Ptolemaic system of astronomy. Everything, it seemed, concurred with the proposition that the created universe is infinitely various, and that it contains secrets (*occulta*) which, by God's permission, humankind is gradually able to uncover and understand. The twin characteristics of Mediaeval and early modern times, *admiratio* and *curiositas* ('astonishment' and 'inquisitiveness') thus seem to receive divine blessing and endorsement.

There was, however, a negative aspect to this. 'So far and no further' was the general rule. The sixteenth-century Jesuit, Martín del Rio, summed it up in a caveat:

> The desire to know is natural to everyone, but this should be restrained by the reins of God's law and of morally proper reasoning. Unless it is held in check, our desire, like a horse without reins, sweeps divine law and proper reasoning away, pell mell. This is a rule which is consonant with both – that we should not wish or try to know those things we

cannot know by the light of nature and which can be known only because God has revealed them to us.

(*Disquisitiones Magicae* Book 6, monition 7)

Earlier in this work, he had told an anecdote which illustrates the point and issues a warning:

> There was someone who used to dine at the same table as [the magician] Cornelius Agrippa, a very inquisitive young man. On one occasion, when he was going out somewhere, Agrippa handed his wife (whom he later divorced) the keys of his study and gave strict instructions that no one was to enter. When a favourable moment presented itself, the rash youth started to beg the silly woman to let him go in, and he would not leave off asking until he got his way. He went into the study, stumbled across *A Little Book of Invocations*, and read it [aloud]. Well now, he was disturbed by a knocking at the door but continued to read. The unknown person knocked again and, as the young man, (who had no experience in these matters), made no reply, a demon entered. 'Why have I been summoned?' he asked. 'What am I being told to do?' Fear blocked the young man's voice, and the demon blocked his throat. Thus the wretched man paid the price for his wicked inquisitiveness.

(Book 2, question 29)

Ritual magic, then, supposes there will be great dangers for those who participate in it. These dangers are moral, spiritual and physical. The moral danger springs from the rewards such magic appears to offer; for penetrating the mind of God in search of knowledge not readily obtainable by other means is likely to breed arrogance and a delusive self-confidence, which may lead the magician to think that because he has survived his contact with superior and inherently unstable forms or entities, he can do so again and again. Cellini's priest experienced no trouble on the first occasion, and indeed told Cellini he had entered magic circles many times, and yet, in spite of the fact that his second attempt with Cellini had nearly ended in disaster, he busily tried to persuade him to help him consecrate a book of magic and ask the demons conjured therewith to reveal to them the whereabouts of great riches buried in the earth. What is more, Cellini agreed to this proposal and was diverted from joining him only by the pressing necessity to finish a complex medal he was engraving for the Pope. Cellini, then, illustrates the other grave moral danger inherent in meddling with ritual magic – that the enterprise is potentially corrupting not only to the morals of him who acts as principal, but also to those of any who assist him.

The potential physical danger attendant upon these rites we have already seen in the case of Neuberg and Crowley; for the threshold between planes of existence, which the magician creates by means of and during his magic rite, is by nature unstable and in consequence presents dangers to both sides of the process – the non-human entities who may become trapped in an alien form of existence and do much damage in their fear and efforts to escape, and the humans who can be attacked or possessed and so rendered ill or mad or dead by prolonged contact with an entity with which they have little in common save the fact that both of them were created by God. Demons, as Paolo Grillando reminds us, may appear to be able to take on human form, but do not do so in reality. Their 'bodies' are mere fantasies, apparent not genuine, and while they can perform certain natural functions, such as moving about, speaking, carrying things and eating and drinking, they are unable to do others, such as growing taller, putting on body weight, suckling a child, producing breast-milk, sleeping, hearing or fathering children (*De sortilegiis*, 1592, question 7). Essentially, therefore, the two species are quite alien to each other, and the demons' ability to assume a human appearance is perilously misleading, since it may trap the real human into thinking he can bargain with or treat the demon as he would another human. Hence the pact which is taken for granted as an overt or tacit expression of the relationship between them. 'Didst thou not write thy name in thine owne blood,/and drewst the formall deed twixt thee and mee,/and is it not recorded now in Hell?' asks the demon Coreb, rhetorically, of the scholar-magician Peter Fabel in the anonymous *Merry Devil of Edmonton* (*c*.1604), leaving Fabel to lament the fatal arrogance 'when men in their owne pride strive to know more/then man should know!/For this alone God cast the Angelles downe' (Induction 27-8, 47-9).

But ritual magic is most dangerous in its threat to the soul. It is not a distinct or discrete branch of magic operating within fixed boundaries, but strays (or appears to stray, because the modern habit of categorising and separating knowledge into self-contained genres makes it seem so), into magical fields less immediately treacherous to the magician. In as much as it seeks hidden knowledge, it partakes of the nature of 'natural' magic, whose aim is precisely that – to discover and then master the secret laws which govern the created universe. In as much as ritual magic claims to demonstrate such mastery, it tends to what Del Rio called 'artificial' magic, that branch of the art which deals in *praestigia*, deliberate and conscious trickery whereby astonishing things are made to happen (or seem to happen) for the diversion or deception of an audience – the kind of thing now called 'conjuring tricks' or 'illusions'. But what characterises *ritual* magic is precisely that it requires evocation of angels or demons so that their assistance may be asked or demanded for the fulfilment of the magician's purposes; and however much he might claim that his purpose was the acquisition of knowledge, hidden beneath his scholarly aspiration might well lie the temptation, voiced long ago in the first-to-third century *Corpus Hermeticum*, to make himself divine:

> Unless you make yourself equal to God, you cannot understand God. Like is understood by like. Make yourself grow to immeasurable immensity, outleap all body, outstrip all time, become eternity, and you will understand God. Having conceived that nothing is impossible to you, consider yourself immortal and able to understand everything... and when you have understood all these at once – times, places, things, qualities, quantities – then you can understand God.
>
> (11.20)

It was an injunction picked up and passed on to the Renaissance magician by Marsilio Ficino:

A human being is a great miracle, a living creature who should be honoured and worshipped: who is familiar with the race of demons as
though he were acquainted with them in the natural course of events:
who changes into a god as though he himself were a god.

(*Theologia Platonica*, *c.*1482, Book 14, chapter 3)

and it is therefore scarcely surprising that the ritual magician tended
to take himself and his art with immense seriousness. If challenged, of
course, he could argue he had Christian precedent. Justin Martyr,
Theophilus of Antioch and Clement of Alexandria were three among
the early Church Fathers who wrote that those who live good
Christian lives will be deified – 'the human soul practises to be a god',
said Clement. Such an argument, however, would have been mistaken
both in its premises and its detail, for Christianity was different from
ritual magic in at least one fundamental practical point: it did not
summon angels or demons as an integral part of its central rites. It was
this aspect of his work which would be liable to bring the ritual magician into immediate danger, and indeed every time he entered a magic
circle he was taking his life in his hands because he was inviting this
interaction of species. In his favour, however, perhaps one can say that
in as far as he was risking his spiritual as well as his physical existence,
he was actually being bolder than modern astronauts, whose physical
dangers are all too obvious but who do not see themselves as latter-
day Fausts, dicing with spiritual damnation every time they venture
beyond the normal constraints of Earth. 'Am I a god? Everything is
growing so clear to me!' exclaims Goethe's Faust as he contemplates
a drawing in a book, which seems to reveal the powers of nature and
its inner workings. His question not only summarises the ritual magician's aim, but also what amounts to his tacit challenge to the genuine
God whose name must not be taken in vain, but which is used over
and over again in ritual magic as an instrument of attempted coercion
of the Deity.

2

Evocation and Ecstasy in the Ancient World

If we look at the surviving *materia magica* from the ancient world, we may be struck by the preponderance of men as its practitioners and clientele. The Byzantines, for example, thought of magic as almost exclusively a male preserve, with the magicians learning how to use and control demons either from older practitioners or from books. Ancient literature, on the other hand, suggests that magic was in the hands of women. This, however, unless we are very careful, may turn out to be misleading, so how should we interpret this apparent discrepancy? Circe and Medea, to take the two most famous literary females who were commonly depicted as magicians, manipulated the laws of nature in order to achieve dominance over men. They did so, however, in a very particular way. Circe fed Odysseus' companions 'wicked drugs' (*pharmaka lygra*), struck them with her staff (*rhabdos*), and this changed them into pigs; and she would have bewitched Odysseus in the same way had he not been protected by a magic herb given to him by the god Hermes, (*Odyssey* 10.233-40, 286-92). Medea killed a rival in love by smearing her garment with deadly, magic poisons (*pharmaka*), and promised to enable an elderly childless king to sire offspring with the help of magic drugs, (Euripides: *Medea* 384-5, 717-18).

There is, however, a difference between the two. Circe was a goddess, Medea was not, and this is why Circe was described as using a *rhabdos* during the course of her transformatory magic. *Rhabdos* may refer to a fairly short stick, such as a staff of office, or a much longer rod, such as a spear-shaft or a shepherd's crook. It is wielded in Classical literature by divinities. Thus, Athene touched Odysseus with her golden *rhabdos* and so restored to him his youthful appearance as well as giving him, Cinderella fashion, new and expensive clothing, while Hermes used his *rhabdos* to put people to sleep at a touch. One is reminded of Allan Bennett's magic staff. Bennett was a friend of Aleister Crowley and, Crowley tells us,

> he used to carry a 'lustre' – a long glass prism with a neck and a pointed knob such as adorned old-fashioned chandeliers. He used this as a wand. One day, a party of theosophists were chatting sceptically about the power of the 'blasting rod'. Allan promptly produced his and blasted one of them. It took fourteen hours to restore the incredulous individual to the use of his mind and his muscles.

> (*Confessions*, 180)

But Circe's *rhabdos* was more an indication of her status, and only in part the means whereby her divine power was directed towards the object of her will. Later literature, (principally Latin), however, despite its acknowledgement of her divinity, in fact represented her essentially as a *venefica*, a worker of poisonous magic. Vergil, for example, tells us she changed Odysseus' companions into pigs by means of magical chants (*carminibus*), and Ovid that she transformed her rival for Glaucus' love by using poisons which had preternatural effects (*portentificis venenis*) and a chant full of strange words. Medea, we have noted, also used maleficent herbal magic. So by the time both women became types of the female magician, their male authors had assigned them to a category regarded as peculiar to women – the worker with herbs and incantations – and the significance of Circe's *rhabdos*, which suggested that she was both divine and of equal status with male deities, was lost during the transition.[1]

Ritual magic, then, in the sense we are using the term here, was essentially a male activity in pre-Christian times as well as later. One distinctive form it took in the Greek and Roman period was necromancy, that is to say, a ritual of evocation intended to raise the spirits of the dead so that they could be asked questions regarding the future and give answers of a particular authority. The rites involved seem to have been reminiscent of what would have been regarded as licit, religious forms, although the place of their performance was likely to have been peculiarly chosen for this type of magical divination, and the time at which they were carried out was usually night. Thus, in Aeschylus' lost play *Psychagogoi* (The Necromancers), Odysseus is told to stand on the grass at the edge of Lake Acheron, slice the neck of a sacrificial sheep, and allow its blood to drain into the water and reeds. He was then to invoke Earth and Hermes, (the latter as escort of the dead), and pray Chthonic Zeus to send up ghosts from the melancholy (that is, black and bitter) water. Children, however, were sometimes sacrificed instead of sheep, and even foetuses were removed and used for divination.

Summoning either gods or chthonic spirits, as opposed to ghosts, might also require elaborate ceremony, not to mention apparatus. The following is an example. First, the magician needed to provide himself with protection against psychic attack. This consisted, not in this instance of a circle, but of a spring of laurel with seven leaves on each of which he was to write certain characters. (These bear a fairly close resemblance to magical characters one finds in later Mediaeval and early modern texts, so their tradition proved to be long-lasting.) The magician also needed a lamp which had not been decorated with red paint or ochre, a piece of linen cloth to serve as a wick, and oil which had been made fragrant with rose or spikenard. It is likely, to judge from the details of the rite, that the magician was going to perform it in a room rather than out of doors, for nearby were to be found a formal chair with a back, (called a *thronos* in Greek), and a couch, with a linen sheet cast over each, although he had also to construct an altar of unburned clay, not necessarily large or high off the floor, to receive a bloodless sacrifice, and there may have also been a table at hand with flour, rain-water, spices, wine, honey and milk upon it, along with some kind of writing materials, perhaps charcoal or, more likely, pen and ink. Finally, next to the altar was a wolf's head so positioned that the magician's lamp could stand upon it throughout the proceedings.

Once all these preliminaries were arranged, the magician, who had abstained from sexual intercourse, avoided anything considered polluting, and refrained from eating fish, (a taboo which indicates the Egyptian origin of the rite), vested himself in a special robe he kept for the occasions on which he worked magic, took in his left hand a staff made of ebony and in his right the protective laurel-sprig, and began the ceremony. The order of proceeding is not clear in the manuscript, but the magician probably offered some kind of initial apotropaic prayer before making seven flat and seven round cakes (presumably quite small), which he then placed on the altar as an offering to the spirit he was to evoke. He poured libations of wine, honey, milk and rain-water, and then burned various aromatic substances including storax, cassia, and balsamum, after which he wrote on a piece of linen cloth two long, magical words, both of which are palindromic, and which he may have chanted aloud before folding the cloth and inserting it into the lamp of rose or spikenard oil and lighting it. The magician was now ready to summon the spirit. He called upon various names – Apollo, Paian, Iao, the archangels Michael and Gabriel, Abrasax, Adonai, Pakerbeth, Aion, Adonaios, Eloaios – and other sources of power to send him a *daimon*, a spirit intermediary between divinities and human beings, who was to answer his questions truthfully and without doing him any harm. The prayer ends with a long, palindromic word hidden in which is a reference to 'Thoth twice great', Thoth being the Egyptian god of learning and magic.

The spirit is now presumed to appear and take its seat either upon the chair or the couch provided. The magician burns more incense and poses whatever questions he has in mind, standing all the while (presumably out of respect). When the time comes for the spirit to be dismissed, the magician shifts his ebony staff from his left hand to his right, and the laurel sprig from his right hand to his left. He extinguishes the lamp, makes a further offering of incense, and then says or chants the final prayer which calls upon various powers to make sure the evoked spirit returns whence it came and, during its departure, does no harm to the magician, (*Papyri Graecae Magicae* I.262-347).

This kind of evocation, whether of a divinity, a *daemon* or a ghost, is and remains typical of one strand of ritual magic. By its words and gestures of power, the apparent veil between worlds is penetrated and non-material meets and converses with material being. But it is important to understand how these words of power were operated, for it is not simply a question of the magician's saying something after the fashion of a wizard's 'Abracadabra' and waiting for marvels to happen. The *Eighth Book of Moses*, a set of Graeco-Egyptian magical texts, provides a good illustration. By performing this ritual, the magician is able to evoke an angel, discover the fate predestined for him, and (if it is bad) supplicate the angel to change it. The rubrics include directions for making certain noises, and these form an important element in the ritual performance, for these sounds are far from meaningless. They imply deliberate breath control and the use of vibrated sound, both of which are basic techniques for enabling the magician to attune his or her subconscious to the non-material world, the most obvious example being the so-called 'Tantric voice' (*rgyud-skad*), an extremely low-register chant with overtone singing employed by monks in the Tantric colleges of Tibet.

Sound was clearly important to the ancient magician – a spell for binding a lover, for example, contains the sentence 'I invoke you by the name which causes fear and trembling, the name at whose sound the earth opens, the name at whose terrifying sound the *daemons* are terrified, the name at whose sound rivers and rocks burst open'. In the Moses ritual the sounds made by the operator are three in type. First there is the hissing of a snake and a popping noise, here associated with a falcon-headed crocodile rising from deep water to greet the sun on four significant days of the year. In this ritual, instructions are given to represent these sounds by drawings, but later comes an extraordinary call in which the magician imitates the sounds of a falcon – CHI CHI CHI CHI CHI CHI CHI, ti ti ti ti ti ti ti – making each note seven times; and this is followed by the instruction, 'Clap three times. TAK TAK TAK, go "pop pop pop" for a long time; hiss a great hiss, that is, one of great length'. The time to be taken over these noises implies a degree of breath control and indeed we see this clearly in a rubric governing the second type of magical sound, vocalisation of god-names. Thus, the Moses ritual directs, 'Draw in spirit/breath with all your senses. Say the first name in one breath to the east, the second to the south, the third to the north, and the fourth to the west', the 'name' (that is to say, the series of names and sounds peculiar to the entity being evoked) being

ŌAŌĒŌ ŌEOĒ IAŌ IIIAAŌ THOUTHĒ THĒ AATHŌ
ATHĒROUŌR AMIATHAR MIGARNA CHPHOURI
IYEYĒOŌAEĒ A EE ĒĒĒ III OOOOO YYYYY ŌŌŌŌŌŌ
SEMESILAMMPS AEĒIOYŌ ĒŌOYE LINOUCHA NOUCHA
HARSAMOSI ISNORSAM OTHAMARMIM ACHYCH
CHAMMŌ.

Now, this collection may look meaningless, and such lists were often dismissed as such by earlier scholars. It begins to make sense, however, if we bear in mind that it represents partly a set of instructions to the magician, (that at this point he is to pronounce the words a certain way, or make certain sounds in a certain way), and partly a gathering of what appear to be barbaric or exotic god- and *daemon*-names. Certain divine names are indeed here – THOTH, HORUS, IAO, SEMESILAM – while other words are magical exclamations (*voces magicae*) either in the form of palindromes or of words slowly diminished – LINOUCHA NOUCHA – a frequent phenomenon in magical incantations, producing a mesmeric, rhythmical recitation of sounds, which is one method of magical vibration. As Paul Valéry expressed it in relation to poetry,

There is no rapport between the sound and the sense of a word... and yet it is the job of the poet to give us the sensation of the intimate union of the word and the mind. One must regard this as a result which is, in the proper sense of the word, 'marvellous'. I say we give to this term when we think of the marvels and wonders of ancient magic. One must not forget that poetry has been for centuries allocated to the service of incantations. Those who devoted themselves to these strange operations were obliged to believe in the power of the word, and much more in the efficacy of the sound of the word than of its meaning. Magical formulae are often devoid of sense, but people do not think their power depends on their intellectual content... They act on us in the manner of musical harmony. The impression they produce depends largely on resonance, rhythm, and the number of their syllables.[2]

The god-names of the Moses ritual may also have numerical significance. In Hebrew, Greek and Latin the letters of the alphabet can stand for numbers, and therefore two words consisting of letters which add up to the same numerical total have a particular relationship with one another. So the names one sees in these incantations may serve a double purpose. They may be significant in themselves and act as calls to the divinity being addressed or evoked; or they may stand as signs for something or somebody else, thereby behaving as veils for words or beings of greater inherent power.

Thirdly, vibration of sounds consisting of repeated vowels is clearly shown here at the beginning and in the middle of the divine names and magical exclamations. They seem to have been voiced on different notes, for the 'name' is immediately followed by 'I call on you, Lord. I sing your holy power in a musical hymn, AEĒIOYŌŌŌ'. These vowels either represent Greek or Egyptian vowel sounds, or notes in the Greek musical scale, or a combination of the two, and this is continued in the next actions, which are to burn incense and say, 'ĒIOYŌ IOYŌ OYŌ YŌ Ō A EE ĒĒĒ IIII', diminishing magical exclamations followed by a set of vibrated notes, each one of which is longer by one beat than the former.[3]

We must therefore imagine such a ritual as being conducted by a man perhaps clothed in white, (a frequent but apparently not required practice), the colour being symbolic of his inner and outer cleanliness.

He will probably burn incense he has made for the occasion under direction from the written rubric, and his prayers and formulae will be punctuated by rhythmical repetitions, non-human sounds or calls, and long, drawn-out noises, half-chanting, half-vocalisation of vowels – all designed to throw him into a psychic or spiritual condition apt to receive and converse with a supernatural or preternatural being, or (in a different ritual) into what one may perhaps loosely call a shamanic state during which his soul or spirit is released to travel in the other-world.

Calling up the gods, the *daemons*, or the spirits of the dead may properly be called the work of the necromancer, but we must be careful not to assume that someone who performed this rite was necessarily an exclusive specialist in the art. Alongside professional necromancers whose function was to lay frightening or troublesome ghosts by sacrificing a black sheep (which had first acted as an indicator of the spot where the ghost's body had been buried), accompanying this with elaborate rituals enabling them to speak to the dead and ascertain why they were angry, there was, for example, Odysseus, who, though no magician, accomplished it under instruction from Circe. Indeed, some of the learned names traditionally quoted in both ancient and later histories of magic – Zoroaster, Pythagoras, Democritus, Bolos of Mendes – were essentially compilers of magical or medico-magical recipes and rituals, along with references to and instructions for what we should call 'conjuring tricks', rather than professional *magi*, although amazing feats were also attributed to them. Others, too, such as Pankrates or Simon Magus or Apollonius of Tyana, became famous for their wonder-working rather than for necromancy or ecstatic magic. Dedicated amateurs such as Vatinius the Pythagorean and Appius Claudius were said to have engaged in necromancy – 'You have undertaken unheard of, vile and immoral rites', said Cicero to Vatinius, 'and you are accustomed to evoke the souls of the dead and to honour the spirits of the dead with children's entrails', (*In Vatinium* 14).

Necromancers also appear in fiction which is clearly based on reality. Apuleius, for example, tells the story of Zatchlas, a famous Egyptian 'prophet' who engages (for a large fee) to bring back to life a corpse so that it may be questioned, while in Heliodoros' novel *Aithiopika*, an Egyptian priest, Kalasiris, confesses that there are two types of magic among his fellow countrymen: one which deals with ghosts and plants and incantations, and a second which looks towards the gods and is concerned exclusively with heavenly things. The reality behind these portraits may be glimpsed on the one hand in Celsus' scathing remarks about market-place magicians who have learned their art from Egyptians and, for a few coins of low denomination, astonish the crowd by exorcising demons, blowing away diseases and evoking the spirits of dead heroes, and on the other in the portrait of a *magus* supplied by the second-century AD satirist, Lucian of Samosata. The following is his account:

Menippos has been disillusioned by various philosophers who promised to enlighten him about the meaning of life. At last, he says,

> I decided to go to Babylon and entreat help from one of the *magi*...
> I had been told that by means of incantations and certain secret ceremonies they could open the gates of the underworld, safely take down anyone they wanted, and bring him back up again.

So off Menippos went, and in Babylon met a man called Mithrobarzanes, who had grey hair and a long, imposing beard, and is described as 'Chaldaean', (implying special skill in astrology), 'clever', and 'marvellous with respect to the art' (presumably here the art of magic). The two of them agreed upon a fee, and the necromantic procedure then began. Starting on a new moon, for twenty-nine successive mornings Mithrobarzanes brought Menippos down to the Euphrates where he washed him and addressed the sun − speaking indistinctly at great speed, and apparently invoking spirits (*daimones*) − after which he spat in his face three times. This done, he allowed Menippos to go home. Both he and Menippos observed a strict regimen during these twenty-nine days. They ate acorns, drank milk, a mixture of honey and water and water from the River Choaspes, and slept out of doors on the grass. Finally Mithrobarzanes thought his client had been sufficiently prepared by their diet, and so he took him down to the Tigris at midnight, purified him, (perhaps by wafting over him smoke from burning sulphur or, more likely, by rubbing his skin with it – the verb implies religious purification, and this was often done with sulphur), wiped him down, (presumably with water from the Tigris), and purged him all round with small torches, a squill and a number of other things.

The squill – here referring to *Urginea maritima* – looks like a large onion and was commonly used as a medicinal plant all round the Mediterranean. One's impression is that Mithrobarzanes was conducting a double purification by fire and water. If the bright yellow form of sulphur were rubbed over the skin, it could symbolise flame, almost certainly through its colour rather than by generating heat. Sulphur may cause mild irritation if applied directly to the skin, but even this slight effect would be annulled by Menippos's being wiped down with water, which is the immediate following ritual action. 'Purging around' almost certainly tells us either that the flaming torches made circles in the air in front of Menippos, or that they were carried around him – one sees these methods of purification in Hindu worship - and the squill was perhaps used in the manner of an aspergillum, a small brush for sprinkling holy water over a congregation, a person or an object. It reminds us of the Psalmist's 'You will purge me with hyssop and I shall be cleansed', (50.9, Vulgate), hyssop being a smallish plant with narrow elliptical leaves, commonly employed by both Jews and Samaritans for sprinkling blood or water.

After these purifications, Mithrobarzanes muttered the same incantation as on previous occasions and then, 'having magicked me from head to toe', he walked around him (that is, created a magic circle) so that Menippos might not be harmed by the ghosts, and took him home, Menippos walking backwards. Once there, Mithrobarzanes put on the robe he wore while conducting magical operations, described as a garment in the Median style, which is likely to be a reference to the *kandys*, a long flowing garment widening from shoulder to hem, with voluminous sleeves which also widened from shoulder to wrist. This was in preparation for a rite of necromancy, the details of which we have noted already with respect to Odysseus – digging a pit, killing a sheep, sprinkling its blood on the earth, and invoking named deities, 'mingling with these [other] names which came from foreign languages and were unintelligible and consisted of many syllables', (*Menippos* 6-9).

Now, none of this should strike us as particularly surprising in the light of the details of rituals we have examined already. Lucian may be a satirist, but in this dialogue he concentrates his fire on Menippos' ingenuousness. He is, it appears, a man thirsty for revelations and has tried all kinds of philosophers before lighting upon Mithrobarzanes. The aim of their association is a descent into the underworld and a safe return therefrom, and although the magician accomplishes this for Menippos, the sum of the wisdom Menippos learns from his quest among the dead can be summarised as 'Don't run after metaphysical speculation. Concentrate on the immediate task of living'. The banality of the advice is deliberate. Lucian is rejecting both speculative philosophy and, by implication, magic as a means of discovering some 'secret of life'. But his portrait of Mithrobarzanes and his rites does not appear to be exaggerated for comic or sarcastic effect, nor does he make Menippos evince any adverse or hostile reaction either to his mentor or the magical operations. Essentially, Mithrobarzanes is a true-to-life picture of a necromancer inserted into a fictional dialogue which has some fantastic episodes, but not in the description of the magic.

If necromancy was one of the ancients' most solemn and characteristic set of rites, however, another formed what turned out to be the principal inheritance of ritual magic transmitted to the modern from the ancient world. Like necromancy, it assumed that between the human and the divine there is an immense distance which teems with supernatural and preternatural entities of all kinds, which may be invoked and evoked; but this branch of the inheritance assumes that the magician's most important task is to negotiate his way through these entities to gain direct intercourse with the godhead. Such intercourse, we learn, can be gained in either of two ways. First, the divinity may be evoked and will therefore make an appearance in some guise to the devotee, an appearance often attended by cosmological disturbances. A good example is the appearance of the goddess Hekate during the course of one of the *Chaldaean Oracles*, texts, perhaps dating from the late second century AD, of a theurgic system which combines religious teachings from Persia and Syria, magic and Platonic metaphysics. The operator is told that after he has repeated a magical formula several times he will see fire, whirling light and hallucinatory visions. Finally, everything will grow dark, the curvature of the sky and the light of the stars and moon will no longer be visible, the earth will shake, and the only illumination will come from lightning flashes. It is then the magician must listen to a voice within the fire, which is that of Hekate herself. So here the goddess does not appear in her own shape, but in that of a formless fire which speaks – much less dangerous for a mortal, as we learn from the Greek myth which tells us that when Zeus granted Semele's wish that he come to her in his own form and not that of a man or animal, she was unable to sustain the sight and was blasted out of existence – and she is accompanied by various non-human entities who glow with a brilliant or golden light.[4]

On the other hand, the magician might wish to journey into Heaven, thereby undertaking an endeavour fraught with immense dangers as the material-and-transient tried to transcend itself and come face to face with the immaterial-and-eternal. Such ecstatic journeys may be (and have been) likened to the journey made by the soul after death, and will recall to the modern reader many accounts of near-death experiences in as much as the latter frequently include descriptions of a post-mortem cosmology and meetings with non-human or divine entities. Narratives of ascents to Heaven have a very long history. There are many examples from both Classical Greek and Roman literature – Lucian's *Menippos* is one of the less serious – and the genre was continued in a multiplicity of both Jewish and Christian texts. Jewish Hekhalot literature of the fifth and sixth centuries AD, for example, gives plenty of evidence of such intentions and endeavours. *Hekhalot*, meaning 'place' or 'sanctuary', is also known as *Ma'aseh Merkabah*, 'the way of the chariot', both terms being references either to a part of the heavenly world through which the practitioner passes on his ascent to the presence of God, or to the divine chariot of Ezekiel 1.4-21. Hekhalot literature consists of instructions to the ritualist regarding ascetic practices – fasting, abstinence from sexual intercourse, daily immersion in water, daily prayer – which will separate him from his usual, everyday existence and prepare him to recite adjurations addressed directly to God, or to angels who are commanded to hear and perhaps descend to earth to teach the practitioner and lend him power to fulfil any of his wishes. These rituals, together with detailed information about names of power – that is the Tetragrammaton, or divine names such as are derived by gematria or notarikon, or names of angelic beings – and seals which the practitioner will show to angels during his ascent to and descent from the heavens, or wear upon his body for protection, together form the written account of this particular mystical system.[5]

The magician may thus go to meet the gods in their own realm to have conversation, ask questions and receive ineffable knowledge otherwise unobtainable. The so-called 'Mithras Liturgy', for example, instructs the operator how to enter into that state wherein he can witness an epiphany of the god Mithras-Helios who will then act as his teacher. The liturgy contains all the technical elements we have been discussing. It begins with a vibrated invocation, AEĒIOYŌ, followed by popping and hissing sounds. It requires breath control. 'Draw in breath from the rays, drawing up three times as much as you can'. The operator calls upon gods by name – SEMESILAM, IAŌ, PEPPER PREPEMPIPI, etc. – and then enters upon an extended invocation by vibrated sounds. 'I invoke the immortal names, living and honoured, which never pass into mortal nature and are not declared in articulate speech by human tongue or mortal speech or mortal sound: ĒOŌ OĒEO IŌŌ ŌE ĒEŌ OĒ', and so forth for line after line of vowel clusters which, by the manner in which they are grouped, clearly indicate rhythm as well as notation and variation in the sound to be made. 'When you have said these things, you will hear thundering and shaking in the surrounding realm'. Thus the magician ascends into divine regions and there sees and speaks to the gods. At the epiphany of the god Mithras, the magician is instructed, 'Make a long bellowing sound' [i.e. like a bull, the animal associated with Mithras], 'straining your belly in order to excite the five senses. Bellow for a long time until you are out of breath'. Then follows a conversation with the god during which, the magician is told, 'you will grow weak in soul and will not be in yourself': and so the experience comes to an end.

For what purpose was the knowledge thus gained to be used? It varied. Hekhalot ritual brought power to the practitioner, which he could then use as he pleased, his pleasure being generally directed, it is clear, either towards his own self-improvement or to the betterment of others. Altruism, indeed, seems to have played a major role in these rituals of power and penetration of Heaven. A fourth-century AD Gnostic text, for example, tells us that the eponymous author, Zostrianos, ascended with the help of divine powers through various regions of a heavenly realm, receiving a sequence of baptisms and occult instructions as he passed onwards until, after his fifth baptism, he becomes 'as a god'. A sixth and final baptism at the hands of a female spirit brings yet more revelation concerning the divine worlds until, having become 'a complete initiate, Zostrianos comes back to the material world where he writes down what he has learned and begins to teach the common people.

There were, however, objections. The philosopher Plotinos, writing just before Christianity became the official religion of the Roman Empire, objected strongly to both the theory and the practice of these endeavours. Divinities, he said, are inviolable and cannot be approached or constrained in the way Gnostic practices claim or, at the very least, imply.

> When [Gnostic magicians] compose incantations addressed to these beings... what are they doing but speaking magical formulae and incantations and supplications as though, if any of us who is reasonably skilled utters in the appropriate manner such things as chants and sounds and exhalations and hissings and so forth, the gods reply and are fetched hither by a word.
>
> (*Enneades* 2.9.14)

Had Plotinos forgotten that he himself had once met an Egyptian priest and, in the Temple of Isis in Rome, witnessed the priest's evocation of a divinity which turned out to be Plotinos' guardian spirit? Perhaps the epiphany had not yet happened when he wrote his polemic, or maybe the tale is just a pious myth. But his criticism of the practice is relevant, for it poses crucial questions relating to the nature of divinity and the relationship between what is uncreated with what is created. Can beings of a much higher order of creation than humanity be constrained, or even persuaded, by some power inherent in words uttered in a special way or in a particular order: and if so, what is that compelling power, whence does it come, and how and why has it been made available to humans?

The 'why' can be seen in Jewish apocalyptic and Hekhalot literature, which partakes of the nature of prophecy and therefore represents a series of records of visions accorded to individual human beings who, in addition to their personal sacrament of immortality which teaches them how to liberate their own soul from the demands of materiality, are thereby enabled to reveal to others less favoured information, reassurance and revelation concerning the reality of God and existence beyond the material, hitherto hidden secrets of the workings of creation, and the nature of life after death. Of all these visions or heavenly ascents, that of Enoch is the best known. It begins,

> And it was shown to me thus in a vision. Behold! Clouds were calling me in my vision, and dark clouds were crying out to me. Fire-balls and lightnings were hastening me on and driving me, and winds, in my vision, were bearing me aloft, and they raised me upwards and carried and brought me into the heavens.
>
> (I *Enoch* 8)

Heaven here, as in so many other writings of a similar nature, is described as a temple in which God sits enthroned and is served by ranks of angels who act as priests, and into whose sacerdotal status Enoch is ordained – the equivalent of Zostrianos's becoming a god and a complete initiate.

But is this, and indeed are the Hekhalot texts and similar literature, the record of actual experience, or are such accounts merely literary constructs based upon the alluring combination of exegesis and imaginative flight? Both Rebecca Lesses and James Davila have argued strongly for the former and maintain that the texts make perfect sense as instructions on how to perform certain rituals intended to control spirits for various ends beneficial to the practitioner; and Davila suggests further that there are valid parallels to be drawn between the Hekhalots' ascetic techniques and those employed by shamans, and between the cosmologies envisioned by each of these cultures. Still, shamanic or not can it be said that the practitioners of such rituals were 'magicians' as opposed, let us say, to religious mystics in the style of St Teresa of Avila or St John of the Cross? The distinction is, of course, to some extent artificial and we must expect our modern habit of categorising to have severe limitations when it comes to our understanding of the fluid interplay between roles, which was a more common feature of earlier modes of thinking. Two characteristics of the Hekhalot, Coptic and pagan practices we have been reviewing, however, do suggest that what their operators were doing can be described as 'magic'. First, the principal end of all these techniques was control of non-human entities and secondly, the format of the techniques included recitation in some form or other of words of power, accompanied by whatever means were thought necessary to attract the spirits' attention and, once attracted, to hold it in thrall. Both these render a performance magical and the performer a magician, regardless of how much religious or mystical content the rite recommends or is given.

Here we enter into something of a minefield of definition. The kind of magical operation I have just been describing was often called 'theurgy', a technical term which goes back to very ancient times, but was understood in somewhat different ways by different writers. If people are to become gods by contemplating Divinity, for example, can mere thinking effect the transformation, or is something else required? The third/fourth-century AD philosopher Iamblichus, whose works were often cited as authoritative by later demonologists, explained, it is not the act of thinking which unites theurgists with the gods, because [then] what would stop theoretical philosophers from achieving a theurgic union with the gods? The truth is quite different. What makes the theurgic union happen is the successful performance of secret actions which are completely beyond the comprehension of those who operate marvels, and the power of silent symbols which are perceived only by the gods.

(De mysteriis 2.11)

In other words, it is the ritual which causes ecstatic union with Divinity. The magician may not understand what he is saying or doing, but that does not matter. If the divine beings whose attention he is trying to attract note particular significance in his actions and the magical instruments he is using, that will be sufficient for the successful accomplishment of his intention.

Later ages, however, would have none of it. The fact that the magician evoked and encountered non-human entities was enough, as far as they were concerned, to condemn his enterprise, and the word 'theurgy' was seen as an attempt to disguise undesirable actions with a palliative terminology.

All magic is divided into white, which people think is licit, and black, which is illicit. So they call the white variety 'theurgy' and the black 'goetia'

wrote Martín del Rio, adding that actually this is an artificial and a farcical distinction. For once, the learned Jesuit is being less than subtle. For if he and his contemporaries, rather like their Mediaeval predecessors, were not prepared, for reasons closely connected with the particular religious and social conditions in which they found themselves, to distinguish between magical operations and between those who conducted them, the ancients not only could but did. When, for example, they discussed the possibility of Jesus's being a magician, Origen records Celsus, an opponent of Christianity, as saying that Jesus learned magic while he was in Egypt and tried out his skills with the help of 'powers', (that is, spirits of some kind), and cast out demons in much the same way as other magicians (*Contra Celsum* 1.28; 2.49). Origen here uses the word *goetes* for 'magicians', a word which always had negative connotations because of its association with necromantic rites or the raising of *daimones* for ill-intentioned or illicit purposes. Justin Martyr, on the other hand, puts in the mouth of a Jewish interlocutor the suggestion that Jesus was a *magos* because he cured the crippled and the blind and, above all, because he raised the dead, (*Dialogus cum Tryphone* 69). Now, a *magos* was originally a priest from Media, who specialised in divinatory interpretation and the conduct of sacrifices – clearly not applicable to Jesus's case. In Greek and Roman linguistic usage, the word became associated with 'foreignness' and thus exotic or undesirable cultic practices, and via continual disdain and suspicion eventually came to be used also of pretentious quacks who tried to dazzle their clients with elaborate, fraudulent ceremonies.[6] What Justin's fictitious Jew clearly meant by 'magos', however, was 'wonder-worker', someone who spectacularly overrode or manipulated the hidden laws of nature to produce remarkable effects, and this more positive association is obviously more likely to be what some of Jesus's contemporaries thought of when they witnessed or heard about his curing miracles.

A prime example of such a person is the man known as Simon Magus, 'Simon the magician', described in the New Testament as someone operating in and around the city of Samaria. According to St Luke, Simon had not only been working magic – not necessarily to be understood in the negative sense attached to 'sorcery' or 'witchcraft' – but was claiming to be a person of importance, and people used to pay him attention because for quite a long time he had been sending them mad (or amazing them – the Greek verb has both meanings) with his acts of magic, although Acts 8 does not tell us exactly what these were. Those details are left to pseudo-Clement, (an author claiming to be Pope Clement I), who says they included making statues walk, bronze or stone dogs bark and mountains jump and fly through the air, (*Recognitiones* 3.60). Indeed, he had astonished people so much that they said of him, 'This man is the Power of God, which is called "great"', (v.10). Celsus, we may recall, had allegedly said that Jesus performed his wonders by means of 'powers', and St Paul writes of groups of preternatural beings created by God, known as 'Thrones', 'Dominions', 'Principalities', and 'Powers', (Colossians 1.16). So were people suggesting that Simon was one of these exalted beings, or even God himself? It is worthwhile comparing him with another first-century AD man of power, Apollonius of Tyana, whose *Life*, as recorded by Philostratos, is a mass of extraordinary anecdote and fable. There is, however, clearly some core of truth in it. After a long time spent in the study of Greek philosophers, Apollonius went travelling in Asia Minor and thence to Persia, always preserving an ascetic mode of life even when lodged in the splendours of the Persian King's palace. From Persia, he went to India where he learned yogic techniques of levitation from Brahmins and exorcised an evil spirit which had inhabited a teenage boy for fully two years past, a cure which began a succession of further, miraculous cures: a lame man, a blind man, a paralytic and a woman who always found child-labour difficult. Apollonius's prescription for her is interesting. 'He told her husband that when the woman was giving birth again, he should come into the room, carrying a live hare in the fold of his tunic, walk round her and, as he did so, let the hare go', (*Vita Apollonii* 3.39). Apollonius, it seems, was knowledgeable in popular magic as well as wonder-working. It is not, however, an aspect of his abilities which receives any emphasis.

From India, (along with Egypt, one of the principal sources of esoteric knowledge in ancient literature), he returned to the west coast of Asia Minor where he gained a reputation as a diviner by correctly prophesying earthquakes in Ionia and a plague in the city of Ephesos. The latter disaster he stopped in its tracks by getting the Ephesians to stone a squalid beggar whom his heightened occult perception had recognised as the plague-demon and therefore the cause of the outbreak. In Ilium (Troy), he evoked the ghost of Achilles and had a long conversation with him, an act of necromancy which may have made some people nervous or suspicious, for the chief priest of the Mysteries at Epidauros at first wanted to refuse to initiate him, on the grounds that he was a *goes*, a magician who practised demonic or harmful magic, but at length was overruled by the enthusiasm of the common people for Apollonius. Further adventures took him to Rome where he raised a young girl from the dead, and to Spain where he predicted the short reigns of Vitellius, Galba and Otho – all Emperors within a single year – thereby reinforcing some people's impression that he was indeed a *goes*. In Egypt he was forced to defend himself and his reputation against the hostility of Euphrates, a philosopher who viewed Apollonius as little more than a subservient lackey of Vespasian, deeply immersed in political intrigue; and there can be no doubt that Apollonius did indeed meddle in affairs of state, for back in Asia Minor he tried to incite rebellion against the Emperor Domitian and at length, after imprudently coming to Rome, found himself imprisoned there on very serious charges.

Indeed, Philostratos felt compelled to defend Apollonius against the general charge of *goeteia*. Having just told us that Apollonius miraculously removed a fetter from his leg in prison, he goes on to say, 'People who are a bit simple-minded attribute things such as this to *goetes*' – as, apparently, did athletes, merchants and lovers – 'so it is not surprising that they go to these cheating word-jugglers and listen to what they say', (7.39); and throughout the long speech before Domitian, which Philostratos puts in his mouth, Apollonius again and again tries to refute this adverse popular view of him. He complained he could not even call the gods to witness he was speaking the truth. 'If I were to call upon Zeus, they would say I was using false and unlawful magic'. Even innocent meetings had been twisted in his disfavour. When he talked to Vespasian in Egypt, he said, they met openly in a temple, whereas by contrast

> when *goetes* have a meeting, they avoid temples of the gods because such places are hateful to those engaged in magic: they cloak themselves in night and the pitch-dark so that they may prevent those who are stupid from having the use of their eyes and ears.

Even his habit of wearing only a linen garment was used against him by the prosecution, because wearing such a robe was the kind of thing a *goes* did; and as for his prophecy that Ephesos would fall victim to plague, apparently 'this goes beyond natural cleverness and is a monstrous prodigy, and I could not have arrived at such an accurate [prediction] had I not been a *goes* and an abominable person!' (8.7.2, 5. 9).

One charge in particular is noteworthy, considering his reputation in many quarters as a magician. 'They say you went into the countryside to meet Nerva,[7] and sliced up an Arcadian child for him while he was having a sacrifice made in order to consult the auspices, to the prejudice of the Emperor [Domitian]', (7.20). At his subsequent trial, Apollonius tried to dismiss the accusation as nonsense.

> In the indictment, your Majesty, a dirge was chanted for an Arcadian boy, accusing me of cutting him open at night. Perhaps the prosecution was told this in a dream, I'm sure I have no idea! This lad, we are told, came from a good family and had the kind of good looks Arcadians have even when they are squalid and unwashed. The prosecution says I cut his throat while he was wailing and begging me with tears not to do it, and that after I had washed my hands in the boy's blood I prayed to the gods to reveal the truth to me... Need I say, your Majesty, how defiling it is even to listen to this kind of thing?
>
> (8.7.12)

Apollonius, however, was surely being either disingenuous or wildly optimistic in his disclaimer that he did not perform hieroscopic sacrifices, for everyone must have known that such things happened and happened not infrequently, and since, as we have seen, he was a man reputed to be a *goes*, the charge would have been perfectly credible to those who heard it.[8]

This combination of wonder-working, miraculous cures and resurrections and accurate divinations, then, coupled with Apollonius' ascetic way of life, mode of dress and authoritative pronouncements on religion and personal conduct, was quite enough to cause people to regard him as a *magos*, if they were favourably disposed towards him, or a *goes* if they were not. But it is also noteworthy that some people went so far as to regard him as a divine being, that is, an actual divinity in human form, or a person who had successfully assimilated himself into the nature of the Divine. Something of the kind, we may remember, also happened to St Paul and St Barnabas just after they had cured a lame man in the city of Lystra. 'When the crowd saw what Paul had done, it raised its voice and said in the Lykaonian dialect, "The gods have taken on the likeness of human beings and have come down to us"', (Acts 14.11). It is scarcely surprising, therefore, that Simon Magus who astonished the citizens of Samaria with his wonder-working should have been called 'a power of God', as though he were in some fashion either a conduit for the Divine or semi-divine himself; and indeed the Church Fathers, Irenaeus and Epiphanios, maintained that Simon's followers believed he was an incarnate god who had come down to earth to save it from the misrule of angels.

But while the Acts does not go into detail about his wonder-working, later Christian literature was prepared to fill in the gap. One key text is the second-century apocryphal *Acts of Peter*, which records a series of magical contests between Simon and St Peter, something after the pattern of the contest between Moses and Pharaoh's magicians. According to this narrative, Simon has gone to Rome, where his extraordinary acts of magic have caused many Christian converts to lapse and come over to him. Simon is living in the house and under the protection of a Roman senator, Marcellus, and when St Peter invites him to a parley, Simon refuses. Whereupon St Peter sends into the house a huge dog which delivers St Peter's message in a human voice. Astonished by this, Marcellus abandons Simon, evicts him from his house and converts to Christianity. St Peter works several more wonders to convince Marcellus that he has made the right choice, and when Simon races to St Peter's house to protest, St Peter strikes him dumb as a punishment for his blasphemies against Jesus. Finally, the magical contest proper begins in the Roman Forum in front of a large crowd and in the presence of the City Prefect, Agrippa. The Prefect orders Simon to kill a young man by magic, and St Peter to raise him to life again. Immediately Simon whispers in the lad's ear and so kills him. Thirty individuals then check the body and certify that the young man really is dead. St Peter tells Agrippa to take the lad's hand and he will live. Meanwhile, a second dead youth, who had died from natural causes, is brought before them, and St Peter brings him to life, too. Lastly, a third dead boy is carried into the Forum and St Peter challenges Simon to restore him to life. Simon accepts and apparently succeeds, for the dead man raises his head, opens his eyes, and bows towards the magician. But the phenomenon turns out to be an illusion. The moment Simon steps away from the bier, the body lies motionless and dead. At a word of command from St Peter, however, the young man stands up, removes the bandages holding his jaw closed, asks for his clothes, and speaks to St Peter, thereby proving he really is alive again.

But Simon was not yet vanquished. For the next few days, while citizens brought their sick to St Peter to be cured, the *magus* evoked spirits in the private houses of those who still had faith in him, worked apparent cures on the lame and blind and raised the dead as he had done in the Forum. Not satisfied with this, however, he issued a challenge to St Peter. Next day, he said, he would leave the earth and fly up to God in front of everyone. So the following day, a great crowd assembled on the Sacred Way to see him do it. Simon climbed to the top of an eminence, looked round, saw St Peter, and boasted he would now fly away; and, sure enough, he did. He rose into the air and began to fly all over Rome. But at a word from St Peter, he fell down and broke his leg in three places, and was taken thence to a *goes* by the name of Kastor who operated on him in an attempt to save his leg. Simon, however, died under the knife and thus left St Peter completely victorious.

Turning Simon into a declared enemy of the Christian religion obviously suggested, if only in subliminal fashion, a link between heresy and magic, and it did not take long before this suggestion was made overt, as when Chromatius of Aquileia compared the raven which Noah sent out of the Ark to its death with Simon who, despite his original repentance, (recorded by Acts), refused to allow himself to be transformed into a good Christian and thus was ejected from the Ark of the Church and so perished (*Sermones* 2.5). Suggesting that someone was a magician, indeed, became a favourite way to discredit a theological opponent. Thus, for example, Eusebius remarked that Marcus of Memphis was extraordinarily skilled in the arts of magic, St Jerome alleged that Priscillian was the devoted pupil of a Zoroastrian magician and had become a bishop through his magical assistance, and Meletios Homologetes pronounced as a general observation that it was not at all remarkable if those opposed to Christ performed magic, because they did so with the help of demons whose purpose was to persuade the practitioners to adhere to their erroneous view that magic is lawful and acceptable to God and their audience or clientele that they should be led willingly into the same grave error.[9]

Similarly, when Islam made its appearance and began to threaten religious stability in parts of the West, Christian biographies often accused Mohammed of trafficking with both magicians and demons after the pattern of Simon Magus. So, in his *De Seta Machometi*, the thirteenth-century Dominican Ramón Martí tells us that Mohammed became a skilled *magus* under instruction, while a century earlier, Embrico of Mainz and Gauthier de Compiègne both say that Mohammed was taught how to be a fraudulent and heretical magician by someone they call simply 'Magus', that he used his magical powers to impose on people's credulity and thus win himself adherents, and that (a curious travesty of Simon's aerial flight) after his death his tomb floated in the air – although Embrico is careful to explain to his Christian readers that this was accomplished by the use of magnets. (*Vita Mahumeti*, vv. 1140-5). The floating tomb and the explanation for it quickly entered European lore. At the beginning of the fourteenth century, Andrea da Barberino wrote an epic, *Guerrino il Meschino*, in which his hero, the mercenary soldier Guerrino, arrives at Mecca, enters the mosque there and describes Mohammed's tomb.

> In the middle of this dome there was an urn in the shape of a perfectly symmetrical coffin about one and a half cubits long and a little more in breadth, according to my guess. It was hanging in mid-air and not in contact with anything. I realised then that I was dealing with a trick thought up by that deceitful man, Mohammed, and I noticed that the

pseudo-church had been constructed, from the centre to the top, of magnetite which is a marine stone whose colour is between black and grey, and which has the property of attracting iron because of its cold-ness...That is why Mohammed's ark (which is made of iron) floats. The magnetite keeps it in place. Those stupid Saracens, however, do not know that it is the magnetite. They think the ark stays in mid-air by a miracle.

Barberino's fantastic description is useful in reminding us of two sig-nificant points. First, the line between magical and 'scientific' expla-nations for all kinds of phenomena was singularly blurred, and we shall find in a later discussion that the distinction made by early modern demonologists between 'demonic' and 'natural' magic in par-ticular was one which troubled their contemporaries and fuelled intense debates on the nature, and therefore the licitness, of knowl-edge. Mohammed's floating coffin is presented here as a type of *praes-tigium*, a trick which depends on certain occult, or hidden, natural powers, presented to the onlookers as a genuine miracle. Secondly, levitation was an equally ambiguous sign of preternatural activity. When the Virgin Mary or St Teresa of Avila or St John of the Cross or the Holy House of Loretto were borne up in the air or flew, the levitation was a mark of their sanctity; and the same is true of Sufi masters in Mediaeval Egypt, who were popularly credited with flying from Delhi to Mecca on a nightly pilgrimage. But when Simon Magus did the same, or witches flew to a Sabbat, or a heretic girl at Rheims escaped the fire by throwing a ball of thread into the air and being pulled upwards to safety in rapid flight,[10] they were assumed to have accomplished it with demonic assistance, their levitation or flight being as it were a mirror-image of the miraculous flight of saints or holy objects.

So what Simon Magus, Apollonius and Jesus appear to have in common is their ability to work miraculous cures and raise people from the dead, although the means they employed seem to have been very different; and for contemporaries, as well as for later generations, the principal question raised by these activities was, by what power did they do them? Miracle, demonic magic, 'natural' magic or *praestigium*? If we put aside for the moment any theological considerations, we can see from the mixed reactions they attracted that, because of these abilities in particular, some people were prepared to look upon each of them as a *magus* – essentially a producer of remarkable effects beyond what was explicable by natural causes, and a person of unusual religious authority – or as a *goes* – a magician in the negative sense, operating by means of evil spirits, or as a deliberate trickster perpetrating fraud upon his audiences, or possibly as a man imbued with qualities of the Divine to such an extent that he was more than merely human and might, indeed, actually be a divinity in human shape.[11] The tradition these represented for successive generations of magicians was awe-inspiring. The dangers inherent in such a tradition, however, were also grave and potentially fatal.

3

The Pattern and Aims of a Ritual Magician

What made a *magus* a *magus* or a *goes* a *goes*? Anyone who wished to enter upon the practice of ritual magic had several traditions to guide him, with Persian, Jewish and Egyptian prototypes, and a large number of textbooks from which, in the event of his not having a personal instructor, he could learn the techniques of his art and the reasons underlying them. These we shall now discuss. Antique, Mediaeval and early modern scholars were agreed that the principal figures responsible for learning and then handing on the art were Ham, son of Noah, and his son Zoroaster.

> He unadvisedly learned and established the system of magical science and passed it on to one of his sons who was called Misraim, and from whom are descended the Egyptians, the Babylonians and the Persians. [Misraim] was called 'Zoroaster' by his contemporaries, who admired and wondered at him as the first authority on the art of magic, and a large number of books on this subject is available with his name attached to them. So he assiduously paid close attention to the stars and, wishing to seem to be a god in people's eyes, he began to draw out from the stars certain things which looked like sparks of fire or flashes of light, and to show them to people, so that the unsophisticated and

ignorant might be lured thereby into stupefaction, [thinking it] a miracle. Wanting to increase popular opinion that he was a god, he engineered these displays on several occasions until it reached a point when the demon to whom he resorted over and over again set fire to him and burned him to ashes.

(Pseudo-Clement: Recognitiones 4.27)[1]

This account, hostile but fairly typical, is noteworthy because it suggests partly that Zoroaster was a fraud, in as much as he wanted to seem to be a divine being, and that he 'engineered' his displays of astral fire – the Latin verb encompasses the notions of striving, building up or constructing, setting something in motion with a deal of effort – and partly that he accomplished his feats with demonic help. He is thus presented as a ritual magician, remarkably learned in the techniques of magic, who, far from being the god-on-earth he wanted his audiences to see, was actually a practitioner of demonic magic, and thus fittingly punished by the evil spirit he pretended to control. Extracts from the books which were fathered upon him circulated and continued to circulate centuries after his death. Cecco d'Ascoli in the fifteenth century, for example, offered such a 'quotation' which, interestingly enough, deals with necromancy and spirits. Zoroaster, he said, used the word 'sky-region' in two ways, one referring to astrology, the other to necromancy.

Especially worthy of astonishment are the sky-regions which give answers by means of the flesh of dead people and the human blood of those who are somewhat inclined to believe in this. Accordingly, you should understand that there are four spirits of great power who stand in places which have been divided crosswise into four, that is, in the east, west, south, and north. Their names are Oriens, Amaymon, Paymon, and Egin. They are spirits of superior rank, and each has under him twenty-five legions of spirits. Consequently, because of their illustrious character, these [spirits] have a natural desire for sacrifices of human blood and the flesh of a dead human or cat.

(Commentarius in Joannis de Sacrobosco sphaeram, 1499, 21)

This is exactly the kind of belief and behaviour to which the twelfth-century Jewish scholar Maimonides was objecting when he said that idolatry arose from the grossly erroneous notion that since God had created the stars and planets to guide people, and since they were in this manner his servants, it must be God's will that human beings show them honour, just as God had done. Therefore, with this idea in mind, people began to build temples to the stars, offer them sacrifices and venerate them in all kinds of ways, hoping thereby to obtain God's favour (*Hilkhot Abodah Zarah* 1.1). Idolatrous blood-sacrifice, indeed, continued to appear in accusations of practising magic for a remarkably long time. Gilles de Rais, erstwhile friend and fighting-companion of St Joan of Arc, was tried and executed for sacrificing children to demons; bulls were still being sacrificed on the Isle of Skye in the eighteenth century; and in Hungary as late as 1963, anthropologists were told that midwives would learn their craft by offering up a human sacrifice, which is reminiscent of Heinrich Institoris's remark in his *Malleus Maleficarum* (1487) that midwives would sacrifice newly-born children to demons, (Part 2, question 1, chapter 13). This aspect of ritual magic, often coupled with astrology and necromancy and always conjoined with the invocation or evocation of spirits, thus lent a sinister undertone to what the operating magician would usually explain as a search for higher knowledge and a more intimate personal involvement with the Creator.

The Jewish strand of the tradition took Moses as one of its central figures, and harked back to Exodus 7-10. These chapters tell us that Moses and Aaron had an audience of Pharaoh and, as God had commanded, Aaron threw down his staff (*rhabdos*) in front of the Court and it turned into a snake. Pharaoh responded by summoning his 'wise men', his 'magicians', and his 'enchanters', and they repeated the marvel with their own staffs, which were then swallowed up by Aaron's magically-produced snake. The words for these groups of people are interesting because they suggest a good deal about what kinds of magical operators the original Hebrew writer and his later Greek and Roman translators thought were involved in this crucial confrontation. The 'wise men' appear in the Septuagint and Vulgate versions as precisely that: men of sound judgement and virtuous philosophy who are capable of passing on their knowledge to others. The Hebrew *hakhamim* means the same, but may also include those who carry a lot of practical information in their heads as well. Now, it will be noted that, in the face of Aaron's apparent magical demonstration, Pharaoh feels obliged to summon three groups of people, 'wise men' and 'magicians' and 'enchanters'. It is the magicians who replicate Aaron's marvel. Are the 'wise men' there as living reference books, to be consulted if necessary for the appropriate words and gestures if the magicians do not know them already? These magicians are reported very differently in the three versions of the text. The Hebrew *hartummim* is an unusual word, peculiar to this group of magical operators, and seems to be similar to the Greek word *magos*, in as much as the author is telling his hearers or readers that these people are foreign and therefore somewhat exotic and mysterious, precisely the flavour of *magos* to readers of Greek. The Septuagint, however, instead of using *magoi* turns them into *pharmakoi*, essentially men who deal with poisonous and non-poisonous plants, and although the word is capable of a more general application, the connotation of working with plants is inseparable from any of its usages. Consequently, it seems to be an odd way of describing the kind of magician who is operating here. The Vulgate is again different and specific. It calls them *malefici*, 'workers of harmful magic', and I presume we are meant, upon hearing or reading this, to take a moral stance against these operators. The context, of course, demands that we do, as well.

Finally we have *lehatim*, the 'enchanters' or 'enchantments' used by the magicians to change their staffs into snakes. The word is, again, an unusual one, so its precise meaning is not easy to fathom. It could be cognate with the 'flame' or the 'flash' of the flaming sword held by the angel at the gate of Eden after the fall. If this is so – and I should emphasise that the Hebrew, Greek and Latin texts with which we are dealing contain all kinds of variants, so any suggestion must be extremely tentative – we may be reminded of the sparks of fire or flashes of light which Zoroaster drew out of the sun and displayed to his audiences. The Septuagint, on the other hand, calls them 'incantations', that is, magical formulae voiced by chanting or singing, while the Vulgate expands the word into *incantationes et arcana*, 'incantations and secret things'. Why 'secret things'? It looks as though the translator has taken *lehatim* to be based on a root meaning 'concealed' (rather than 'flash' or 'flame') and has therefore understood it to refer to secret gestures or perhaps unintelligible words. If the word refers to people rather than magical operations – and this is perhaps more likely - it would, of course, simply tell us that these people were using a flashing flame or voicing arcane spells to achieve the required metamorphosis.

May we, then, (given all the textual uncertainties), catch here a glimpse of three different psychologies, produced by three different historical periods and cultural ambiences, reacting to magical demonstrations by ritual magicians? In Hebrew the magicians are exotic and 'flashy', theatrical in their response to Aaron's challenge; in Greek the magic is linked to chanted spells and to plants in which lies dormant a power of transformation (one thinks of Circe changing Odysseus's men into pigs); while in Latin the magic is effected by chanting and unintelligibility accompanied (perhaps because we are now dealing with a Christian translation of the Jewish text) by an undertone of perceived evil.

How is it that Pharaoh's magicians reproduced some of the marvels God worked through Moses? What did this contest mean to them? Was it merely a struggle between magical practitioners for the attention and favour of Pharaoh, as the Egyptians would have seen it, or, in the Jews' case, a series of wonder-workings in fulfilment of God's threat against Pharaoh's intransigence? It was a question which exercised St Augustine, and while he did not deny that Pharaoh's magicians were able, at least in appearance, to perform wonders equal to, and indeed the same as, those of Moses and Aaron, they did so, he says in *De civitate Dei* (10.8), with the help of demons, just as Moses and Aaron were helped by angels. The Egyptians' motives, however, were entirely wrong, and in consequence what they did, though spectacular, was ultimately worthless. Holy people, he maintained, work openly and rely upon the authority of God; magicians use their invocations as lures to deceive their audience and subjugate people to their will. Holy men seek God's glory in the working of miracles; magicians seek their own. Good Christians do such things for the public good; magicians make private contracts (*De diversis quaestionibus LXXXIII*, no. 79).

This demonstration of the Jews' superior power over nature is followed by God's infliction of various disasters upon Egypt. As in the case of the transmuted staffs, the first three 'plagues' – rivers turned into blood, frogs overrunning the land, and an abundance of lice – are actually effected by Aaron, not Moses. Aaron uses his staff as a conductor or sign of power, and the catastrophes follow. But they are also replicated by Pharaoh's *lehatim*, (the Septuagint's 'enchanters' and the Vulgate's 'workers of harmful magic'.) Perhaps for this reason Moses takes over from Aaron and disables the enchanters physically by making them fall prey to the outbreak of boils which constitutes another of the 'plagues'. From then on, the magicians play no further part in the process, and the magical contest is over.

Unlike Aaron, Moses does not wield a staff each time he inflicts a plague upon the Egyptians. To raise boils, for example, he casts up ashes into the air – a curious pre-figuring, in a way, of the powders said to have been thrown up by early modern witches to bring blight upon crops – and to cause hail, he merely points his hand towards the sky. Nevertheless, he too does have a staff which he can use in what would have appeared to contemporaries to have been a magical fashion. By stretching it out over the land, he brought a plague of locusts, and later in the desert he struck a rock with it and the rock gushed water. Indeed, in a 'rehearsal' for his encounter with Pharaoh's magicians he had thrown his staff on to the ground, at God's behest, and it had turned into a snake. Then, 'Take this staff in your hand', said God, 'and you will work marvels with it'. Then tradition of the magical operator's staff, therefore, was well established and proved to be very long-lasting. One thinks of the high priest criticised by Hosea (4.12) for using his staff as a divining-rod to answer questions with the help of a spirit; of St Patrick who used his *bachail* (staff or crozier) to draw a circle on the ground and so discover the entrance to

Purgatory, to drive snakes from Ireland and to revivify a dead man; of Richard Graham, a Scottish magician at the heart of the alleged magical conspiracies against the life of King James VI, who showed his friends, the Earl of Bothwell and the Scottish Chancellor, 'a stick with nicks in it, all wrapped abut with long hair, either of a man or a woman, and said it was an enchanted stick'; and of two European Protestant clergymen, Isenberg and Krapf, who were travelling through Ethiopia and noted in their journal on 11 April 1842 a local belief that when a stick of acacia wood, known as 'the staff of Moses', was swung in front of a woman in labour, her delivery was the faster and easier for it.

The prolonged series of 'plagues' was therefore quite enough to establish Moses in popular legend and consciousness as a superior magician and repository of secret knowledge. In the first century AD, for example, we find the Roman encyclopedist Pliny the Elder telling his readers that one branch of magic was derived from Moses and other Jewish practitioners, 'many thousands of years after Zoroaster' (*Naturalis Historia* 30.11); and magical literature of the first few Christian centuries is full of titles attributed to him – 'The Diadem of Moses' (containing spells for love and invisibility), 'The Eighth Book of Moses', 'The Key of Moses', 'The Archangelic Teaching of Moses', 'The Tenth Secret Book of Moses', 'The Secret Moon Book of Moses' – while his name also appears as a Name of Power on amulets and a number of phylacteries.

Equally important in the tradition of Jewish prototype magicians was King Solomon, for Hebrew, Greek and Arabic traditions associate him with the power to summon and control demons. An apocryphal psalm belonging to the Qumran texts makes him an exorcist, able to invoke and then dismiss all manner of spirits who are causing harm to his people, while the Hellenistic *Testament of Solomon* describes him putting a powerful demon to work on cutting stones for the building of the Temple.

> I, Solomon, rose from my throne and saw the demon bristling with fear and shuddering and quaking. I said to him, 'Who are you? What is your

name?' [This, as we have seen, is a crucial piece of information for the magician because once he knows the spirit's name, he can control him.]
The demon said, 'I am known as Ornias'.
I said, 'Tell me in which part of the zodiac you exist'.
The demon answered and said, 'In Aquarius. I throttle those who are born under Aquarius and have invoked the Virgin of the zodiac because they lust after women. I also appear in dreams and change myself into three different shapes. Sometimes [I am] like a man who lusts after the bodies of little boys who, like women, do not have a beard, and when I have sexual intercourse with them, they suffer a lot of pain. Sometimes I become a winged creature in the heavenly places. Sometimes I display the appearance of a lion. While I am an offspring of an archangel, the Power of God, I am rendered of no effect by the Archangel Uriel.' When I, Solomon, heard the name of the archangel, I uttered a loud prayer and extolled the God of Heaven and Earth. Then I marked [the demon] with a seal-ring and assigned him to the work of cutting stones for the Temple. (2.1-5)

Solomon's ring with its seal was famous not only in Greek but also in Jewish tradition. One version tells us that, unable to use iron tools in the building of the Temple, Solomon sought the advice of rabbis who told him to find the *shamir* – a fabulous worm which could bore through any kind of stone – by binding together a male and female demon and forcing them to tell him where it was. This he did and was told that the great demon Asmodeus had that information. Apparently, each day Asmodeus used to drink water from a private well dug in a mountainside. So Solomon sent thither Benaiah son of Jehoiada with a chain and a ring, both engraved with the Tetragrammaton, some wool and some bottles of wine. Benaiah rained the water from Asmodeus' pit, and dug another which he filled with wine; when Asmodeus uncovered this pit, he drank the wine and fell asleep. Benaiah was thus able to chain the demon, who could not escape on account of the Tetragrammaton engraved on it, and in this state, with much difficulty because of Asmodeus's attempts to trick and confuse him, brought the demon to Jerusalem and King

Solomon. Told that Solomon wanted the *shamir*, Asmodeus tried to temporise and caused Benaiah to be sent yet again on a complex mission. This time, too, he was successful, and Solomon kept Asmodeus with him, in chains, until the Temple was complete. But once that was done, Solomon's caution slipped and he asked Asmodeus about his power over human beings. Asmodeus offered to demonstrate it if Solomon would remove the chain and give him the ring – which Solomon unwisely did. Immediately, Asmodeus swallowed the ring, spread his wings and hurled Solomon a great distance through the air. It took him a long time to get back to Jerusalem, and when he first arrived the Sanhedrin thought they were dealing with a madman. But eventually they were convinced of his true identity and gave him back the chain and ring – it is not explained how they got hold of them – thus restoring him to his former power. When Asmodeus saw him once more in possession of the chain and ring, he was overcome by fear and fled. (*Babylonian Talmud: Gittin* 68a-b).

The ring and its seal were thus an important source of Solomon's power, and they could be reproduced with equally potent effect, as when Eleazar exorcised a malignant demon by holding under the nose of the man it was possessing a ring under whose seal was lodged a certain root, as recommended by Solomon. The man sniffed it and the root drew out the demon through his nostrils, whereupon the man collapsed and Eleazar commanded the demon never to return, at the same time mentioning Solomon by name and repeating incantations which Solomon had composed (Josephus: *Antiquitates* 8.46-7).

Control of and command over demons was one of the aims and marks of a ritual magician, and according to this Solomon was a paradigm *par excellence*, more imitable than Moses. The Koran, too, notes this command of his and notes further his control of the winds (21.81-2; 34.12), an important glance at his fabled wisdom, for possession of the ring which had been given to him by an archangel enabled him to learn the secrets of Heaven and thus understand God's creation in all its diversity.

[God] himself gave me an accurate knowledge of those things which exist, so that I might know how the world has been put together, and the powers of the [four] elements; the beginning, the completion, and the intervening period of the seasons, the different transformations which take place as they reoccur, and the upheavals of the seasons; the annual cycle and the ways in which the stars are arranged; the distinctive characteristics of living creatures and the bad moods and tempers of animals, the force of the winds, the thoughts and purposes of human beings, the different kinds of divining-rods (virgultae), and the powers of roots. I acquired knowledge of whatever has been concealed and whatever appears without warning,[2] because Wisdom, the craftsman who has made everything, taught me.

(Vulgate: *Liber Sapientiae* 7.17-21)

As Josephus said, Solomon surpassed the ancients in wisdom, even the Egyptians who were said to be cleverer and wiser than any other human beings. Thus, Solomon provided yet another key feature of the ritual magician, an extensive knowledge of the hidden workings and laws of nature.

This knowledge of his, needless to say, was written down in a large number of books bearing his name as author or originator, much after the fashion of Moses. They form a remarkably diverse collection. Late in the sixteenth century, for example, a Jewish physician, David de Pomi, noted that a volume by King Solomon dealing with the secret properties of herbs had been prohibited by the rabbis because of the extraordinary information the King imparted therein.[3] But much more typical were books of magic dating from a much earlier period. Thus, we have the fourth-century AD *Hygromanteia*, supposedly written by Solomon for his son Rehoboam, which contains practical instructions on how to make various magical implements, how to summon spirits, two techniques of divination, a list of the angels and demons presiding over every hour of every day, prayers to be addressed to the planets and the symbols and plants belonging to the planets. It is thus a slightly curious mishmash of practical, astrological and symbolical information pertaining to the practice of ritual magic, and as such is fairly representative of its type.

It is worthwhile our looking briefly at two Mediaeval examples whose influence extended far beyond their own time, since the one, *Clavicula Salomonis*, was used as source material by a nineteenth-century magical society, the Hermetic Order of the Golden Dawn, while the other, the *Lemegeton*, throws light on certain magical activities of the sixteenth-century English *magus*, John Dee.

The *Clavicula Salomonis*, 'The Key of Solomon', (although the title could also be translated as 'The Rod' or 'Wand of Solomon'), is divided into two parts. The first is a curious mixture of practical instruction for the ritual magician and banal ceremonies aimed at enabling him to find stolen objects, make himself invisible and so forth. It begins by detailing for him the relationship between hours and days and planets, and the necessary rigorous preparation he and his pupils or assistants will need to undergo before commencing any ritual work – nine days of sexual abstinence, plain food and serious conversation, a ritual bath on the seventh day accompanied by prayer, wearing a clean linen garment and then three days of fasting and prayer, before they all retire to the place where the rite is to be performed. There they bathe again, recite a confession of their sins which the magician, after the manner of a priest, absolves – although one should bear in mind that, given the widespread involvement of the clergy in ritual magic, it is quite possible the magician actually might be a priest – and then, each person carrying one of the magical impedimenta to be used in the ceremony, they go to the assigned place and prepare to consecrate a magic circle.

Instructions for such a consecration follow, along with prayers and a number of invocations to the proper spirits and angels, each prayer more potent than the last. At this point, the spirits should appear and the magician is told he will see extraordinary things relating to all branches of knowledge and everything which may be happening in the world. Finally, the book tells him how to give the spirits licence to depart. This is most important. Unless he is sure the entities he has evoked have actually gone back to their own appropriate sphere or lane, he risks leaving them trapped in an environment to which they do not properly belong, and this entrapment will only confuse or anger them. This, it has been suggested, accounts for the disturbing and highly unpleasant happenings at Boleskine, Aleister Crowley's Highland retreat on the shores of Loch Lomond. His evocation of spirits there was successful, but he failed to control those which he raised and, on at least one occasion, left Boleskine with a ritual uncompleted, thereby abandoning spirits he had not ritually dismissed with dangerous consequences for the house and the neighbouring area.

The remaining chapters of Part I contain details for the construction of pentacles, the precise time at which they should be drawn, the different colours of inks for the pen, how to make garters out of stag-skin, and the words and characters to be written on them, how to make a carpet, (an unusual requirement).[4] Interspersed with the chapters in Part I, however, are others dealing with what can only be called magical trivia: operations for finding stolen objects, making oneself invisible, stopping a hunter from killing game, filching treasure from the spirits who are guarding it, seeking favour and love, and performing what we should call 'conjuring tricks', *praestigia* intended to make objects disappear before the eyes of an audience. This mixture of seriousness and frivolity we have noted before in connection with Marlowe's Faust, and Benvenuto Cellini; and indeed there does appear to be something distasteful at best, blasphemous at worst, about the magician's assumption of a semi-sacerdotal role, rigorous physical and spiritual preparation, and his use of prayer addressed directly to the Creator along with his invocation of Names and Signs of Power, with the declared end and intent merely to uncover a theft or obtain someone's love. E.M. Butler expressed this unease in forcible, downright terms:

> The discrepancy between the lofty tones of the prayers and conjurations and the puerility of the 'secrets'; the inconsistency, to put it mildly, between the comminatory sermon on the misuse of the pentacles and the actual use recommended show a divided mind on the part of the author or compiler of the *Key of Solomon*... The self-interest skulking in the very heart of magic, violently suppressed throughout the course of the rite of conjuration, shows itself in all its pettiness, ruthlessness

and abject lust for power in the ignominious 'secrets'... Perhaps in no other magical manual is the tragic dualism between the aspirations and achievements of magic, between the religious convictions and its secular temptations more vividly illustrated than here.

(*Ritual Magic*, 62)

It is a case worth making and has much to recommend it in those instances such as Marlowe's Faust where a moral point is being driven home to the audience. But in the case of the *Clavicula*, I think Butler has overlooked one important point. It exists, not in one but in several manuscripts – as, indeed, do other works of a similar kind – and these vary considerably in their versions, as one might expect. Chapters which appear in one manuscript do not appear in another, and so it is impossible in most cases to argue that the gallimaufry one is reading represents the uncontaminated, unrevised and original intention of the first author; and one's suspicion that oddities have been added here and there is strengthened by the appearance of alternative workings to some of the *Clavicula*'s instructions. In the chapter on how to recover stolen goods, for example, one manuscript adds a prescription for finding a thief by suspending a sieve over water, spinning the sieve one way with one hand and stirring the water to stop its movement, at which time the face of the thief will become visible in the water. This, and a further working with a sieve, are very common examples of practical 'folk' magic and have nothing to do with the kind of ritual operation with which the *Clavicula* is principally concerned. There is a similar kind of addition to the chapter on invisibility, and the method for preventing a hunter from killing game is entirely without ritual dependence in the sense we have been using the word in this study.

The *Lemegeton*, often called 'The Lesser Key of Solomon', is divided into five parts. The first gives a list of spirits, their status, appearance and particular powers and abilities – Bael makes one invisible, Agares causes earthquakes, Vassago foretells the future and uncovers lost or hidden objects, and so forth. The range of things these spirits can do or in which they can instruct the magician is very wide but entirely practical, and represents a kind of wish-list of someone who would like to be able to alter the natural course of events with a wave of the hand. The spirits, we are told, teach the liberal arts, philosophy, astrology and the secret powers of plants. They can cure disease, change people's shapes, procure love – one even makes men fall in love with men and women with women – reconcile enemies, cause battles, transport people over great distances, foretell the future, make people invisible, build and destroy houses and towns, create disasters at sea, uncover theft and, in a manner reminiscent of Prospero in Shakespeare's *The Tempest*, cause music to be heard in the air, although the source of it is unseen. Several aspects of this list – transvection, divination, curing the sick, working magic for good as well as ill – are familiar from the accusations of witchcraft brought against large numbers of men and women during the sixteenth and seventeenth centuries in particular, and it is worth remembering that the details of these indictments were not pulled out of thin air or necessarily induced by the pain of torture or the pressure of bullying. This wish-list of abilities was common currency among the learned as well as the unlearned, and had been so for a long time. What all the desired abilities have in common, as prosecutors of every kind of magician were quick to point out, is the mediating assistance of spirits, and it is their participation in the magical process which made the process itself undesirable and illicit.

The *Lemegeton* gives the names of seventy-two spirits altogether, a significant number because it is the equivalent of the *Schemhamphoras*, the seventy-two names of God Kabbalistically derived from certain verses in Exodus 14. Instructions are given relating to the form of Solomon's ring, a triangle intended to restrict the movements of the evoked spirit – we may recall that Aleister Crowley and Victor Neuberg constructed such a triangle beyond their protective circle during their ritual in the Algerian desert – and to the construction of restraining and protecting lamens and a circle, and finally a series of conjurations to evoke the spirit.

All this belongs, significantly, to a part of the book subtitled 'Goetia' which is, in effect, demonic magic. The second part, 'Theurgia-Goeta' should, therefore, be a mixture of ritual magic intended to remove the magician, whether in body or spirit or both, from this physical plane of existence to one which is purely spiritual or even divine, and ally this with demonic magic. In fact, it consists of the names of spirits ruling the principal and intermediate points of the compass, along with their signatures. Now, the first part also includes the sigils of spirits and these, bizarre and indeed crude as they may appear to modern Western eyes, are essential to the working of this type of magic. The difficulties attendant upon drawing non-material beings into manifestation on the physical plane which is not naturally theirs are immense, and these signatures provide not only a recognisable point of contact for the spirits to home in upon, but also a guarantee to the human operator that the spirit he has conjured is the one he intended to evoke, since the spirit will have been drawn by its own signature and not by that of someone else.

The third part is called 'The Pauline Art' which, once again, gives lists of angels and the seals which are to accompany their invocation. The seals are different from their signatures, in as much as they show the planetary signs appropriately grouped for the day and hour of working, and the character belonging to the spirit who is (astrologically speaking) in the ascendant at that time. A special incense, too, is to be compounded of pepperwort, nutmeg, lignum aloes, saffron, cinnamon, myrtle and mastic, these being the spices and herbs attributed to the seven planets. The purpose of this part of the *Lemegeton* is to instruct the magician in the necessary preparations and invocations for scrying in a crystal, and he is promised strange sights therein, including that of his personal spirit. This is a magical exercise we shall discuss in greater detail in connection with John Dee, who left detailed accounts of his contacts with spirit-worlds via consecrated crystals.

Finally comes the fourth part, 'The Art and Magic of Almadel'. This provides instructions for the making and use of a magical table-top made from pure wax, coloured according to the direction of the magical focus – east (white), south (red), west (green), and north (black mixed with green). The wax is to have three squares inscribed upon it, one inside the other. The outer square has holes in each corner to carry candles and their holders; under the middle square are placed four legs to support the whole, while the central square is intended to carry a golden seal during the ritual operation. The two outer squares are inscribed with divine names and pentacles, and the third with a hexagram, in the centre of which is a triangle bearing three names of God. Below the table is sufficient clearance for a thurible which will allow incense fumes to rise directly underneath this inmost square. A golden triangle inscribed with the same divine names as those of the triangle in the centre of the hexagram constitutes the seal. Specific angels are to be evoked. They will appear on top of the central seal, wearing robes of the appropriate colour – white, red, green, black-green – and the magician is instructed to wear a robe of the correct colour, too. The instructions provide suitable invocations, tell the magician what he should expect to see when the spirits appear, and offer advice about what he should not as well as what he should do. Again, this part of the *Lemegeton* has a bearing upon John Dee's conversations with spirits, since he too received detailed instructions on how to make and engrave the magical table which was to support his scrying stone.

If Zoroaster represents the Persian strand of this particular magical tradition, and Moses and Solomon the Jewish, the Egyptian is perhaps best represented by the Egyptian god Thoth, known by his Hellenised name of Hermes and called 'three times great' (*trismegistos*) in a translation of an Egyptian form often applied to him. (Egyptian has no superlative, so the adjective simply means 'very' or 'exceedingly great'). Thoth was credited with the invention of writing and acted as a guide to the souls of the dead – hence his later association with Hermes who fulfilled the same function in Greek religion. Between the third and fifth centuries AD, Graeco-Roman intellectuals were fascinated by mystical religions, astrology and magic, and these they wove into systems of thought and theurgical practices intended to enable the individual to reach a more intense personal experience of God and a greater understanding of the created universe. This syncretism found powerful expression in a corpus of Greek texts known as the *Hermetica* or *Corpus Hermeticum* which, as the title suggests, was fathered upon

Thoth-Hermes in Hellenistic Egypt, and though far fewer than the 20,000 or 36,555 books attributed to him by Seleucus and Manetho,[5] these documents (some of them fragmentary) were considered to be the product of a figure more significant by far than Moses or Solomon, Pythagoras or Plato, and hence the record of a theology more ancient than any other in existence. In consequence, their influence on later occult speculation was immense. The *Corpus* was known to the Arabs, who added to its literature, and to Byzantium wherein it generated further monographs and commentaries; but the West had to wait until 1462, when Cosimo de Medici commissioned Marsilio Ficino to translate into Latin a copy of the Greek text he had just acquired for his manuscript collection.

One can see the relationship between one of these texts, the *Poimandres*, and those others describing methods of projecting the spirit from the body, by noting its introduction:

> One day, when I had been concentrating on the things which exist and my concentration had soared upwards and my bodily senses had been suspended, as happens when someone falls asleep after eating too much or physically working too hard, I had the impression that a being of infinite size was calling me by name and saying to me, 'What do you want to hear and see? What do you want to learn and know, in as far as you can understand?'

This, of course, may have been an experience brought on by meditative rather than magical techniques; but the 'suspension' of bodily senses is expressed by a Greek verb (*katekhein*) meaning 'to hold in a firm grip, arrest, take possession of', frequently used in magical contexts where a magician wants to bind and thus assume complete control over spirits and *daimones*, and so it is possible that the Hermetic narrator's trance has been induced in this way. Certainly there is enough apparent magic elsewhere in the *Corpus* and other 'Hermetic' writings fathered upon Trismegistos for such a reading to be valid. The dialogue called *Asclepius*, part of the authentic *Corpus*, for example, discusses among other things statues which can be filled with life and made to work and predict the future, a reference to Egyptian cult statues and those *ushabti* figures buried with the dead to serve and tend their *ka* in the after-life, a theurgic practice which St Augustine deplores at length in his *De civitate Dei*, and one which was clearly still well-established in North Africa during the third and fourth centuries. Divinities, he tells us, were invited to occupy statues of themselves as though they were the statues' souls, but then were imprisoned inside them, like captives chained in a cell.

It was a magico-religious tradition which lasted well beyond antiquity. In the *Picatrix*, originally an Arabic text of the tenth century but which was translated into Latin during the thirteenth, this notion has been preserved and expanded:

> [Certain magicians] maintain that Hermes... was the person who built a city east of Egypt, which was twelve miles long and in which he constructed a fortification with four gates in its four quarters. On the eastern gate he placed the figure of an eagle; on the western gate, the figure of a bull; on the southern gate, that of a lion; and on the northern he built the figure of a dog. He made disembodied spirits (*spirituales spiritus*) enter them, and these would speak by projecting voices[6]... Around the perimeter of the city he arranged various images of all kinds, and by the power [inherent in them] the people who lived there were rendered virtuous and shone [free] from ugly filth and distressing diseases.
>
> (Book 4, chapter 3)

It was the kind of thing, we may remember, that Simon Magus was accused of doing by Clement of Rome, and it will be considered at greater length when we come to discuss automata and the various reactions to them; and it can also be seen in the plethora of anecdotes from the Middle Ages and early modern period, telling us how magicians imprisoned demons in rings and bottles in order to have their services on call. The Jesuit Martín del Río tells us of one such example:

> A certain lawyer from Bordeaux kept a servant-spirit in a glass bottle. When he died, his heirs did not want to keep the bottle but did not

dare break it, either. So they came to the Jesuit college to ask advice. The Fathers told them to bring them the bottle and they would smash it on the ground in their presence. The heirs brought the bottle, but begged the Fathers not to break it while they were still there because they were afraid of seeing something frightful. So the heirs withdrew and the Fathers hurled the bottle as hard as they could into an oven which happened to be lit at the time. They heard nothing more than a brief hiss as the two elements met.

(*Disquisitiones Magicae* Book 4, chapter 2, question 6, section 4)

Between them, therefore, Zoroaster, Moses, Solomon and Hermes Trismegistos provided a set of paradigms for the ritual magician and (via the books foisted upon their names over the centuries) a detailed body of knowledge both practical and theoretical to which he could turn and which in some measure he ought to have mastered before embarking on his perilous enterprises. These, however, also presented the magician with a continuous series of moral choices. On the positive side, they encouraged him to investigate the mysterious laws and sympathetic relations governing the created universe and so gain a closer, more intimate knowledge of the mind of God. Mastery of these laws and understanding of these sympathies would enable him to work wonders beyond the natural, unaided abilities of human beings such as curing the seriously ill or maimed, or raising the dead to life – all of which had precedents not only in the life of Jesus but in those of the Apostles and other major saints, and so were guaranteed moral respectability. Moreover, techniques for passing directly into the presence of God or into heavenly converse with angels conferred a personal blessing and stimulus to virtuous life and conduct. One thinks, for example, of the *Sworn Book* of Honorius of Thebes, dating from the first half of the thirteenth century, which seeks (in spite of its overt hostility towards the Church) to provide its readers with a ritual whereby he or she may gain the beatific vision and thus a share in God's omniscience. It is not easily done. Twenty-eight days of rigorous preparation are required, during which the operator must go to confession, hear Mass and communicate, fast, pray, and finally, on the day of the ritual itself, prepare a bed of hay surrounded by a magic circle, wear black clothing, (an unusual requirement), and after prayers and exhortations, retire to sleep during which the vision of God will come.

On the negative side, however, lay the temptation to excessive curiosity and overstepping of the bounds acceptable to God, by which investigation of the workings of the universe became blasphemous and acquisition of hitherto hidden or occult knowledge merely fed the magician's vanity and made him arrogant. Such a lapse into pride, notorious as the worst of the seven deadly sins, would encourage him to work wonders for their own sake in order to show off his newly acquired skills and so dazzle his audience; and this in turn opened the road to fraud for those who wished to pretend their knowledge and abilities were far greater than they were. What is more, the magician who had given way to this sinister use of magic would inevitably lay himself open to invasion by evil spirits whose promises of co-operation might well prove irresistible, with fatal consequences for their human host in this world and the next.

It is interesting, therefore, to see how the light and the dark sides of ritual magic appear in the history and the fictional literature of the Middle Ages and the Renaissance. The two most obvious examples of men who straddled both are Merlin and the original of Marlowe's and Goethe's Faust. Merlin was a figure with possible roots in historical reality. One of the works which sets the pattern of his later reputation is *Historia Regum Britanniae* (1136) by Geoffrey of Monmouth, who depicts him as the offspring of a human mother and a demon–incubus. According to this version, Merlin had the gift of accurate prophecy, could see things hidden beneath the earth, was able to raise Stonehenge by the art of magic and change people's appearance. Geoffrey's *History* proved hugely popular and its various themes were repeated, translated and developed by other writers, notably, of course, by Sir Thomas Malory in his *Morte d'Arthur*, where he makes magical statues for King Arthur, a magical sword for Galahad and accurately prophesies the future. The wildest imaginative exercise perhaps belongs to the thirteenth-century Burgundian poet, Robert de Boron, who produced an account of Merlin which allows us to see parallels between him and both Christ and Anti-Christ – Merlin was born of a demon and a virgin, Anti-Christ also of a demon and a virgin, Christ of God and the Virgin Mary; Merlin was a wonder-worker, so was Anti-Christ, and Christ worked miracles – and so forth; and once printing enabled literature to spread at a more affordable rate than manuscript, there was no stopping the flood of fictional portraits, all repeating in one guise and another the outlines of Geoffrey's original, ending with T.H. White's novel, *The Sword in the Stone* (1938) and Merlin's metamorphosis into Gandalf in Tolkien's *Lord of the Rings*. The accretion of legend, however, as in the later case of Faust, concealed a touch of reality. For, according to a suggestion made by Nikolai Tolstoy, Merlin had begun as a druid living in Lowland Scotland at the end of the sixth century AD, and his membership of a pagan priesthood easily gave rise to the notion that he was a magician and a prophet, which is how later English writers in particular tend to portray him.

Faust, likewise, began as a real individual. A letter from Abbot Johann Trithemius to Johannes Virdung, dated 20 August 1507, describes someone known to both of them, a George Sabellicus, 'Faust the Younger', who was travelling round some of the German cities boasting that he was 'the fount from which necromancers flow, an astrologer, a second *magus*', (the first, presumably, being Simon), 'someone who practised divination successfully from the palm of the hand, earth, fire, and water'. In Gelnhausen he claimed extensive, indeed complete, knowledge of Plato and Aristotle; in Würzburg, that he could replicate Christ's miracles as often as he might be asked to do so; and in Kreuznach, that he was the most learned man in alchemy who had ever lived. Further records from the next two decades depict him as a palmist, astrologer, necromancer and sodomite – this last a reference to an accusation of pederasty from 1507 which may or may not have been true. Martin Luther knew of him and, significantly in view of Faust's later legend, seems to have associated him with the Devil since, upon hearing his name, he said, 'The Devil does not cause magicians to work against me'. Faust is here called Schwartzkünstler, 'black artiste', that is to say, someone who fabricates within the dark side of magic, a designation of a piece with all the reports made of him. The hostility, however, is to be expected since he appears to have been a great braggart, (rather like Paracelsus who likewise irritated his contemporaries exceedingly), and most of the evidence mentioning him comes from Protestant sources whose antipathy to magic was likely to have been coloured by anti-Catholic propaganda, regardless of their individual and personal convictions on the subject.

It is also worth observing that the stories about him became more and more elaborate as time went on, and that it is from these that Faust's reputation as an important *magus* tends to be derived. At the beginning of the sixteenth century, notices of him paint the picture of a professional huckster-magician specialising in divination and the casting of horoscopes. But by 1548 (while he was still alive) he has turned into a magician with demons at his command, whom he employs to set a monastery in turmoil after he has been refused a drink of wine; he has tried to fly, like Simon Magus, and like him has fallen painfully to earth, an incident supposedly taking place in Venice where 'he wanted to provide a public spectacle'. He was said to have lectured in the University of Erfurt and to have summoned before his students the ghosts of various famous Greeks such as Hector, Odysseus, Agamemnon and finally the one-eyed giant Polyphemus whose appearance was so frightening that the students' hair stood on end. Faust, says the account, had great difficulty in getting this spirit to go away, (a reminder of the ever-present dangers of evocation). This account from Zacharias Hogel's *Chronical* ends with Faust confessing to a Franciscan friar who wanted to save his soul that he had pledged himself absolutely to the Devil by means of a bond written in his own blood, and that in consequence he was unable to seek forgiveness of God for the acts of magic he had been performing with Satan's aid. He died, according to another Protestant source, Johann Wier, in his bed in a town in the Duchy of Württemberg, 'his face turned round as far as it would go, and there is a report that in the middle of the night before this happened, the house was shaken repeatedly'.

Stories such as these proved irresistible. From at least 1570 onwards they were collected and published, frequently with moralising commentaries warning against pride, ambition, unsuitable attempts to go beyond the bounds of allowable knowledge, the dangers attendant upon dealing with evil spirits, and so forth. From Germany the legend quickly spread, with translations of the *Spies Faustbuch* (1587) appearing in Dutch, French and English before the end of the century, and it was this English version which served as the source for Marlowe's play. Performances, either of Marlowe's version or an adaptation of it, toured parts of Western Europe throughout the seventeenth century thus ensuring the perpetuation of the most extravagant account. The eighteenth century added to these performances the full range of mechanical stage-tricks at its command – the programme for October 1767 in Frankfurt promises the appearance of monsters, spirits and furies at Faust's conjuration, the destruction of Jerusalem, 'surely a fine spectacle' and transformation scenes from cemetery to pleasure garden and from pleasure garden to Hell, not to mention a ballet of furies and a grand fireworks display as Mephistophilis draws Faust into the jaws of Hell. Thus, a real historical person regarded locally as a braggart and a fraud is transmuted into a Gothic horror figure, and the serious dangers of an art which seeks to penetrate and then bridge quite different planes of existence in ways which, in an instant, could lose their legitimacy and turn into a fatal challenge to God, are minimised and allowed to dwindle into theatrical effects.

Likewise, Shakespeare's Prospero operates as a ritual magician in his world-upon-the-stage, and as the stimulus for mechanical stage-illusions in the theatre. *The Tempest* begins, for example, with a shipwreck and is followed by Prospero's first appearance, clad in his magic garment, when he admits he is responsible for both the wreck and the storm which caused it. He claims, in fact, an almost complete control over nature, one he describes later in the play:

> I have bedimm'd
> The noontide sun, call'd forth the mutinous winds,
> And 'twixt the green sea and the azur'd vault

81

Set roaring war: to the dread rattling thunder
Have I give fire, and rifted Jove's stout oak
With his own bolt; the strong bas'd promontory
Have I made shake, and by the spurs pluck'd up
The pine and cedar; graves at my command
Have wak'd their sleepers, op'd, and let 'em forth
By my so potent art. (5.i.41-50)

We find similar opportunities in Calderón's play *El Mágico Prodigioso* (1637). Cipriano, the main character, is a young pagan scholar who meets the Devil disguised as a traveller and defeats him in philosophical argument. The Devil vows revenge and causes Cipriano to fall in love with a virgin, Justina, who rejects him as a lover, whereupon Cipriano exclaims that he would give his soul to the Devil in order to possess Justina, an offer the Devil immediately accepts. Returning to Cipriano in the guise of a shipwrecked traveller, he promises to teach him magic in return for shelter and, to demonstrate his power, causes a mountain to disappear and raises a vision of the sleeping Justina. He also creates the sight of a treasure-ship arriving safely in port despite a massive storm, and while it would be unwise to discount entirely the purely commercial aspect of these plays, we should bear in mind that one of the principal functions of the stage-magician was to provide opportunities for this kind of technical display. Indeed, Barbara Traister has pointed out that the magician as 'creator and director of spectacle, pageant, and masque' was a standard figure on the London stage for several years preceding the first performance of *The Tempest*.[8]

Nevertheless, their theatre-within-a-theatre also represents a real concern which had exercised inquirers for some considerable time. Given that several modes of being co-existed, that they frequently, if only temporarily, penetrated each other's plane and that the spiritual forms were much more varied than the human, more knowledgeable and more powerful, how can one be sure that a visual, audial or even tactile experience is real as opposed to illusory? As Marsilio Ficino had pointed out late in the fifteenth century,[9] there exists a fifth element beyond those of earth, air, fire and water, an extremely subtle spirit which provides the medium whereby cosmic influences may be drawn down and imprinted upon the human imagination – the internal faculty for creating images which are real in as much as they are echoes of a cosmic reality, but can be false in as far as they may be created especially to deceive, as when Mephistophilis raises the 'ghost' of Helen of Troy for Faustus.

But how closely do these stage-magicians actually mirror reality? How did the genuine ritual magician of the period behave, and was his aim merely wonder-working or did he conform more closely to the patterns set by the Persian-Jewish-Hermetic prototypes we were discussing earlier? He needed to be learned, of course, and either be rich himself or have ready access to funds, because the paraphernalia of ritual magic were expensive. He also needed time to practise his art. The lengthy preparation frequently required for a single ceremony meant that he could not have been tied to the exigencies of heavy labour or craftsmanship; and the energy needed for ritual magic of the complexity we are discussing was surely not in the gift of the poor. Frequently, therefore, we find that the ritual magician belonged to the aristocracy. Enrique de Aragón, Marqués de Villena (1384-1434) is an obvious example. Famous in his own day as a student of astrology and magic – he was the author of an unfinished treatise on the evil eye, *Libro del aojamiento ó fascinologia* (1411) – and for his extensive library which included fifty 'libros de malas artes' burned by Bishop Lope de Barrientos after Villena's death, the Marqués quickly became a figure highly praised for his immense learning in occult subjects in Spanish literature, and his legendary status, like that of Faustus, increased vastly the further the actual man receded into history. In his *Visita de los Chistes* (1622), the poet and novelist Quevedo tells us the story of how, in a dream, he came upon a bottle in which small pieces of flesh were boiling and dancing. Slowly they joined themselves together until they completed a man who then identified himself as Villena, explaining that he had had himself dismembered and put into a bottle in order to achieve immortality. It is an old story told and re-told of Vergil, Faust, Roger Bacon, Paracelsus and Cornelius Agrippa, and probably has its origin in a Greek tale about Medea who cut up an old ram, threw the pieces into a cauldron, and magically produced a young lamb from the concoction.

A much more sinister example, however, is Gilles de Rais, Baron de Retz and, after 1429, Marshal of France. He fought alongside Ste Jeanne d'Arc, but in the early 1430s began to run into financial difficulties and sought ways out of these by practising alchemy – an obvious expedient – and necromancy, this last principally as a means of achieving control over spirits, one of the main aims of a ritual magician. He was arrested in 1440 and put on trial both by the Church and by the State, and it was the state which sentenced him to death by hanging for offences including the murder of a large number of children. The ecclesiastical court dealt with the counts of heresy and ritual magic, and several erstwhile colleagues and acquaintances came forward to offer evidence against him. One was Eustache Blanchet, a priest aged about forty who testified to Gilles's daily practice of alchemy. He also said that one day he saw Gilles and another cleric, Francesco Prelati, an experienced student in the occult arts, go into a lower room [in the Castle of Tiffauges] where they and Eustache himself stayed the night. At one point, Eustache heard Gilles say in a low voice, 'Come, Satan!' or 'Come!' in the plural, along with several other words Eustache did not hear properly and could not remember; and not long after these words had been pronounced, a cold wind suddenly blew through the castle, which made Eustache afraid, for it occurred to him that Gilles and Francesco were invoking demons. Conversation about seven weeks later with Jean Méric, castellan of Rocher-sur-Oyon, revealed that common gossip in the region was saying that Gilles

> was killing and having other people kill a large number of children, and was writing a book in their blood with his own hand, and that once the book was finished he would capture any fortress he wanted, and that no one could stand in his way once he had this book which had been written in this manner.[10]

Eustache's evidence was supported and amplified by Etienne Corillaut, alias Poitou, aged about twenty-two, a member of Gilles's household. He testified that at Tiffauges, in the presence of Gilles, Francesco Prelati, Eustache Blanchet, Henriet Griart and himself, a circle was drawn with the point of a sword, to which were added crosses, signs and characters which Etienne thought looked like armorial bearings, perhaps because the circle had been divided into four parts, like a family shield. Etienne, Eustache, and Henriet were carrying a large quantity of incense, a magnetic stone, an earthenware pot, torches, candles, fire and other things he could not now remember, which Gilles and Francesco placed in certain parts of the circle.

> A big fire was lit in the earthenware pot in which there was a lot of charcoal. Then Francesco drew other signs or characters like armorial bearings on the wall of the chamber, at the corner of the door, and lit another fire near these latter signs. Francesco also had the four windows of the chamber opened so as to form a cross.

Then Gilles told Etienne, Eustache, and Henriet to leave the chamber to stop anyone from seeing or hearing what was going on, and telling others about it. Etienne says he did not know what went on in the chamber after that, but was told by Eustache and Henriet that they heard Francesco speaking in a loud voice, (although they did not understand what he was saying), and that they heard a sound like that of a four-footed animal entering the building.

Late the following evening, Gilles ordered him to leave the castle with Francesco. They went to a small meadow about quarter of a mile from Tiffauges, Etienne full of fear because he knew that Francesco was going to invoke a demon, since they were carrying with them the same apparatus as had been used the previous day in the castle chamber. When they arrived in the meadow, Francesco made a circle on the ground with a knife, added crosses and characters, and lit fire in an earthenware pot. He forbade Etienne to make the sign of the cross, and then told him to step with him into the circle. There Francesco made his invocations. Etienne thought he heard the name *Baron*, which Francesco said in a loud voice, and, contrary to what he had been told, he secretly made the sign of the cross. Francesco had already testified to the ecclesiastical tribunal and revealed the precise conjuration he used on these occasions. 'I invoke you, Baron, Satan, Belial, Beelzebub, by the Father and the Son and the Holy Spirit, by the Virgin Mary and all the saints, to appear here before us, to speak to us, and to carry out our will.' The spirit Baron, he said, had appeared on ten or twelve occasions in the form of a handsome young man aged about twenty-five and had brought Gilles various pieces of magical material, including a black powder which caused him to enjoy good fortune as long as he carried it about his person.[11]

Now, even though technically speaking the ritual magic was being performed by the priest, Etienne's participation was an integral part of the whole. The division of labour between the two, however, emphasises yet again the sacerdotal or quasi-sacerdotal nature of the ritual magician. It is not enough merely to dress as a priest. He must behave as one, too, or employ a real priest for the purpose. But sometimes a priest might be employed because the patron, although a priest himself, was too elevated to undertake the work. When Pope Urban VIII felt threatened by the approach of a lunar eclipse, he had a magico-astrological ceremony performed for his benefit in the Lateran Palace. Tommaso Campanella, a Dominican responsible for directing the ritual, describes for the benefit of others what should be done under similar circumstances.

How to avoid the evils threatened by an eclipse. First take every pain to live temperately, according to reason and as closely to God as possible, by dedicating yourself to Him by means of prayer and holy rituals. Secondly, close up your house entirely so that no one else's air may enter therein. Sprinkle the house with rose-flavoured vinegar and waft it with aromatic odours. Make a fire and burn thereon laurel, myrtle, rosemary, cypress, and other aromatic woods. There is nothing more powerful than this for dissipating the poisonous operations of the sky, even if these are administered by the Devil. Thirdly, decorate the house with white silk cloths and branches of fern. Fourthly, burn two lights and five torches to represent the planets, so that their places may be filled on earth at the time they are absent from the sky, just as one sets up a lantern at night to supply the lack of the Sun when he departs at night, so that there may be no lack of light when daylight has been removed. Make representation of the planets from a mixture of aromatic substances, and once you have made copies of the twelve signs of the zodiac (according to the principles of philosophy and not of superstition as the common people believe) you may proceed. Fifthly, have with you friends and associates whose horoscopes have not been subject to the evil of an eclipse. Apotropaic procedure does a lot of good, as does procedure which imitates the desired outcome. The former drives away the event you do not want and the latter invites the event you do want. Sixthly, have people play music belonging to Jupiter and Venus in the room, so that it can break up the evil character of the air; and let symbols of beneficent things exclude the power of maleficent stars. Seventhly, since the symbols of each star are found in stones, plants, colours, odours, music, and movements... provide those which attract the power of beneficent stars and put to flight that of maleficent stars. Liquors distilled under planetary influences should be drunk, as they have a great deal of power. You should do all this for three hours before the start of the eclipse and for three hours after it, until such time as the beneficent stars have arrived at the angles and absorbed their strength.

(*Astrologorum libri VII*, 1630, Book 7, chapter 4, article 1)

Astrological magic of this kind was not an invention of the early modern period, of course. It had been in existence for a very long time. The Roman historian Ammianus Marcellinus tells us about the trial of two such magicians, Patricius and Hilarius, before the Emperor Valens in AD 371-2. According to Hilarius' testimony, they made a small ceremonial table from sticks of laurel, consecrated it with dire and secret incantations – presumably 'secret' here means either that the formulae the magicians used were obscure or recondite, or that they were spoken in a low murmur or whisper – and then they set about making it work. The general aim of the ceremony was to divine some future event. The particular aim of Patricius and Hilarius was to discover who would be next Emperor after Valens. The procedure was as follows:

> The house was cleansed with fragrant smells from Arabia [i.e. incense], and in the middle of it was set up [the table] on top of which was placed a round dish made from various kinds of metal, without any superfluous ornamentation. Round its outer rim were expertly engraved the written forms of the twenty-four letters of the [Greek] alphabet, and these were separated from each other by carefully measured intervals. Then a man clothed in linen robes and wearing slippers made likewise from linen, and a cord wound round his head, and carrying twigs from an auspicious tree, uttered solemn incantations and obtained favourable omens from the divinity who is the source of predictions. Then, with an expert knowledge of the ritual, the priest stood over the metal vessel and held over it, suspended by a fine linen thread, a ring which had been consecrated by secret formulae. This ring swung randomly over the marked intervals, its movements rendered jerky because they stopped for a moment at individual letters, and [so] composed hexameters appropriate to the questions asked of it.
>
> (29.1.30-1)

The biggest difference between this and the ritual performed for Pope Urban is, of course, their intention. With Marcellinus, in spite of the elaborate procedure undertaken in preparation for the climax of the ceremony, we are very close to what is, in effect, a simple act of divinatory magic made complicated by preliminaries which may be regarded as desirable but are not integral to the act of magic itself. In the case of Pope Urban's ritual, the aim is re-alignment of planetary influences so as to form a protective shelter for the Pope against malign astral agencies threatening him in the immediate future. Consequently, the ritual is an integrated whole and each part of it is necessary to achieve the intended goal, a manipulation of the occult forces of nature, along with their preternatural governors or presiding spirits; and it is this rather than the details of the ritual performance which makes Pope Urban's ceremony an act of 'ritual' magic proper, rather than an act of magic with extended ritual attached. Similarly, when the performance is intended to summon spirits, either good or bad, the ritual fulfils a number of essential roles. It is formulated in particular ways so as to attract the attention of individual spirits; it protects the operating magician during the time the non-human and human planes are co-existent and inhabitants of one have penetrated that of the other; and it maintains the spirits' presence in a fashion calculated to preserve human safety while containing the instability inherent in that same presence, so that communication between human and non-human becomes temporarily possible.

The impression of matter-of-factness given by stage performances of *The Tempest, Dr Faustus, A Midsummer Night's Dream* and the like, where spirits and angels and demons and fairies appear in human or near-human shape and converse with the human characters almost as though they were themselves human at slight remove, is extremely misleading. The same impression is given by many accounts of Satan's appearing to people subsequently charged with witchcraft. He comes as a man, talks to them, makes a bargain with them, and then disappears. Were it not for his sudden vanishing from sight, he might almost be a *rentier* or a lawyer. Such accounts or stage performances, however, disguise the true nature of what is being suggested. The immensity of the disruption to natural law involved in having a spirit obtrude, even in appearance, never mind in coherent speech and dialogue, into a plane of existence not its own is properly acknowledged only by exorcists and ritual magicians. Playwrights (and later, writers of other fictional genres) are constrained by the requirements of their craft to present the picture they do, and this in turn, of course, influences the manner in which their audience conceives and reports the appearance, shape and behaviour of spirit beings. It is a question worth pondering how much the meetings with Satan or other evil spirits reported in court proceedings against accused witches may owe to a memory of stage performances either seen personally by the defendant or drawn from second-hand accounts of such performances.[12]

Deliberately summoning spirits, then, is actually a very dangerous business, regardless of the magician's intention in so doing, although curiously enough, ingenuousness may provide a protection as reliable as that of a magic circle. I am thinking here of the experiences of John Dee. Dee (1527-1608/9) is a man sometimes misunderstood. He frequently appears in encyclopedias of witchcraft, for example, even though he was not a witch himself and had nothing to do with witchcraft. He was, rather, a magician after the style of Gilles de Rais in that he provided the intention, the impetus and the facilities for magical ceremonies which aimed to invoke and thereby allow him to enter into converse with spirits, thereby playing an active part in the magical operation. He was also, and most famously in his own day, a scholar and an alchemist. His scholarship ranged over mathematics, cartography, botany and cryptography, and he was also, as one might expect, a competent astrologer. Used for a while by Elizabeth Tudor as an occult consultant, he found, for a while at least, a prestigious niche in the remarkable gathering of occult scholars and practitioners assembled by the Holy Roman Emperor Rudolf II at Prague, before retiring to England, obscurity and poverty. But he is now most famous for his conversations with angels, a long series of encounters, lasting principally from 1581 to 1587, which he recorded in meticulous detail.[13]

His medium of contact was two-fold: a crystal and a scryer. Dee himself had not, or did not develop, the gift of sight, so he employed a number of men who had, the two most talented being Barnabas Saul, whose name is the first to appear in Dee's records of scrying sessions, and Edward Kelly, alias Talbot, who remained his principal scryer and then alchemical partner for the good part of a decade. Dee's *modus operandi* was as follows. In a private room set aside especially for the purpose, Dee uncovered one of the 'shewstones' which provided a focus for the spirits and the stage, so to speak, on which they paraded in answer to his entreaties. One such stone is illustrated in a rough drawing Dee made in his *Mysteriorum Libri V*, the manuscript record of these conversations.[14] Dee would pray and then prepare himself with pen and paper to record the whole proceedings, while his scryer looked into the crystal and spoke aloud what he saw therein and heard the spirits say. The following (modernised) extract from the entry for 22 December 1581 – the earliest of the conversations – will give a notion of what they were like:

> After my fervent prayers made to God, for his merciful comfort and instruction, through the ministry of his holy and might angel, named Anael, (if it were his divine pleasure) I willed the scryer (named Saul) to look into my great crystalline globe, if God had sent his holy angel Anael, or no. And Saul looking into my foresaid stone... for to espy Anael, he saw there one which answered to that name.

A note in the margin sounds a note of caution. Dee calls the apparition 'an illuding intruder', that is to say, a spirit which is playing tricks on him or trying to deceive him. So Dee had it challenged and, sure enough, the intruder disappeared to be replaced by another spirit. This one was very beautiful, clothed in golden yellow, with blazing beams streaming from his head, and eyes like fire. He wrote many Hebrew letters in the stone, but Saul was not able to read them, and so could not convey them to Dee who would have been able to do so. Other sights came and went in the crystal beside the spirit, including a star and a long-headed white dog. Dee then addressed the spirit through Saul. One must bear in mind how laborious these conversations must have been: Dee posed a question, the scryer repeated it to the crystal, the spirit answered the scryer, and the scryer then told Dee what he had been told or shown, and Dee wrote it all down before proceeding to his next question.

This first conversation was conducted in Latin, the language appropriate for learning and for magic:

DEE: In the name of Jesus Christ, who are you?
ANAEL: All power is situated in me.
DEE: Which [power]?
ANAEL: Good and bad.
[Two letters, M and G, appeared in the stone. These either meant nothing to Dee, or for some reason they spurred him to ask further

91

questions, all of which dealt with hidden or buried treasure. This topic, however, irritated the angel, who rebuked him.]

ANAEL: Don't trouble yourself [with that]. These are things of no account.

[Whereupon a large number of dead men's skulls appeared on the left of the angel.]

ANAEL: Where is *your* power?

DEE: Why do you ask about any power I may have?

ANAEL: Why? [Make it known to me.]¹⁵

[Dee then got up, put another crystal ball set in a frame beside the one Saul was using, and asked Anael if any good angel had been assigned to this second 'mirror' (as he puts it).]

ANAEL: Yes.

DEE: Who?

Anael answered by displaying the Hebrew letters for Michael.

DEE: Is that the good angel of whom mention is made in the Scriptures?

ANAEL: It certainly is.

DEE: Can he appear, so that I can see him and engage with him?

ANAEL: Yes.

[Whereupon a character looking rather like a conjoined J, A, and T appeared in one of the crystals.]

DEE: What do you wish to signify by this?

ANAEL: It is the character of the other angel.

DEE: Why are you showing me this, and why now?

ANAEL: For an important reason.

The record now changes to English. Anael tells Dee to finish for the time being and to resume in the new year, and after a few final instructions from the spirit, Dee says in Latin, 'Glory be to the Father, and to the Son, and to the Holy Spirit: as it was in the beginning, is now, and ever shall be, world without end, Amen'; and so the session (or 'action', as Dee calls it) comes to an end. Dee notes further that he has not recorded everything which took place on this occasion – thereby explaining the odd disjunction here and there – 'but these may suffice'.

About two weeks later, on 10 March 1582, Dee had his first angel conversation via a new scryer, Edward Kelly, who was to remain his principal and most talented medium till the end. During this action he received initial instruction on how to make a table to support a large wax seal (*Sigillum Dei*, 'the seal of God') elaborately engraved, on top of which the shewstone would be placed. The table was about four feet square, constructed from 'sweet' wood, its top painted with angelic names, a pentagram and other emblems, in blue, red, and gold. The four legs of the table rested upon wax seals which in turn stood upon a large piece of red silk, while a red silk hanging with tassels at its corners was draped over the top, covering not only the surface of the table but also the *Sigillum Dei* placed at its centre. This big wax disk, known also as *Emeth* (Hebrew for 'truth'), with its engraved heptagon, pentagram, divine and angelic names, thus formed a hidden focal point for the spirits, a beacon, as it were, directing them into the shewstone. The use of a similar table we have seen already in the divinatory rite described by Ammianus Marcellinus, and the fourth part of the *Lemegeton*, it may be remembered, provided detailed instructions for the inscription and colouring of a large wax table-top to be used in ceremonies intended to evoke particular spirits. So Dee was not being asked to do anything especially unusual, in magical terms.

Likewise, on 14 March, the Archangel Michael described a ring which Dee was to wear during his spirit conversations.

> MICHAEL: I will reveal thee this ring which was never revealed since the death of Solomon... Lo, this it is. This is it, wherewith all miracles and divine works and wonders were wrought by Solomon...
>
> DEE: Then he laid the ring down upon the table and said, Note. It showed to be a ring of gold with a seal graved in it, and had a round thing in the middle of the seal, and a thing like a V through the top of the circle, and an L in the bottom, and a bar clean through it. And it had these four letters in it, PELE.

Solomon's ring, as we have seen, was a famous conductor of power and must be regarded here as part of the standard personal equipment

of a ritual magician. Dee may have needed intermediaries for his converse with the spirits, but it is clearly he and not the scryer who is
being regarded as the principal agent of the operation. Dee was also
told to make a *lamen*, a small magical breastplate made from gold, tri-
angular in shape (thereby referring to the Trinity), and inscribed with
various sigils. Dee associated this with the Urim and Thummim worn
by ancient Jewish priests – an interesting identification of his role as
magus with that of a priest which, as we have also seen before, seems
to have been concomitant with the psychology of the magical practitioner. Moreover, he was supposed to make a special rod or staff –
the final distinguishing instrument of a magician – but although he
complied with every instruction the various spirits gave him, he does
not seem to have placed any great emphasis on these personal impedimenta. Perhaps once they were made, he simply wore them or carried them at certain points in his opening and closing ceremonies, and
for the rest concentrated on recording the immense cascade of occult
information his scryer had to cope with every session.

The spirits which appeared in the shewstones hardly conform to
the traditional types evoked by other magicians. Apart from the
archangels Michael and Uriel, there were hundreds who made only a
brief appearance before taking their leave.

> There stood up another, and opened his bosom, and showed on his
> breast bare (being like silver) a small 'h', and he pointed to it, and over
> it was the number of 22…Then came one in with a garment all bloody.
> He was like a child. He had a ball in his hand of perfume which smoked:
> and he hath upon his forehead a little 'h'…Then stepped one forth like
> a water running round about him, and he crieth miserably [in Latin],
> 'O blessed is thy name, O Lord. The number has perished with them'.
> A little 'o' with 18 over it appeared.
>
> (*Mysteriorum Libri V*, Book 2)

Others spent longer conversing. One such was a pretty girl aged seven
or nine who seemed to come out of the shewstone and play amid the
piles of books in Dee's study. She told Dee her name was Madimi and

that she would be beaten if she let him know where her home was. This child-like character vanished, however, when she appeared to him in Prague, and she terrified him with apocalyptic prophecies of impending disaster generated by Satan who was angry with Dee and intent on destroying him.

But perhaps the most significant and lasting legacy of all these many sessions was the spirits' revelation of what Dee calls 'the language of the angels' or 'the speech of God'. (Modern scholars have side-stepped these designations and called it 'Enochian'). It began with the vision of a book whose leaves consisted of complex squares, some as large as 49 x 49, which contained the sacred language in its own alphabet – twenty-one characters, each with its own name. Once these had been communicated to Dee, the rest of the book followed, a wearying process which involved Kelly's dictating each word letter by letter, an added complication being that much of the material appeared to him backwards. No wonder, then, if Kelly sometimes felt the strain.

2 April, 1583, Tuesday.

EK felt his head as if it were on fire.

A VOICE [in Latin]: Thus I am accustomed to cleanse people's mistakes. Say what you see.

EK: I see letters, as I said before.

A VOICE: Move not from your places, for this place is holy. Read.

EK: I cannot.

DEE: You should have learned the characters perfectly, and their names, that you might now have readily named them to me as you should see them. Then there flashed fire upon EK again.

A VOICE, speaking to EK: Say what thou thinkest.

EK: My head is all on fire.

It took thirteen months full of interruptions from spirits who talked about other things, or from non-angelic entities, before Dee had the full extent of the angelic material. This consisted of (i) *Liber Logaeth*, which transmitted the spirit language; (ii) *De heptarchia mystica*, which contained seals for forty-nine angels who presided over aspects of the natural world, and also prayers to be said to designated angels at designated times; (iii) *48 claves angelicae*, which consists of eighteen invocations of spirits and a longer nineteenth, 'the key of the thirty airs'. The opening of this last will give the modern reader a notion of what the angelic language looks like when transcribed in English letters.

> Madriax ds praf lil chis micaolz saanir caosgo od fisis balzizras Iaida: Oh you heavens, which dwell in the first air are mighty in the parts of the earth and execute the judgement of the Highest.

Other books reveal the names of the presiding angels of various regions of the world and further tables containing letters and numbers from which Names of Power may be generated; some books, however, were destroyed in Prague in 1586 at the command of the spirits themselves. The angelic language is puzzling in many ways. It is written from right to left, like a Semitic language, and yet it is not Semitic; and the form of its letters reminds one vaguely of Amharic, although there is no good reason to suppose that either Dee or Kelly based the appearance of the angelic alphabet on the Ethiopic *Book of Enoch* – the most likely source for knowledge of Amharic at the time. The phonetic patterning of what we have – and this, it should be stressed is relatively little, a number of invocations and phrases amounting to a vocabulary of about 250 words – is similar to that of glossolalia. Modern psychological research into 'speaking with tongues' suggests that 'glossolalists are more submissive, suggestible, and dependent in the presence of authority figures than non-tongue-speakers... [and] they always thought about some benevolent authority person when they began to speak in tongues';[16] but neither of these is really applicable to the relationship between Dee and Kelly. Dee was certainly an authority figure, but he relied very much upon Kelly during the transmission of information from the spirits. To be sure, he directed and thereby to some extent controlled the exchanges, but essentially the relationship between the two men was a partnership, and Kelly's highly strung, sometimes near-hysterical outbursts during the sessions

1 Moses and Aaron performing the snake miracle before Pharaoh

2 *Left* Hermes Trismegistus

3 *Above* Faust signing the contract with the Devil in blood

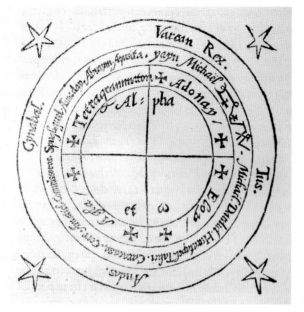

4 Magician's circle

5 *Above* Cornelius Agrippa

6 *Right* The characters of evil
spirits, from *The Fourth Book of
De Occulta Philosophia* attributed
to Cornelius Agrippa

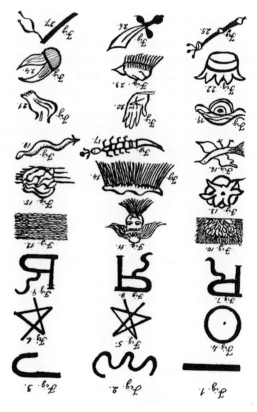

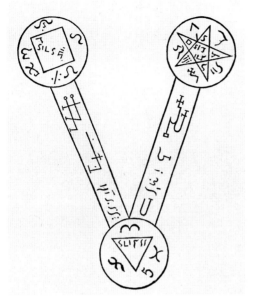

7 *Virgulta divina*: a divining rod to uncover buried treasure

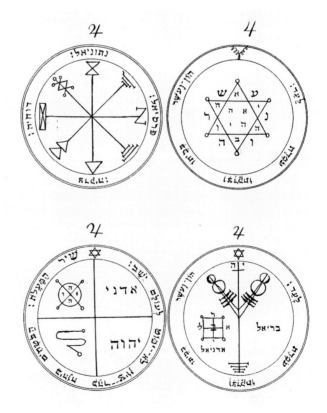

8 Four pentacles of Jupiter, showing divine names and angelic sigils

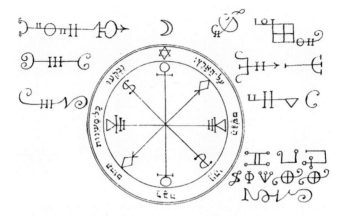

9 Pentacle of the moon and angelic signatures

10 Magic squares relating to Mars, from Cornelius Agrippa,
De Occulta Philosophia

11 Ritual magicians evoking the spirit of a dead person. From Ebenezer Sibly, *A New and Complete Illustration of the Occult Sciences*, c.1795

12 Ritual magician in a circle. From Daniel Defoe, *A Complete System of Magick*, 1729

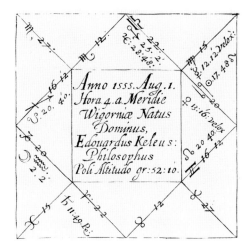

13 Edward Kelly's horoscope

14 Bird automata. From *Heronis Pneumatica*, ed. W Schmidt, 1897

15 Christophe Wagner's magic mirror

16 Eliphas Lévi's most famous illustration, the Baphomet of Mendes, from *Le Dogme et Rituel de la Haute Magie, c.*1856

17 Warrant of the Horus Temple

18 *Right* Application form for the Hermetic Order of the Golden Dawn

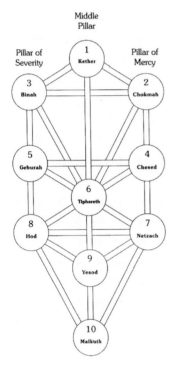

19 *Above* The Kabbalistic Tree of Life

20 *Right* A magician in his oratory. Engraving from *The Astrologer of the Nineteenth Century*, c.1825

precluded the degrees of submissiveness and dependence modern research seems to suggest are commonly present in glossolalists.

The language is thus reminiscent of things we know, yet unidentifiable with them. Could it be a cipher? Cryptography was a common enough preoccupation of the period, especially for anyone engaged, however distantly, in government service, as Dee undoubtedly was. But the clearest argument against this, as Donald Laycock has pointed out, is that the 'Enochian' airs are recorded with English translations following. Obviously, there is no point in writing a piece in code and then providing an open version along with it; nor, had Dee merely wished to write ciphered messages, would he have needed to expend so much time and effort on surrounding them with angels and spirit visions. Once more, therefore, the exact nature of the angelic language eludes us.

So the important question now arises, what was the aim and sum of all this occult knowledge? Actually, Dee himself in a preface to the *Mysteriorum Libri V* explains why he undertook this kind of endeavour:

O God Almighty, thou knowest and art my director and witness herein, that I have from my youth up desired and prayed unto thee for pure and sound wisdom and understanding of some of thy truths natural and artificial... For as much as many years in many places far and near, in many books and sundry languages, I have sought and studied and with sundry men conferred, and with my own reasonable discourse laboured, whereby to find or get some inkling, glims, or beam of such the foresaid radical truths. But (to be brief), after all my foresaid endeavour, I could find no other way to such true wisdom attaining but by thy extraordinary gift...And seeing I have read in thy books and records how Enoch enjoyed thy favour and conversation, with Moses thou wast familiar, and also that to Abraham, Isaac, and Jacob, Joshua, Gideon, Esdras, Daniel, Tobias, and sundry other, thy good angels were sent by thy disposition to instruct them, inform them, help them, yea in worldly and domestical affairs: yea, and sometimes to satisfy their desires, doubts, and questions of thy secrets. And furthermore, considering the shewstone which the high priests did use by thy own ordering, wherein they had lights and judgements in their great doubts...Therefore, seeing I was sufficiently taught and confirmed that this wisdom could not be come at man's hand or by human power, but only from thee, O God, mediately or immediately,[17] and having always a great regard and care to beware of the filthy abuse of such as willingly and wittingly did invocate and consult in divers sorts spiritual creatures of the damned sort, angels of darkness, forgers and patrons of lies and untruths, I did fly unto thee by hearty prayer, full oft, and in sundry manners.

Human book-learning had proved unsatisfactory; only angelic help could open God's book of nature, and only reading it by the light of the original, Adamic language with the constant help of prayer and in constant awareness of possible deception by evil spirits could provide the kind of exegesis Dee was craving. Hence the names and the 'calls'. These would enable Dee to achieve direct communication through which he might be taught the necessary means whereby a fractured and decaying natural world could be restored to wholeness and harmony – his ultimate goal. One may notice a parallel with Dee's other great preoccupation, alchemy. During the Middle Ages and early modern period alchemy was an entirely practical discipline whose aim was to hasten the naturally improving processes of nature by precipitating matter through stages of decay and decomposition into a new birth whereby it would become 'perfect', in the Latin sense of 'completed' or 'fulfilled', and having once achieved this state, the new-born matter could then be used to heal any sickness in the rest of nature. Dee's aim was therefore in the highest degree lofty and altruistic, and if we ask ourselves why he devoted so much time and effort to these spirit conversations, (which he, let us remember, experienced largely at second hand through his scryers), it is worth recalling Dee's own distinction between wisdom, which he said is a gift from God, and knowledge, which comes from creation and created things. Having essayed the latter and found it wanting for his purpose, he then tried to achieve the former by the most direct route he and his contemporaries knew.

His reliance upon Saul and Kelly and other scryers was, of course, crucial, especially upon Kelly, whose character was far from exemplary, or even pleasant. He was some thirty years younger than Dee and although he had attended Oxford University (under the surname 'Talbot') while decently educated he was clearly not as learned as Dee himself. He did not know enough, for example, to have manufactured the complexities and internal consistencies of the angelic language at top speed over several months, and to have delivered it in such a complicated fashion, although it is also true that Dee discussed with him more than once the techniques of *gematria*, *notarikon* and *temurah*, which deal with the transposition of letters in words according to specific Kabbalistic rules. These transpositions, however, refer to Hebrew words and depend on the prior existence of those words. Applying them to the angelic language therefore likewise presupposes the prior existence of the angelic words and adds another layer of complication to the business of their transmission via the crystal if we are to suggest that Kelly was consciously practising fraud. Besides, Kelly's emotional outbursts during the weeks and months of scrying, his frequent reluctance to continue (out of which he had to be argued by Dee), and his admission to the authorities in Prague that he did indeed see visions in the crystal, even though such an admission endangered his life in view of the hostility the visions generated in those who had it in their power to punish him for them – all these need to be taken into account when we try to assess how genuine a medium Kelly was.

The fraud argument is, in fact, suspect. It may spring from late-modern unease at accepting the early-modern concept of a world created and controlled by God and dominated by hierarchies of non-human entities, and from the notion that, because Kelly was an unsavoury character,[18] he could not have been a genuine medium or a person who really believed in the truth of his mediumship – a *non sequitur* we should try to avoid. We cannot actually prove him a fraud, and so we are left with Dee's trust in him. Dee, of course, wanted to believe and relied on his being truthful; and we must certainly not forget that over the time they were together Kelly got to know Dee's interests and cast of mind, had access to his extensive library and could easily have tempered or inclined his revelations in accordance with what he learned therefrom, and knew Dee might wish to hear. Nevertheless, interpreting, expanding, altering or otherwise tampering with visions is not the same as having no visions at all or manufacturing visions from nothing. Telling lies, in effect, is the essence of modern talk of 'fabrication' and 'fraud' anent Kelly's work with Dee. In the end, we have to fall back on Dee himself. He lived with Kelly for years and worked with him every day. He was *intimately* aware, in fact, as we are not, of Kelly's faults and unstable character. But when it came to the business of scrying (which is, after all, the bond they had in common), Dee, who cannot be dismissed as a credulous fool in relation to any other aspect of his life, and indeed was likened by one contemporary to an Atlas on whose shoulders rested the scientific universe, trusted Kelly's gift as a medium and was prepared to place the most important enterprise of his life in Kelly's hands.

Benjamin Woolley sums up Dee's position very well:

> Plenty of evidence shows that Dee had to some extent fallen under Kelley's spell. But so did men like Dyer, Cecil, Rozmberk, and Rudolf. However, Dee's faith in Kelley cannot be solely ascribed to the skryer's charms. The sophistication of the Enochian language, the huge cast of spiritual characters, the flamboyant personalities and the sheer quantity of material, all conjured up from a stone, without recourse to prompts or pre-written scripts, were compelling.
>
> (*The Queen's Conjuror*, 327)

4

Natural Magic and the Blurred Borders of Deception

Dee's discovery or reception of the angelic language was timely and chimed well with one of the preoccupations of the period, for language itself was a matter for concern and heated debate. 'Human beings were endowed with language in order to proclaim truth', wrote Erasmus in 1523, but just what that truth might be, and whether words were the best method of expressing it was increasingly being called in question. Anxiety on the point was caused partly because of the Humanists' and reformers' desire to establish ancient texts in their pristine purity and thus give themselves and others direct access to the truths they were believed to contain; and partly because increasing use of vernacular tongues was not only stimulating a similar interest in vocabulary and grammar, but also making people aware of the rapid changes which were taking place in both as people experimented with new concepts which required (or were deemed to require) fresh coinages to express them. The French grammarian Henri Estienne caught the negative aspects of this:

> One finds so much absurdity (indeed even more) in several other expressions which, nevertheless, please some people, for no other reason than that they are said in contravention of all reason; and actually, if this

silly (indeed mad) wish for novelty continues to gain ground and knocks down everything wherever it passes, I am very much afraid that in the end one will be obliged to call the head 'the foot', and the foot 'the head'.[1]

Uncertainty about language was threatening. The old notion that language provided the most reliable vehicle for logic whose aim was to discover that truth which existed before the Fall was rapidly proving untenable. New certainties grounded in reason were required, and different solutions proposed. John Dee, for example, sought an expression in symbolic form, the *monas hieroglyphica*, to which he devoted a whole book of explanation, written in twelve days during a kind of trance in January 1564. The sign is illustrated in the frontispiece to his book. It is revealed, so to speak, in the doorway of a temple, surrounded by an ovoid shape representing the 'egg of creation' familiar to scholars from Orphic religious texts. The Oval is embraced by four zodiacal figures – Cancer, Capricorn, Taurus, and Leo: signs of water, air, earth, and fire. Cancer is supported on each side by a Hermes or Mercury. The *monas* itself in the centre of the oval consists of a crescent moon slipped through a sun dominating the cross of the four elements, which rises from the centre of the zodiacal sign Aries. Within this complex, however, can also be seen the signs of the seven planets, beginning with the moon at the top, then Mercury, Venus, the sun, Mars, Jupiter, and Saturn. It may also be seen as Mercury dominant over or rising from Aries. In addition to these zodiacal indicators, the attentive spectator can notice a series of numbers. The point within the circle = 1. The points where the crescent intersects the circle = 2. The horizontal line of the cross = 3 because it has three points, one at each end and one in the middle. The two equal arms of the cross = 4 because there are four outer points. 4 + 3 = 7, a significant Pythagorean figure. The four outer and four inner points of the cross = 8, which is the symbolic figure of Christ. The four arms of the cross remind us of the four qualities of the four elements: earth, air, fire, water – cold, dry, hot, moist. The point within the circle represents God, the Creator. He is surrounded by all the elements and signs which make up his creation; and we are reminded by the cross of the sacrifice made by Christ to save that same creation.

Could it be suggested, therefore, that symbols, if universally understood and accepted, might under certain circumstances provide a reliable substitute for words? Unfortunately there were problems. Symbols were actually highly abstruse and so not altogether acceptable as a universally comprehensible tongue, and the circumstances under which they could operate successfully were far too limited for descriptive purposes. No adequately detailed account of the cosmos, or any novelties which might be noticed therein, could be given by symbols without the assistance of words. But we need to bear in mind, in connection with this, the gradual spread into general use, from the beginning of the sixteenth century, of those particular symbols known as Indian numbers (often called 'Arabic' because they were mediated via Arab learning in southern Spain). The old notation consisting of Latin letters – M = 1,000, D = 500, C = 100, and so forth – was overtly and intimately connected with words; the new notation was not. Consequently their increasingly widespread use represented a real, conscious jolt to the common psyche, for the new usage liberated number from its dependence upon different alphabets – Greek, Latin, Hebrew – and offered people what seemed to be a universal tongue which would remain the same, regardless of which language was being spoken or written round it, and had the capacity to develop into an expression of the universe and its laws accessible to all, undeviating from fact, and free from the long-attendant symbolism of words and letters.

Increasingly, then, it seemed as though the great desideratum might be found in mathematics. Descartes, for example, was prepared to entrust himself to them. 'The only principles I accept or need in physics', he wrote, 'are those of geometry and pure mathematics. These principles explain all natural phenomena, and enable us to provide absolutely reliable demonstrations regarding them.' (*Principia philosophiae*, 1644, part 2, paragraph 64) The consequence of this, of course, is that the physical phenomena to which he refers are reduced to matter which can be defined in mathematical terms. Consequently,

because physical phenomena can be measured mathematically, con-
clusions reached about their composition, nature and behaviour may
be regarded as reliable and certain, while anything which cannot be
so defined is not physical and must be attributed to the human mind.
Descartes' delight in the possibilities of mathematics was a popular
view during the Renaissance and early-modern period, but Giordano
Bruno, a radical thinker in his own right whose cosmological insights
anticipated modern cosmological thinking in several important ways,
was unwilling to subscribe to it, pointing out that the astronomer
Ptolemy had been a remarkable mathematician but that this had not
saved him from making very serious mistakes in his model of the
cosmos. Imperfection, Bruno argued, characterised everything
throughout the universe, not just creation beneath the moon, and in
consequence the power of mathematics and geometry to provide a
completely reliable account of physical reality was actually limited.
Within those limitations they were extremely useful tools. Beyond
them, however, intuition and reason operated far more successfully.
The Dutch mathematician and astronomer Christiann Huygens also
expressed his reservations in a letter to Pierre Bayle on 26 February
1693, in which he likened Descartes' *Principia philosophiae* to a work
of fiction and said that, having been swept away by it when he was
fifteen or sixteen years old, he now believed almost nothing Descartes
had said about physics, metaphysics or meteorology.

The Latin word *mathematica*, we also need to remember, had a different range of meanings from the modern 'mathematics'. On the one
hand, it referred to arithmetic, geometry and astrology, and in consequence a mathematician was someone who dealt principally with
numbers, measurement and the stars and planets. How these three
coincided in natural philosophy is described in the opening para-
graphs of Bruno's *De magia mathematica* (1589):

> God flows into the angels, the angels into celestial bodies, celestial bodies
> into the elements, the elements into things mixed, things mixed into the
> senses, the senses into the mind, and the mind into the living creature.
> The living creature rises through the mind to the senses, through the

senses into things mixed, through things mixed into the elements, through the elements into the heavens, through these into demons or angels, and through these into God or the workings of God. In this way there is a descent of God or from God through the created world to a living creature, and the ascent of a living creature through the created world to God. God is at the summit of the ladder; the Kabbalistic Jacob at its base and foundation. The ranks of the created things in between decide how high up the ladder they are according to their numbers through which the higher operative powers descend to things below and those below mount to the higher. (This ascent and descent through the exit and entrance of the two gates of Cancer and Capricorn, one of which is said to belong to the gods, the other to human beings, has been described by ancient authors of an abstruse philosophy).

Everything has its place, and its place is numbered. This arithmetic and geometry of creation was by no means peculiar to Bruno. It can be seen, for example, in Origen's remark that God made the world in accordance with some definite number which he determined in advance, because it is unimaginable that created things have no kind of limit. This owes much to the Pythagoreanism which dominated both the concept of number and of the creative process, succinctly expressed by the Arab philosopher and mathematician, Nichomachus (floruit AD 100) in his *Introduction to Arithmetic*:

> Everything in the universe, which nature has arranged in accordance with a systematic plan, seems, both in the part and the whole, to have been settled and arranged in accordance with number by the fore-thought and mind of the Creator of everything. The model was estab-lished like an outline pattern from the prevalence of Number pre-existent in the mind of God, creator of the universe – Number which was simply a concept, entirely without material form, and yet the everlasting essentiality, in order that time, movement, the sky, the stars, every kind of astral revolution, every one of these things, might be produced in accordance with it, as from a workman's plan. (1.6.1)

This plan gave rise to a unified whole – 'the [divine] intelligence liberates its own goodness multiplied by means of the stars, turning itself upon its own unity', as Dante expressed it[2] – and because both the process and the result of God's creative act was envisaged in terms of a craftsman making an object, it became logical to try to explain this via mystical numbers and geometry. Both these mystical numbers and their attendant geometry sprang from Pythagoras's tetractys ($1 + 2 + 3 + 4 = 10$). One is the source of all number, while not being a number itself, and is therefore analogous to God. Two is even and divisible and corresponds geometrically to the straight line. Three defines a triangle and surface, and four, a solid body. Progression from one to four thus allows us to envisage the generation of the created universe, while the sum of those four numbers sets a limit to the creative process, in as much as $10 = 1 + 0$ which $= 1$; and thus generation returns to its ultimate source. It was a way of looking at and understanding creation which lasted well beyond the Mediaeval period. Even books ostensibly devoted to arithmetic looked at numbers as signs with meaning greater than mere computation. Pietro Bongo's *Mysticae numerorum significationis liber* (1585), for example, is, as its title suggests, devoted to explaining the symbolic meaning of numbers; William Ingpen's *The Secret of Numbers According to Theologicall, Arithmeticall, Geometricall, and Harmonicall Computation* (1624) is filled with Kabbalistic references; and the alchemist Thomas Vaughan drew his readers' attention to the significance of number in the basic elements. 'I advise the reader to be diligent and curious in this subsequent part of the discourse', he wrote,

> that having once attained to the fundamentals of science, he may the better understand her superstructures... Know, then, that every element is threefold, this triplicity being the express image of their author, and a seal he hath laid upon his creature. There is nothing on earth, though never so simple, so vile and abject in the sight of man, but it bears witness of God, even to that abstruse mystery, his unity and trinity... I speak of celestial hidden natures known only to absolute magicians,

whose eyes are in the centre, not in the circumference: and in this
sense, every element is threefold.

(*Anthroposophia Theomagia*, 1650, published under the
pseudonym 'Eugenius Philalethes').

Number was therefore both explanatory and symbolic, and the
number of objects used in a given situation, or the number of times
an action was done or a word or phrase was said, not only symbolised
that original generative process, but also recreated parts of it for the
moment, just as the Mass recreated or re-enacted the sacrifice of Jesus
upon the cross by virtue of the miracle of transubstantiation lying at
its centre. Thus, at an episcopal Mass, Honorius of Autun tells us:

> there are seven deacons because the Apostles chose seven deacons for
> the ministry; and because the seven gifts of the Holy Spirit produce the
> sacraments of the Mass; and seven deacons act as ministers because
> seven disciples were working as fishermen after the resurrection, and
> [Jesus] invited them to eat with him. By the seven subdeacons are
> understood the seven columns of the house of wisdom; and by the
> seven acolytes, the seven lights and tabernacles, or the seven candle-
> sticks referred to in the *Apocalypse*.

(*Gemma animae*, chapter 9)

This kind of recreative symbolism extended everywhere. Most of the
mazes constructed in northern French churches, for example, consisted of an eleven-track pattern set inside an octagon, because the
number eleven signified sin, discord, and lack of completeness, while
eight denoted baptism and rebirth through Christ. In fifteenth-
century music, we find notes in a motet so arranged that groups of
thirty represented Judas's betrayal of Christ for thirty pieces of silver,
or that a rhythmic pattern was established to mimic the proportions
of Solomon's temple; while in the Credo of Josquin Desprez's *Missa
Hercules dux Ferrarie* (c.1505), the tenor suddenly starts to retrace his
musical steps, each note in turn, until he reaches *et caro factus est* ('and
he was made flesh'), thereby signifying to the listeners that everything

begins and ends in Christ.[3] This exquisitely refined type of musical symbolism, however, powerful as it was, more or less died out in the sixteenth century. It was perhaps too obscure and too difficult an art for any but the most attuned and attentive listener to comprehend and absorb.

But another esoteric musical tradition based on mystical numbers did survive as a magical technique. It began with Pythagoras mediated by Aristotle, and was concisely explained by Cicero in a text which was widely read from the first to the eighteenth century:

> 'What', asked the dreamer, 'is this sound, so loud and so pleasing, which fills my ears?'.
> 'The sound you are hearing', replied [Scipio], 'is that which is caused by the impulse and movement of the spheres themselves. It is distinguished by unequal intervals which, however, are separated precisely according to a fixed proportion, and modifying high notes with low causes an agreeable variety of sounds in a regular manner. Such great movements cannot be roused by silence, and it is natural that the spheres at one extreme make a low sound, while those at the other extreme[4] make a high sound. Consequently, the highest orbit of the sky, the one which carries the stars, whose revolution is faster than the others, is moved by a high, shrill sound; whereas the lowest, which is that of the moon, is moved by a very low sound. The ninth sphere, the earth, remains unmoved and always keeps one place, since it has embraced the central spot of the universe.'[5]
>
> (*Somnium Scipionis* 5)

Not surprisingly, then, Marsilio Ficino would go on to argue that music could be used to bring down astral influxes into the terrestrial world and thus influence human beings via its harmonies or dissonances, (which is why chanting rather than merely saying an incantation was more likely to stimulate this effect, as I suggested in my earlier discussion of Greek ritual texts); and this brings us to the second major association which people made with *mathematica*. They were very closely linked with the practice of magic. Roger Bacon (*c*.1214-1292/4) offered an etymological explanation in the fourth part of his *Opus Maius* where he distinguishes between different kinds of mathematics according to whether one derives the word from the Greek *mathesis* ('learning', 'knowledge'), or *mantia* ('divination') – an inaccurate distinction, in fact. The former he calls true mathematics, the latter false. But then he goes on to subdivide magic into five types, divination (*mantike*), mathematics (*mathematica*), working harm by magic (*maleficium*), trickery (*praestigium*), and casting lots (*sortilegium*), and says that 'mathematics, therefore, is the second part of the art of magic and takes upon itself the contemplation of heavenly things, spoiled with characters, incantations, invocations, the sacrifices of a pagan religion, and various mischievous delusions'. Bacon's 'true' mathematician is thus someone who deals with number and measurement and astronomy, while his 'false' mathematician is, in effect, a worker of astrological magic. 'This type of *mathematicus*', he says, 'calls upon demons to assist in the arranging of heavenly bodies by invocations and sacrifices, something which is entirely impious.' Hence the reason for Cornelius Agrippa's insistence that mathematics were essential to both the understanding and the practice of magic:

> The various branches of mathematics are so necessary to magic, and have such an affinity with it, that whoever practises it without them goes completely astray, labours in vain, and has no hope of achieving the end he desires.
>
> (*De occulta philosophia* Book 2, chapter 1)

Now, there was an ancient theory which said that numbers may be regarded as signs for other things, and therefore as constituting a part of those other things which means they are capable of exercising power over them.[6] So numbers may have a relationship with entities and verities existing on planes other than that of the senses, and consequently can be used as links between the worlds and, if arranged correctly, are capable of revealing truths which would otherwise remain hidden and inaccessible. One such arrangement is the magic square, and Agrippa gives several examples to show how these particular arrangements are linked to the seven planets. Thus, the square relating to Mars consists of a five-sided square containing twenty-five numbers, five in each line and diameter, whose total is sixty-five, the grand total of the square itself being 325. There preside over this square divine names, and the numbers in the square, when related to letters of the Hebrew alphabet, yield the sign or 'character' of Mars and his spirits, with an Intelligence for good (GRAPHIEL) and a Demon for evil (BARZABEL). To bring success in battle, the magician is meant to inscribe this square on a lamen or sword made from iron, or on a cornelian, to stop the flow of blood, and so forth.[7]

This is one form of *magia mathematica* – an ambiguous phrase which may mean 'mathematical magic', but is more likely to mean 'astrological magic': hence the relationship with the planets – and constitutes a fuzzy area in the spectrum of the occult sciences. Magic squares clearly operate in conjunction with non-human entities, just like lamens which are engraved simply with words and non-numerical signs and characters. But Agrippa was insistent that with number, and its allied concepts 'weight', 'measure', and 'harmony', we enter a realm occupied by natural, as opposed to demonic magic. This aspect of magic Martín del Rio divided into two, *operative* and *divinatory*, by which he meant magic which produced wonderful effects and that which uncovered hidden things ranging from buried treasure to the future itself. Since he distinguishes these from demonic magic, we must assume he meant that this kind of magic worked by natural means, with the operator relying upon licit acquisition of knowledge rather than illicit assistance from spirits. Even so, this 'natural' magic may not be deemed always to have worked entirely without external help, and we should pause before we start assuming we are about to enter the territory of 'science' as we understand it.

Let us see how the term 'natural magic' was interpreted by Giambattista della Porta in his *Magiae naturalis sive de miraculis rerum naturalium* in 1558 (using the English translation of a hundred years later):

Now it is meet to instruct a magician both what he must know and what he must observe, that being sufficiently instructed every way, he

may bring very strange and wonderful things to pass. Seeing magic...
is a practical part of natural philosophy, therefore it behoveth a magician, and one that aspires to the dignity of that profession, to be an
exact and a very perfect philosopher. For philosophy teaches what are
the effects of fire, earth, air, and water, the principal matter of the
heavens; and what is the cause of the flowing of the sea, and of the
divers-coloured rainbow; and of the loud thunder and of comets, and
fiery lights that appear by night and of earthquakes; and what are the
beginnings of gold and of iron; and what is the whole witty force of
hidden nature.

Then also he must be a skilful physician, for both the sciences are
very like and near together, and physic, by creeping in under colour of
magic, hath purchased favour amongst men. And surely it is a great help
unto us in this kind, for it teaches mixtures and temperatures, and so
shows us how to compound and lay things together for such purposes.

Moreover, it is required of him that he be a herbalist, not only able
to discern common simples, but very skilful and sharp-sighted in the
nature of all plants; for the uncertain names of plants and their near
likeness of one to another, so that they can hardly be discerned, hath
put us to much trouble in some of our works and experiments. And as
there is no greater inconvenience to any artificer than not to know his
tools that he must work with, so the knowledge of plants is so necessary to this profession that indeed it is all in all.

He must be as well seen also in the nature of metals, minerals, gems,
and stones. Furthermore, what cunning he must have in the art of dis-
tillation which follows and resembles the showers and dews of Heaven,
as the daughter the mother, I think no man will doubt of it; for it yields
daily very strange inventions [discoveries] and most witty devices, and
shows how to find out many things profitable for the use of man: as,
for example, to draw out of things dewy vapours, unsavoury and gross
scents or spirits, clots, and gummy or slimy humours, and that intimate
essence which lurks in the inmost bowels of things, to fetch it forth,
and sublimate it, that it may be of the greater strength. And this he must
learn to do, not after a rude and homely manner, but with knowledge
of the causes and relations thereof.

He must also know the mathematical sciences, and especially astrology, for that shows how the stars are moved in the heavens, and what is the cause of the darkening of the moon, and how the sun, that golden planet, measures out the parts of the world and governs it by twelve signs; for by the sundry motions and aspects of the heavens, the celestial bodies are very beneficial to the earth, and from thence many things receive both active and passive powers and their manifold properties...

Moreover, he must be skilful in the optics that he may know how the sight may be deceived, and how the likeness of a vision that is seen in the water may be seen hanging without in the air by the help of certain glasses of divers fashions; and how to make one see that plainly which is a great way off, and how to throw fire very far from us – upon which sleights the greatest part of the secrecies of magic doth depend.

These are the sciences which magic takes to herself for servants and helpers, and he that knows not these is unworthy to be named a magician. He must be a skilful workman, both by natural gifts and also by practice of his own hands, for knowledge without practice and workmanship, and practice without knowledge, are nothing worth. These are so linked together that the one without the other is but vain and to no purpose.

(Book 1, chapter 3)

This extraordinary range of requirements shows that natural magic extended into areas we should not call 'magic' at all, and yet we seize upon the practical aspects of Della Porta's list and ignore at our peril the potential for preternatural activity underlying them. Notice, for example, how Agrippa introduces a short chapter entitled *De magia mathematica*, which is actually devoted to automata:

There are other very perceptive imitators of nature, and very daring investigators of it, who give assurances that they can produce things resembling those in nature by means of natural powers, using only mathematical methods and engaging influxes from the heavens. Examples are bodies which move or speak and yet do not have the powers of living creatures, such as the wooden dove of Archytas, which used to fly, and

the statues of Hermes, which used to peak, and the bronze head made
by Albertus Magnus, which they stopped from speaking.[8]

The external help here consists of rays from the stars, and thus counts
as 'natural' rather than 'demonic'; and yet these rays infuse mechanical or material objects with power and thereby enable them to behave
in ways other than natural. It was part of the puzzlement attending
automata. We have already seen that pseudo-Clement credited Simon
Magus with fabricating walking statues and barking dogs made from
brass or stone, but the idea of such things was very much older than
that. Homer says that Hephaistos, divine smith to the gods, had bel-
lows which worked themselves, female slaves made of gold who
obeyed his commands, and tripods which were able to move of their
own accord. Hesiod tells us that the gods made human beings from
various metals, and Plato that Daedalus created statues which had to
be tied down lest they run away. None of these represents actual
automata, of course. They are poetic devices intended to illustrate the
power of the gods, unless we allow a possible exception in the case of
Daedalus's statues. But the concept of moving statues, or statues which
emitted sounds, was very powerful, and by the first century AD engi-
neers – notably Heron of Alexandria – had managed to turn the concept into reality. A favourite device consisted of a bird or birds perched
upon the edge of a vase or bowl representing a pool. Water was forced
to flow into an airtight compartment, and the displaced air was obliged
to escape into a narrow pipe which produced a particular musical
note. Different sizes of pipe would emit different notes. Hence the
possibility of having several birds and an harmonious set of notes.

A variant upon this kind of device used steam instead of water.
Water was used to make automata move, too, and the first-century BC
Roman engineer Vitruvius said that water-pressure could also be used
for the same purpose. Interest in automata and the mechanical sciences underpinning their remarkable performances continued to be
intense among Byzantine and Arab authors, and it is clear that they
were manufactured not only to delight but also to impress. Liutprand
of Cremona, who visited the Byzantine Court in 948 and 966, was

received by the Emperor in state, and noted that a gilded tree made of bronze was standing where the Emperor could see it, and various kinds of birds, also made of gilded bronze, filled its branches. These birds were singing in accordance with their different species. Lions covered with gold acted as guardians of the throne and struck the ground time and time again with their tails. Their tongues moved and they roared aloud. Editions and translations of earlier Greek works on *pneumatika* (wind-driven machines) and automata were readily available throughout the Byzantine and then the Renaissance periods. In consequence, knowledge of how such contrivances worked and how they might be adapted and diversified was also widespread, and we find examples destined to please and astonish at noble courts and universities.

Thus, in April 1581 we find Montaigne visiting the Villa d'Este in whose famous gardens he heard

> the singing of birds, which are the little bronze pipes one sees on organs, and emit a sound like that from the little earthenware pots full of water, which children blow through the 'beak', a device similar to that of organs. Then by other means they make an owl move. It appears on top of a rock and all of a sudden the singing ceases because the 'birds' are afraid when it is present. Then it goes away again, and this happens time and time about, as often as you want.[9]

If these were self-evident *divertissements*, not altogether realistic, John Dee's flying beetle was not. Dee's initial reputation came from his ability to produce wonderful machines, a fame based on his time as an undergraduate at St John's College, Cambridge, where he made a piece of stage machinery for a performance of Aristophanes's play *The Peace* – a large wooden dung-beetle which flew up into the air with a man and a basket of food on its back – 'whereat was great wondering and many vain reports spread abroad of the means how that was effected'. (*Compendious Rehearsal*, 1592) In the Deutsches Museum in Munich there is an automaton dating to *c.*1560. It is the figure of a bearded man clad in what appears to be a long robe. Its foot (only one is visible) makes the figure walk in a rectangle, its hands make circular move-ments, its head moves back and forth, its mouth opens and closes, and its eyes roll backwards and forwards as long as the automaton is in motion. The exact purpose of this figure, however, is not clear.

The notion of automata is a powerful one, since it reinforces the ambiguity inherent in natural magic. How far do these objects reflect human ingenuity alone, and does there come a point in their con-struction where assistance other than human is required? Do their creators, in other words, run the risk of entering a grey area in which demonic help is both actively sought and used? Take the example of the famous bronze head reputedly made by Roger Bacon. After his death in c.1292, stories began to spring up which suggested he had made such a device by magical means, and this tale was seized on by Robert Greene in 1594 for his comedy *Friar Bacon and Friar Bungay*. Tantalising references to the head are made from as early as the second scene, but then towards the end of the play, in scene 11, Greene pro-vides the audience with a set piece of magic and low comedy. Bacon enters upon the stage with a magician's staff and book, and the bronze head itself. He is accompanied by his servant, Miles, who is to keep watch and call him when the head begins to speak:

> Bacon:
> Miles, thou knowest that I have dived into Hell
> And sought the darkest palaces of fiends,
> That with my magic spells great Belcephon
> Hath left his lodge and kneeled at my cell;
> The rafters of the earth rent from the poles,
> And three-formed Luna hid her silver looks,
> Trembling upon her concave continent
> When Bacon read upon his magic book.
> With seven years' tossing nigromantic charms,
> Poring upon dark Hecate's principles,
> I have framed out a monstrous head of brass,
> That, by th'enchanting forces of the Devil,
> Shall tell out strange and uncouth aphorisms,

And girt fair England with a wall of brass.
Bungay and I have watched these threescore days,
And now our vital spirits crave some rest…
Therefore, I charge thee by the immortal God
That holds the souls of men within his fist,
This night thou watch; for ere the morning star
Sends out his glorious glister on the north
The head will speak. Then, Miles, upon thy life,
Wake me; for then by magic art I'll work
To end my seven years' task with excellence.

(7-22, 28-34)

Here are many of the elements we have come to expect of the ritual magician: the priestly status, learning, magic staff, book, a long period of preparation (in this case, sixty days), control over nature and association with spirits, specifically the 'fiend' Belcephon, whom Bacon has evoked and bent to his will, and the bronze head, half automaton-half resonating chamber through which a demon voice might choose to speak, and which was made, we are to understand, with the help of a demon. Of course, since, as we saw earlier, the real Bacon actually disapproved of magic, it is clear that Greene's play provides another rewriting of history such as happened to Merlin and Faust. The effect of stage plays on the popular perception of magicians, in fact, has its modern parallel in the refashioning of historical incidents or figures by some Hollywood films. But the point of these and similar portrayals, of course, is not to recreate history, but to represent myth in accordance with popular inclination (one could almost say 'need'). The natural magician may be extraordinarily skilled and clever, and can deliver by his art all kinds of wonders; but the ritual or demonic magician, who perhaps does no more in actual fact, *appears* to be his superior precisely because he is calling upon powers much greater than his own, powers which by *their* nature are unstable. The frisson provided by such magicians is irresistible, hence the constant urge to see beneath the learned explanations afforded by natural magic the guiding hand of an angel or a demon.

With automata, then, we see 'natural' magic converging with 'mathematical' and 'demonic' magic, and Agrippa lets us know how careful we must be when we come across the term 'mathematician' in the Middle Ages or early-modern period. The term 'magic', he said, embraces every branch of speculative learning which deals with creation and with mathematics (i.e. numbers, measurement and astronomy/astrology), and conjoins with them the capabilities and significances of religion in its different aspects. Natural magic he then defined as that which contemplates the powers of everything in nature and in the heavens, corrals them using a person's curiosity as a kind of hunting net, investigates the sympathetic links between them, and so draws forth into the open the secret powers which lie hidden in every created thing. Mathematical magic he regarded as that which enables particularly acute imitators of nature,[10] who are prepared to be bold to the point of rashness in their investigations of her, to use mathematical disciplines aided by influxes from the heavens to create things which resemble works produced by nature, such as bodies which can move or talk. (*De incertitudine et vanitate scientiarum*, 1582, chapters 41-43) When John Dee was described as a 'mathematician' therefore, it was difficult for people to separate his ability to calculate, measure and engineer from the possibility that there might be inherent in his calculations or in the product of those calculations influences other than purely intellectual; and we may care to bear in mind that, given Dee's personal interest in non-human realms and the ways in which they might be contacted, such a separation would have been neither logical nor necessary.

Now, this brings us to that division or type of magic known as *praestigium*, deception or trick or illusion. Agrippa discussed these as well. He called them artificial, demonstrations of skill, cunning devices, pieces of dexterity intended to create illusions, the means whereby magicians produce apparitions and reproduce the marvels done by itinerant or fairground performers. Then he makes the important point that *praestigia* are not achieved by goetic enchantments or conjurations or the deceits of evil spirits, but rather by vapours from certain fumigants, lights, doctored drinks, images in mirrors and so forth

– 'the drugs and instruments of the magic art and the natural power of the heavens'. *Praestigium* is thus essentially human-made 'magic', such as that described by Chaucer in *The Franklin's Tale*, where 'trege-tors' (people who cause rapid changes to take place) perform during a feast and make it look as though a barge is being rowed up and down on water within the great hall, or cause the spectators to think they see a lion, or flowers springing up, or a castle, all of which dis-appear from their sight in an instant. (vv. 1142–51) *Praestigium* can also be produced simply by manual dexterity as Martín del Rio, for exam-ple, knew perfectly well when he wrote of begging jugglers, itinerant performers and tightrope walkers who were thought to achieve their effects by incantations, whereas they actually did so because of the dexterity of their hands and feet, and Del Rio recorded a whole series of *praestigia*, ending with a magic lantern.

> Iron objects, silver platters and similar things of great weight are put on top of a table and then, without the assistance of a magnet, a cord, a hair, or other means, are drawn from one end of the table to the other, jumping up and down as they go. Someone pulls out a playing card from the rest of the pack without letting anyone else see it, and then its face is changed three times while the person still has the card in his hand. There are mirrors which seem to show things from far away places. In the space of three hours a real shrub is made to grow a span's length from the table, and trees with leaves and fruit suddenly appear. Lanterns lit with a special flame make all the women present look as though they are naked, and reveal those parts which nature tells us should remain concealed; and while the women are unclothed, they perform a ritual dance as long as a lantern, which is hung up in the middle of the room, continues to burn. The lantern has certain char-acters inscribed on it and is filled with hare's fat.
>
> (*Disquisitiones Magicae* Book 2, question 6)

The remark about mirrors is here almost a throwaway, but in fact mir-rors represented a focal point for Mediaeval and early-modern curios-ity and investigation, since they posed questions about how we see things and what can be deemed real and what false. Greek and Roman theory, for example, maintained that images seen in mirrors actually flowed from the onlooker or reflected object, and consisted of very small bodies called *simulacra*, 'appearances', and some such notion, allied to the concept of sympathetic magic, may account for certain individuals going up to the altar after Mass to stare into the chalice and so cure themselves of jaundice. But what we see in a mirror we must also interpret, and therefore appearances really can be deceptive, since we may be inclined to 'see' in a mirror those things we should like to see, rather than the sights which are actually there. Thus, in *Harry Potter and the Philosopher's Stone*, Harry Potter looks into a mirror and sees the images of his dead mother and father apparently alive, although backward writing round the mirror should have warned him: 'I show not your face but your heart's desire'. It is a very old mistake. As Johannes Hartlieb observed in 1456, 'I have seen magi who claim they are able to manufacture mirrors in such a way that anybody, man or woman, can see in them whatever he or she desires'. *(Buch aller verbotenen Kunst, Unglaubens und der Zauberei*, chapter 86)

Interpreting what we see is indeed difficult. As St Paul says, 'we see through a mirror in an enigma', and the quality of early mirrors reinforces the point. Polished gold, silver, bronze, or obsidian surfaces present the onlooker with blurred reflections; concave glass mirrors and the silvered glass mirrors of the thirteenth century distorted their images, while in the sixteenth century mirrors of steel and of glass were still liable to present a somewhat misleading image to the person who used them. Small wonder, then, if people who were not accustomed as we are to seeing their appearance frequently in a large number of reflective surfaces both within and outwith the house should be intrigued by these extraordinary instruments of revelation, and find it puzzling to interpret what they saw, or thought they saw, therein. Could it be possible that the complex images in the mirror not only reflected immediate reality, but also realms beyond the physical and images from the past and future too? Many of the Church Fathers – Gregory of Nyssa, St Basil, St Ambrose, St Augustine – seized upon the mirror as a metaphor for discussions of truth and deception, real appearances and false illusions. 'Speculation' (a word derived from the Latin word for mirror, *speculum*), considered both the visible and the invisible worlds, the speculator's relationship with them being like that of a mirror which is capable of reflecting the world apprehensible by the senses and the insensible world of which creation is a reflection, just as humankind was made in the image of God and thus, however poorly and distortedly, reflects him in some measure.

But if the mirror could reflect reality, whether of this world and time or of others, it could also be used by the unscrupulous as a reflector of illusions. In 1398 the theological faculty of the Sorbonne issued a set of condemnations of superstitions and magical practices. Its fourth article noted that there were those who 'endeavour by means of the arts of magic to enclose, constrain, or imprison demons in stones, rings, mirrors, or statuettes', the object being to have them there ready at all times for consultation. So it is no wonder that Hartlieb condemned the naivety of certain priests who would make children look into the polished surface of the paten and report what visions they saw there, on the grounds that because they were using (or rather misusing) a sacred vessel, only angels and not demons could appear therein (chapter 95). Needless to say, there were many sceptics who wondered whether the distortions they knew were in any given mirror did not give rise to some, at least, of the things people saw there, as Chaucer noted in *The Squire's Tale* when he remarked that people said the sights in a magical mirror might be caused simply by 'angles and sly reflections' (vv. 225-35). Agrippa was inclined to agree:

> There's a cunning trick to certain mirrors, which means that the images we want [to produce] are produced in the air at a distance outwith the mirrors. Then people who have no experience of this kind of thing see them and think they are seeing the disembodied forms of demons or of souls, when in fact these things are nothing but likenesses (*simulacra*) related to themselves and devoid of any life.
>
> (*De occulta philosophia* Book 1, chapter 6)

In other words, the onlookers are simply seeing images of themselves projected from the mirror and fail to recognise them. That word *simulacra* reminds us of the Greek and Roman theory which said that the images in a mirror actually consisted of self-generated sights. No wonder, then, that Noel Taillepied, a French Capuchin writing in 1588, maintained that the mind could play tricks and make us see in mirrors things and people which are no more than figments of our imagination; or that thirty years earlier, the French mathematician Jean Pena was prepared to suggest that any ghostly apparition can be explained by reference to mirrors.[11]

Mirrors, then, could reveal what was true and make one see what was false. They were capable of being interpreted and of being manipulated. Automata parodied life, by what means the onlooker might or might not know. If the mechanism was on show, it was clear what was making the figures move. If the mechanism was hidden, explanation was not so easy. Sylvia Berryman makes the important point that 'it is not *a priori* obvious what kind of effects can be achieved by mechanical means. Experience of the actual, not imaginary account of the possible, teaches us what mechanics can achieve';[12] and indeed it is what Agrippa was saying when he wrote that those who had no experience of mirrors (*imperiti*) mistook thrown images of themselves for those of demons or ghosts. Without a sight of ropes or cogs or water or steam, the automaton becomes an object of legitimate wonder, a *mirum*, 'an astonishing thing', and the onlooker is entitled to look for non-mechanistic explanations of what she or he is seeing, whether vague 'natural powers', (which would amount to natural magic), or personal non-human forces (which would amount either to miracle or to demonic magic).

We can misunderstand this frame of mind and mode of perception if we are not careful. Let us take as an example the famous case of the Rood of Boxley Abbey. In his *Chronicle of England during the Reigns of the Tudors*, Charles Wriothesley recorded for 1538:

> This year, also in February, there was an image of the crucifix of Christ, which had been used of long continuance or a great pilgrimage at the

Abbey of Boxley by Maidstone in Kent, called the Rood of Grace, taken from thence and brought to the King at Westminster, for certain idolatry and craft what had been perceived in the said rood; for it was made to move the eyes and lips by strings of hair, when they would show a miracle, and never perceived till now. The Archbishop of Canterbury had searched the said image in his visitation, and so, at the King's commandment, was taken thence, that the people might leave their idolatry that had been there used. Also the said rood was set in the market place first at Maidstone, and there showed openly to the people the craft of moving the eyes and lips, that all the people there might see the illusion that had been used in the said image by the monks of the said place of many years time out of mind, whereby they had gotten great riches in deceiving the people thinking that the said image had so moved by the power of God, which now plainly appeared to the contrary.

On Sexagesima Sunday the image was exhibited again at St Paul's Cross in London and Bishop Hilsey of Rochester preached a sermon against idolatry, after which he demonstrated to his audience how the image had worked, and then broke the wires himself before allowing 'the rude people and boys' in the crowd to destroy the image completely.

Now, it is clearly important to our understanding of this episode that we ask ourselves who is recording it and why are we being told about it, and the answers are perfectly straightforward. The sources are Protestant and the intention is anti-Catholic propaganda. Yet the matter is obviously not as simple as that. We are given the impression that the crowd in London was angered by the revelation of how the rood was made to move, but 'rude people and boys' clearly did not constitute the whole audience, and we have no means of telling who these rude people and boys were – Protestant converts exhibiting genuine indignation? Place-men arranged and paid to deliver a satisfactory climax to the Bishop's sermon? – and what did the rest of the Bishop's audience think? What was the opinion of the Maidstone crowd which was the first to be shown the workings of the image? Before we try to answer this, let us consider another example of an automaton. It is taken from Thomas Ady's *A Candle in the Dark* (1654).

A juggler, knowing the common tradition and foolish opinion that a familiar spirit in some bodily shape must be had for the doing of strange things beyond the vulgar capacity, he therefore carrieth about him the skin of a mouse stopped with feathers, or some like artificial thing, and in the hinder part thereof sticketh a small springing wire of about a foot long, or longer; and when he begins to act his part in a fair or a market before vulgar people, he bringeth forth his imp and maketh it spring from him once or twice upon the table, and then catcheth it up, saying, 'Would you be gone? I will make you stay and play some tricks for me before you go'; and then he nimbly sticketh one end of the wire upon his waist, and maketh his imp spring up three or four times to his shoulder, and nimbly catcheth it, and pulleth it down again every time, saying, 'Would you be gone? In truth, if you be gone I can play no tricks or feats of activity today'; and then holdeth it fast in one hand, and beateth it with the other, and slyly maketh a squeaking noise with his lips, as if his imp cried, and then putteth his imp in his breeches, or in his pocket, saying, 'I will make you stay, would you be gone?' Then begin the silly people to wonder and whisper; then he showeth many slights of activity, as if he did them by the help of his familiar.

Here we are told that the conjuror's audience was stupid – 'vulgar people' and 'silly people' imply that they are uneducated and naïve to the point of foolishness – but can we rely on Ady's version of events? Thomas Ady was a physician who wrote his 'treatise concerning the nature of witches and witchcraft', as its subtitle goes, in order to impress on his readers his conviction that the English were 'so infected with this damnable heresy of ascribing to the power of witches that seldom hath a man the hand of God against him in his estate, or health of body, or any way, but presently he crieth out of some poor inno-cent neighbour that he or she hath bewitched him' (p.114); and from whom had the English acquired this nonsensical idea that witches have power to harm? From Catholics, and the Pope in particular. Indeed, 'the Popish religion', he said, 'is altogether upheld by witch-craft'. Obviously, the point of his conjuror story is to show that the common people are stupid enough to be misled by the simplest of *praestigia*, and therefore run the danger of being drawn into Catholicism again unless the government is sufficiently alert to prevent this from happening.

In the light of these tendentious accounts, therefore, we should take care to side-step the religious propaganda and ask ourselves whether the common people really were as naïve or stupid as the propagandists have been suggesting. Pageants, for example, regularly provided machinery which let clouds bearing God ascend and descend, and celebrations in churches at Easter or Pentecost saw figures of Christ raised up and the Holy Spirit in the form of a dove descend. Jean-Baptiste Thiers (1636-1703) records that it used to be the custom at certain altars when Mass was said for the souls of the dead that from the moment of consecration until the end of communion small fireworks would be set off to indicate that souls were being released from Purgatory and flying straight up to Heaven (*Traité des superstitions qui regardent les sacremens* 4.260); and there are holes in the west front of Wells Cathedral opening on to a singers' gallery within, which allowed the voices of seven choristers to ring out across the cathedral green whence they were answered antiphonally by others. The congregation outwith the cathedral would have seen only the brightly-painted statues of angels from whose immediate proximity the singing would have seemed to emanate. What these various devices suggest is that people were well used, both in the Middle Ages and later, to devices of one sort or another calculated to present opportunities for a suspension of disbelief, in essence a suspension not dissimilar to that which a modern audience brings to a conjuror or illusionist. Is the modern illusionist trying to deceive the audience? Yes. Is the audience aware of this, and do people willingly accept it as part of the performance? Yes. In what way, then, were the monks of Boxley *guilty* of deception? The answer depends on whether their audience was aware of the machinery which worked the rood and happily complied with its presence as the means whereby their imaginations were stimulated to a more intense devotion. Cynical exploitation of essentially stupid believers, however, is likely to be the least satisfactory explanation of this and similar devices, although it may flatter our sense of superiority to think otherwise.

This brings us back to Agrippa's comment on the properties of mirrors. The *imperiti*, those who have no experience of their possibilities, may be prone to misinterpret specular phenomena. Congregations which saw the ropes and pulleys attached to clouds and statues of Christ and figures of doves were self-evidently not being hoodwinked. Those who did not see the internal workings of the Boxley Rood had a choice of interpretation. The image could be a mechanism, or its movements might be the result of natural or demonic magic. Elias Ashmole records an example of this from the early sixteenth century:

> In the time of King James the 1st there was one [ ] Cantelow of Funthill, whom the country thereabout did repute a great wizard. Several odd stories go yet of him, but one to this purpose. A difference had been between the minister of Orston (or near Orston) and him; and shortly after, when the minister was in bed and going to his repose, he should hear in his chamber chimney the noise of a great passing bell, but without door it was not heard. This noise continued every night for divers months, to the parson's great vexation. Some did think it might be a trick contrived by a great virginal wire strained, but it was never discovered.
>
> (Royal Society ms. folio 363)

Natural magic, as we have seen, could simply mean that an image was being made to move by natural means unknown to or unperceived by the general public. Only 'demonic' magic supposed that those means were preternatural and sinister. As early as 1487, the Dominican Heinrich Institoris had explained this set of choices. *Praestigium*, he said, can be done in three ways. First, it can be achieved without the aid of demons, simply by human dexterity; secondly, people can use the natural power in natural materials to create illusions; and thirdly, one can rely upon demonic assistance to produce illusions. Now, demons are able to effect these illusions in several ways. If a human being can exhibit physical dexterity, a demon can do so even better. Demons know the hidden powers of natural substances more intimately than humans and can therefore use natural magic to even greater effect. (Notice that these two 'demonic' methods are demonic only in the sense that they are being used by demons instead of humans). A demon can disguise himself or a human being as something else, such as a lump of gold or a wild animal. He can work on the organs of sight and create a false impression, or upon the imagination which will perform a similar transformation and cause the senses to perceive something which is not there, or to mistake one thing for something else. (*Malleus Maleficarum* Part 1, question 9)

Deception by means of natural magic is thus quite difficult to define, for natural magic, (like every other form of magic), is open to demonic intervention and this intervention may not necessarily employ fantastical, wonder-working methods. For us, interpretation of what we see tends to be somewhat restricted because we tend to search for some mechanical explanation founded upon the physical order of things. Is the person or object or action 'real'? If not, is it an illusion or a trick? If the former, what is causing it – a play of light, a malfunction of the eye or brain, disease or drug? If the latter, are we aware of the trick and do we acquiesce in its being performed? If not, is the performer 'guilty' of some offence against us? For earlier periods, on the other hand, the blurring of lines between various magical techniques meant that explaining to oneself or to others how any particular marvel had been achieved was extremely problematical, and seeking refuge in an explanation dependent on purely human and deliberate deception would have been shutting one's eyes to a whole range of other, equally valid possibilities.

5

Wizard or Witch? A Problem for the Authorities

If there were difficulties in the past in distinguishing various kinds of reality from various kinds of illusion, people also found problems in trying to classify the different kinds of magical practitioner. Daniel Defoe wrote in 1727:

> Raising the Devil has been thought by some to be a Branch of *Witchcraft* rather than Magick... but the Point is not fully decided. It seems both the Worthy Professions have pretended to it, and perhaps both have attain'd to practise it, and so it may be reckon'd among the *Occult Sciences*, in common to the Practitioners of both kinds. [But if people do raise Satan], then they are no more Magicians, but Necromancers, and downright Dealers with the Devil, [and if they genuinely have power to produce the Devil himself, or at least the appearance or apparition of the Devil], then I say, they are no more Magicians, but Witches, Wizards, Necromancers, or what else you please to call those people that have an immediate Conversation with the *Devil*.
>
> (*A System of Magick*, Part 2, chapter 6, pp.379, 389)

Defoe, as we can see, is thoroughly confused. But he is trying to deal with a question which ought to concern us. Calling someone a 'ritual magician' runs the danger of being confusing because, taken by itself, it seems to imply that other magicians do not use ritual, and this, of course, is not so. The picture of the ritual magician we have been eliciting from our material has, so far, indicated the relevance of the following points: (i) the ritual magician is either a priest or someone who adopts a priest-like role in the performance of his (usually 'his') ritual; (ii) the ritual itself is complex, often requiring elaborate impedimenta and a lengthy period of personal, physical and spiritual preparation by the magician himself; (iii) during the course of the ceremony, spirits of one kind or another will be both invoked and evoked, and God himself may be called upon to act as guarantor of the efficacity of the ritual; (iv) the ritual magician's aim is threefold: to work wonders, to achieve a more immediate and better understanding of the mind of God, and to enter in body or in spirit into the divine presence, or into that of some angelic being. He may wish to accomplish all three ends on a single occasion, but it is more likely that his intention in working the ritual is focused upon one of these goals.

The principal ambiguity in these considerations, of course, is how complex or elaborate the operator's ritual has to be before one classes him as a ritual magician. An illustration may help. The Inquisitor-General of Spain issued an edict in 1536 requiring all Christians to declare certain points to the Inquisition.

First, if they had heard that any person had familiar spirits, and that he invoked demons in circles, questioning them and expecting their answer, as a magician, or in virtue of an express or tacit compact; that he had mingled holy things with profane objects, and worshipped in the creature that which belongs only to the Creator.

Secondly, if he had studied judicial astrology to discover the future, by observing the conjunction of the stars at the birth of persons.

Thirdly, if any person in order to discover the future had employed geomancy, hydromancy, aeromancy, pyromancy, onomancy, necromancy, or sorceries by beans, dice, or wheat.

Fourthly, if a Christian had made an express compact with the Devil, practised enchantments by magic, with instruments, circles, characters, or diabolical signs; by invoking and consulting demons, with the hope of a reply, and placing confidence in them; by offering them incense, or the smoke of good or bad substances; by offering sacrifices to them; in abusing sacraments or holy things; by promising obedience to them, and adoring or worshipping them in any manner.

Fifthly, if any one constructed or procured mirrors, rings, phials, or other vessels, for the purpose of attracting, enclosing, and preserving a demon, who replies to his questions, and assists him in obtaining his wishes; or who had endeavoured to discover the future by interrogating the demons in possessed people; or tried to produce the same effect by invoking the Devil under the name of holy angel or white angel, and by asking things of him with prayers and humility; by practising other superstitious ceremonies with vases, phials of water, or consecrated tapers; by the inspection of the nails, and of the palm of the hand rubbed with vinegar; or by endeavouring to obtain representations of objects by means of phantoms, in order to learn secret things, or which had not then happened.

Sixthly, if any one had read or possessed, or read or possessed at present, any manuscript or book on these matters, or concerning all other species of divination, which is not performed by natural and physical effects.

Three of these six requirements describe behaviour particularly appropriate in a ritual magician: evocation of demons from a circle; the use of paraphernalia designed for Church worship rather than magic, Names of Power, characters, signs, incense; adoration of evoked demons with sacrifices, prayers, and explicit submission to their superior status; and the attempt to obtain foreknowledge of the future or knowledge of 'things hidden' (*occulta*) directly from non-human entities. Possession of written magical texts, while not necessarily confined to the learned, tends to suggest that an educated person is taking a special interest in this topic; so the weight of the Inquisitor's concerns seems clearly to lean against those who operate in a sacerdotal fashion with the intention of gaining knowledge they are not entitled to have by means they are not entitled to use. Overt idolatry, which is the thrust not only of this Inquisitor's fears but also of the theological commentaries produced later in the sixteenth and early seventeenth centuries, thus appears to be the principal uniting factor in any definition of a ritual magician as opposed to the covert or tacit idolatry observable in other operators.

Does this suggestion hold up under scrutiny? In 1398, Jehan de Bar was accused of several articles of magic, found guilty, and burned in Paris. He had been practising magic over an extended period of time – he himself confessed to eighteen years, 'and particularly the last two years' – and had been employed as a known magical practitioner by some remarkably well-placed people including the Duke of Burgundy whom de Bar sought to bring completely under his own control by making an image of the Duke and consecrating it with the help of demons. The twenty items to which he confessed included worshipping demons and offering them sacrifices; wearing and using clothing, images, and books consecrated to the art of magic; invoking demons during the celebration of Mass; consecrating rings, mirrors and images; evoking demons, and enclosing one in a crystal (claiming that the demon was in fact a good angel); promoting magic as a good and licit art, and maintaining that kissing or wearing an object offered or dedicated to evil spirits is not idolatrous. There is also mention of an overt pact (*convenance expresse*) with the Enemy, a covenant which would by itself have brought him within the purview of idolatry and heresy since, as both St Augustine and St Thomas Aquinas maintained, all acts of magic were founded upon communication with demons and this communication, being made by mutual agreement for mutual advantage, necessarily implied the existence of a pact whether overt (as in Jehan's case), or tacit. An idolater, therefore, Jehan was by contemporary definition, so it is hardly surprising he was burned. Now, while we do not know what was his profession, his behaviour during his rituals was undoubtedly priest-like, and he does say at one point that he got priests to invoke demons; so if he was not a priest himself, he was able to call upon their services for magic, just as Gilles de Rais made use of Francesco Prelati.[1]

Invocation and evocation of non-human entities does seem to characterise the ritual magician in whatever century. Early in the fifteenth,

the Benedictine Johannes Nider recollected a member of his Order
who had once been a 'nigromancer', as he calls him.

> These days he lives in the Schottenstift Monastery in Vienna, but when
> he was still a layman he was a very famous nigromanticus. He had
> demonic books dealing with necromancy, and for a very long time
> lived his life according to their precepts, in pitiable and debauched
> fashion. [Saved by his devout sister's prayers, he repudiated his demons
> and became a monk.] He told me once that when he was a novice, he
> endured a good many torments from the demons he had abandoned...
> [and one night], while he was carrying a lamp, he sensed that a demon
> was with him. With a violent blow, the demon struck the lamp from
> the novice's hands and set about doing him a fair amount of harm.
>
> (*Formicarius*, c.1437-8, 5.4)

What, we may ask, has nigromancy or necromancy to do with this
Benedictine's past behaviour? Nider tries to explain. *Lazy*, a character
in his dialogue, asks the *Theologian* 'if there is a difference between
'nigromancers' and 'workers of harmful magic' (*malefici*), and if so,
what it is they do. The Theologian replies that 'properly speaking,
nigromantici are people who ostentatiously demonstrate by means of
superstitious ceremonies that they can raise the dead from below the
earth so that they can speak of hidden things' (*occulta*), and the two
examples he gives are those of the Witch of Endor and Simon Magus,
who did indeed either summon up a ghost or temporarily revive a
corpse. But then he goes on to say

> by a change in usage, however, people are called 'nigromancers' if they
> predict the future by making pacts with demons and putting their trust
> in rituals, or if they make known hidden things thanks to demonic rev-
> elation, or if they use harmful magic to cause their relatives and neigh-
> bours pain and are, in their turn, often caused pain by demons.

The likelihood, then, is that in his lay life the brother was a professional magician, attempting to read the future or give directions to

hidden treasure by performing rituals intended to raise demons who would answer his questions – exactly the kind of services rendered by Jehan de Bar and so many others like him to the noble or regal families of Europe during the fifteenth century. The key to calling them *nigromantici* as opposed to *malefici* seems to lie in their ritual summoning of demons (often, if not invariably, accompanied by an overt pact), as opposed to their aims in doing so. Witches, of course, foretold the future too, uncovered buried treasure or found lost articles, and did harm to their nearest and dearest, usually, according to expert sixteenth-century opinion, after entering into a pact with Satan who either helped them himself or allowed one of his lesser demons to do so. Witches, however, did not summon these beings by elaborate ritual. Indeed, Satan most often came to them of his own accord and made an offer which constituted the pact between them, should it be accepted. As far as Nider was concerned, therefore, the Benedictine's nigromancy lay in his possession of learned books on the subject, and in his practising what they contained to invoke demons, to judge by his later experience.

Likewise, nearly two hundred years later, Philibert Delneau, a Burgundian priest, was hanged on charges of practising magic (April 1624). A spirit, sometimes in the shape of a man and sometimes in that of a child, had been appearing in the château of Brandon, and Father Delneau, who was known as a student of magic, was sent for, whether in his capacity as a priest or as a magician is not altogether clear. Once arrived in the château, Father Delneau made several invocations to evil spirits, after which he told the seigneur that there was a treasure hidden in the grounds, watched over by a demon called Mamenon. He then provided the seigneur with characters and formulae which would help him to conjure Mamenon himself, and added a letter written in his own hand to prove he had actually spoken to the demon. The seigneur, however, left to his own devices, met with no success in uncovering the treasure and, still troubled by the spirit which continued to haunt the château, causing a great deal of noise and disturbance, abandoned his attempts at magic and, quite probably out of pique, had Father Delneau arrested.

At first the priest denied everything; but the letter in his own hand-writing was evidence too strong against him to be resisted, and so he began his confession. He had started to practise magic, he said, while he was still a schoolboy, learning the craft from a man named Cordatus. One day Cordatus, Delneau and two other schoolboys entered a magic circle and Cordatus evoked three beautiful young women who proceeded to excite them to sin and lasciviousness. Nothing further happened until after Delneau had been ordained and appointed to the cure of Anost, were he met a gentleman fallen into penurious circumstances who offered to teach him magic and, in particular, how to conjure demons. Delneau said he agreed out of curiosity and, once instructed in the art, went into a wood to put it into practice. There he stood at a crossing of two paths, made his invocations and was rewarded by the appearance of the Devil who came to him in the form of a very tall, dreadful-looking man clad in a black garment. The Devil spoke to him in a harsh, raucous voice and asked him what he wanted. Delneau's reply reminds us of the apparent frivolity which overtakes human beings in such a situation, as we saw in the cases of Cellini and Faust. He simply wanted, he said, a magical charm which would give him success in hunting. He received it, but it turned out to be useless because he and the Devil parted without making a pact. Still, Satan did promise he would appear whenever Delneau called him.

Remaining points in Delneau's confession form a curious mixture. A villager suffering from impotence asked Delneau's help, and Satan advised saying Mass backwards. This Delneau did, the responses being given by a disembodied voice which Delneau took to belong to Satan himself. For a while, Delneau did not invoke the Devil, but when at length he did, the two of them entered upon a pact which was supposed to last Delneau's lifetime. The new relationship allowed Delneau to cure bewitched persons by means of herbs and disgusting, obscene prayers; but when, on one occasion, Delneau was celebrating Mass and inadvertently spoke the words of consecration, (something he had been careful to avoid doing hitherto), the Devil beat him so badly that he felt the pains for several days afterwards. Delneau also confessed to attending the witches' Sabbat, sometimes in body and sometimes in spirit, and he gave a general description of what went on there. But this is clearly an attempt by the arresting authorities to make him fit, procrustean-fashion, an established pattern of offence which could be dubbed 'witchcraft', whereas it is most likely, as we may gather from the other items in his confession, that he was actually a ritual magician, not a witch in the conventional sense. Nevertheless, his offences, even omitting those which related to the Sabbat, were quite sufficient to condemn him and he was hanged the day after his trial.

He belongs to what we can now recognise as a very familiar pattern for magicians, the priest who evokes spirits in order to use them for purposes he could not manage to achieve successfully on his own. What is somewhat unusual about Delneau's case is his account of his seduction into experimentation with magic during his schooldays. The name of the older man, Cordatus, sounds like a pseudonym, or perhaps a professional tag, since it is merely the Latin word for 'sensible, judicious, endowed with intelligence'; and the incident of lascivious behaviour between Delneau and two other schoolboys *déjà assez grands* (which implies they were past the age of puberty and already strapping youths), and three beautiful young women, sounds like a straightforward sexual adventure, with Cordatus acting as supplier or pimp, which has been rendered a touch more exciting and mysterious by the addition of magical details. But we try to explain, or rather explain away, such evidence at our peril. We are quite without any of the necessary information which would enable us to make an informed judgement, and there is always the possibility that the incident never happened at all, or that it took place in a way much nearer that which Delneau describes than we might care to acknowledge. It does, however, provide a possible key to explaining why Delneau appears to have succumbed so easily to the suggestion of the gentleman from Poitou, who offered to instruct him in magic and the invocation of demons.

It is interesting to ask how people such as the Benedictine monk and Father Delneau were regarded by their contemporaries, and how well or how ill they fitted into the general picture of magical practitioners. For the range covered by magicians was large in the spectrum of magical operators as a whole, and each time one thinks one has managed to produce a reasonable definition of one particular type, somebody turns up to modify the pattern. Invocation and use of non-human entities, for example, seem to be two distinguishing marks of the ritual magician. But others, who were clearly not magicians in this sense, also had attendant spirits. Eugene Torralva was one such. Born in Cuenca, a provincial capital south-east of Madrid, he went to Rome when he was fifteen and entered the household of Francesco Soderini, not long afterwards Cardinal de Volterra. Torralva studied medicine, qualifying in *c*.1501 when he met a man who had been a Jew, a Muslim, a Christian, and finally a believer in 'natural religion'. Contact with this man, who had highly unorthodox opinions, unsettled Torralva's faith, although he continued to go to church and behave as a Catholic. While in Rome, however, he also met a Dominican who told him he had acquired the services of a good angel called Zequiel. Zequiel served only one human master at a time, did not make any pact, and would leave anyone who attempted to force him to answer questions. His principal gift was remarkable prescience. The Dominican offered to pass on Zequiel to Torralva out of friendship, an offer Torralva accepted. Zequiel then appeared to Torralva in the form of a young man with blond hair, clothed in a flesh-coloured garment and a black over-robe, and promised to transfer to his service for as long as he (Torralva) should live.

The flesh colour is unusual. Presumably Zequiel would thus appear naked under his outer robe. Since angels did not have bodies of their own, but had to manufacture them out of air, or borrow them, this colour may simply be a way of indicating that he looked as though he had flesh. The black outer robe is also likely to have been symbolic, a sign that in spite of his claiming to be a good angel, Zequiel was actually evil. Torralva, however, maintained, as a proof of Zequiel's heavenly provenance, that the angel never spoke against religion or urged him to commit a sin and indeed accompanied him to church, and stuck to his belief in Zequiel's essential goodness until torture made him change his mind.

Between 1502 and 1525 Torralva lived time and about in Italy and Spain, for most of that time enjoying the protection of Cardinal de

Volterra and a growing reputation as a good physician. He studied chiromancy – not necessarily as an occult discipline, but perhaps to further his medical knowledge – and Zequiel taught him the secret powers of several plants which, much to the angel's annoyance, Torralva then used to increase his income. But the most notable result of their relationship showed itself in Zequiel's accurate prophecies of future events, especially those which had political implications, such as the sack of Rome in May 1527. This last Torralva witnessed for himself. He was in Valladolid when Zequiel told him it was going to happen and, upon his asking to be taken to Rome to see such an important event, was transported thither through the air on a knotted stick. It was not the first time he had been magically transvected. In 1513, for example, Zequiel whisked him from Rome to Venice and back so quickly that his absence went unremarked. But Torralva's presence at the sack of Rome proved his undoing; for he could not keep his mouth shut and, on his return to Valladolid, proclaimed publicly what he had seen. Naturally, as soon as the truth of what he was saying was realised, his fame as a great magician increased (so much so, in fact, that Cervantes mentions this incident in *Don Quixote*), and it was this burgeoning reputation which led to his arrest by the Inquisition at the beginning of 1528 while he was visiting his native city of Cuenca.

Having collected sufficient evidence, the local inquisition found itself split on his case and applied to the Council of Castile for further advice. The Council directed that Torralva be tortured – but in limited fashion, taking into account his age and rank (and perhaps the fact that he was personal physician to the Admiral of Castile who always supported him). Torture produced a change in his view of Zequiel. Torralva was now willing to admit that Zequiel was an evil spirit, but not that they had entered into any kind of pact, or that he himself was guilty of practising magic. Faced with this new declaration, the inquisitors decided to treat Torralva with compassion and suspended his trial for a year in the hope that passage of time would produce admission of those points he was denying. In January 1530, however, his youthful dalliance with unorthodox religious opinions caught up with him as a witness informed the Inquisition of them.

Under instruction from the Council, two learned priests were appointed to bring about his conversion and were partly successful, in as much as Torralva confessed sorrow and expressed repentance for his sins, but unavailing in as much as he said he could not promise not to communicate further with Zequiel, because the spirit was more powerful than he. In March 1531, Torralva was finally sentenced to abjure all his heresies and to suffer imprisonment, a sentence which lasted for four years until the good offices of the Admiral got him released back into his service.

The angel is interesting. In addition to his original Dominican master and Torralva, Zequiel had apparently been seen by Cardinal de Volterra too, and this had piqued the curiosity of the Archbishop of Toledo who asked for a sight of him, but was refused by Zequiel himself, the refusal being diplomatically softened by a prophecy that the Archbishop would become a king, a prediction fulfilled insofar as he became Regent twice during an interregnum. Don Diego de Zuñiga, a close friend of Torralva's, who later denounced him to the Inquisition, once thought he saw something indefinable pass near Torralva while they were out walking, and was told it was Zequiel. Once again, however, the spirit refused to make an undoubted appearance. But whether others apart from Torralva actually saw Zequiel or not, no one seems to have expressed any doubts about the reality of his existence. The inquisitors themselves accepted the truth of what Torralva told them about him, and were principally concerned to make sure Torralva broke off all communication with him. (Our opinions on the reality or unreality of Zequiel are, of course, beside the point. What matters, from the historian's point of view, is what Torralva and his contemporaries accepted as true, how they incorporated such beliefs into their interpretation of the multifarious worlds about them, and how they dealt with the consequences of those beliefs.)

Torralva's attendant spirit is by no means unique. Girolamo Cardano, for example, openly admitted to having a guardian angel, although it usually manifested itself via intuitive impulses or loud noises rather than by taking recognisable shape; and people of reputedly saintly life were sometimes conscious of angelic presences apparently special to them, as in the case of Sister Giglia di Fino whose angel spoke and acted through her body while her soul was else-where, enraptured at the sight of God, and wrote down a meditation which she passed on to a local priest. Her ecstasies, levitations and cures, however, brought her to the attention of the Holy Office in 1628, and gradually, as information about her guardian angel came under close scrutiny, the suspicion grew that she was actually a char-latan and that her 'angel' was no more than Satan who was trying to have Sister Giglia taken for a saint so that he might perpetrate greater evil thereby.[2]

In such a case, the authorities had little difficulty in interpreting correctly what was going on. But in others, they experienced prob-lems they either could not or would not take the trouble to under-stand or unravel, and plumped for the simplest, most familiar solution. Thus, we have Chonrad Stoeckhlin, a horse wrangler in the moun-tains of Allgaü in the territory of Augsburg, who was visited by an angel dressed in white with a red cross on his (or her) forehead and who, in 1578, rapt Stoeckhlin away in spirit to Purgatory, an experi-ence which seems to have been repeated on several further occasions. Twenty years later, in January 1598 we have the case of Andrew Man, accused in Aberdeen of 'using and practising divers sorts of witchcraft and sorcery'. Among the fifteen items of his dittay [indictment], and in several places in his separate confession made the previous October, we find him giving details of a spirit he calls 'Christsonday':

> The said Andrew confesses that Christsonday came to him in the like-ness of a fair angel, and clad in white clothes, and said that he was an angel; and that he [Andrew] should put his trust in him and call him his lord and king; and marked him on the third finger, which mark he still bears. Also the said Andrew confesses that Christsonday rides all the time he is in their company [Andrew claimed to be a lover of the Queen of the fairies, to ride with them, and meet them on certain days] and has carnal dealing with them; and that all honest men and women, and he [Andrew] himself, kissed his arse.

Christsonday's behaviour is remarkably ambiguous in these testi-
monies, both of which, of course, are hostile to Andrew and are therefore reporting what he said about the spirit in a manner detrimental
to him. On the one hand, Christsonday showed Andrew the fires of
Hell and warned him 'he should get a touch thereof' and that he himself should be put therein. He also prophesied that on the Day of
Judgement he will be acting as a prosecuting counsel, that every person
will have his or her own dittay, that the good will be separated from
the wicked, and that on that same day, 'the fire will burn the water
and the earth, and make all plain, and... Christsonday will be cast into
the fire because he deceives earthly people'. Other, less apocalyptic
pronouncements included the prediction that 1598 would be a hard
year, but that the next fourteen would be good. On the other hand,
in the hostile phrases of the dittay,

> thou confesses that the Devil thy master, whom thou terms
> Christsonday, and supposes to be an angel and God's godson, albeit he
> has a quarrel with God and swings towards the Queen of Elfen, is
> raised by the speaking of the word *Benedicite* [Bless!], and is laid again
> by taking a dog under thy left armpit in thy right hand, putting that
> same hand in his mouth, and speaking the word *Maikpeblis*.

(This last is a puzzle. It may be meaningless, of course, but it could be
a peculiar version of the Gaelic *MacPìobull*, 'Son of the Bible' – scarcely
a clarification in itself). Moreover, the rides and meetings with fairies,
which Andrew confessed having made on All Hallows' Eve in 1596
and on Rood Day (5 May) in 1597, are recorded as though they were
conventions of witches, with Andrew acknowledging he 'saw
Christsonday come out of the snow in the likeness of a stag', presumably because his interrogators were accustomed to the notion that
Satan tended to assume animal form at the Sabbat.

The mark Christsonday was supposed to have made on the third
finger of Andrew's right hand, 'which thou has yet to show' – an interesting comment from the dittay: witches' marks were easy enough to
discover by pricking – is as odd as the rest of the matter alleged against

Andrew. Marks in the Bible are capable of indicating divine protection, as in Ezekiel 9.4 which says that a mark was placed on the foreheads of the righteous to preserve them from destruction; or they may be an outward show of someone's wickedness, such as the mark of Cain (Genesis 4.15) or the mark of the Beast (Apocalypse 16.2; 19.20). Witches' marks, obviously related to the latter, being left upon a witch's person by Satan's grip, usually appeared on the arms or legs or sides of Scottish witches. A mark on the finger was highly unusual. Andrew may have included this detail without prompting, but its appearance in his confession and dittay is strongly suggestive of his being a witch, and this chimes rather suspiciously with the general thrust of his interrogators' obvious inclinations. It goes with the confession that those who attended a fairies' convention kissed both Christsonday and the fairy Queen on the arse, a detail borrowed straight from the standard account of a witches' Sabbat.

But perhaps Andrew's interrogators were misled by the other charges against him. He was accused of accurately foretelling the future, curing humans and animals, removing bewitchment, drying up a cow's milk and blighting corn – all standard items of complaint against witches; and Heinrich Institoris had warned readers of his *Malleus Maleficarum* (1487) that one witch is able to cure anyone who has been made the victim of maleficent magic at the hands of another witch. So Andrew's removal of such a condition could easily be seen as a sign that he himself was a witch in the conventional sense of demonological treatises. Re-interpreting fairies as demons is a fairly obvious way of denigrating long-standing beliefs in localised non-human entities and thus demeaning practices connected with them as superstitious, although we should not misunderstand this reinterpretation as necessarily implying lack of belief on the interrogators' part; it is more likely that they will have seen credence in fairies as an undesirable distraction from worship of the one, true God, and a potentially dangerous opening through which Satan could enter a community and draw people into much more lethal behaviours. What will have confused the interrogators far more is the figure of Christsonday, just as Stoeckhlin's angel worried his inquisitors. The demonologist Jean Bodin maintained that genuine angels could indeed appear to human beings, urge them to behave well, and allow them foreknowledge of the future, (as Christsonday did for Andrew); but he added that it was sometimes not easy to tell the difference between a good angel and a bad one, and that the touchstone was whether the angel allowed his or her human companion to perform any kind of magic, for this was absolutely forbidden by divine law. (*De la démonon-amie des sorciers*, 1580, Book 1, chapters 2 and 3) According to this criterion, Andrew's spirit was certainly a demon in disguise, because Andrew frequently performed magical operations, both beneficent and malefic.

In Andrew's case, then, we can see that the evidence placed before them would incline his interrogators and then his assize [jury] to interpret what they read and heard as ordinary witchcraft with a number of bizarre variations. In Stoeckhlin's case, by contrast, the re-interpretation seems have been imposed on his confessions by violent torture, as though the authorities were determined to deal with the extremely unusual aspects of his testimony by lopping and stretching it until a narrative of witchcraft emerged. Thus, for example, his frequent trance flights in company with what he called 'the phantoms of the night' became a witches' transvection to the Sabbat, and his angels took on a sexual role in their relationship in order to fit, however badly, the concept of a *succubus*. We have seen, too, that Eugene Torralva's angel enabled him to fly from Spain to Italy upon a knobbled stick, and Torralva could count himself lucky that the Inquisition, as so often, resisted the pressure to turn any unusual narrative into witchcraft, although even they would have been happier had Torralva confessed to a pact with Zequiel, and spent some considerable time urging him to agree he had made one. In the end, however, the Inquisition confined itself to punishing Torralva for heresy. Both Andrew and Chonrad were executed as witches.

But if there was constant pressure to see these people with their attendant angels or demons as witches, can we detect anything in the cases of men who were never mistaken for anything other than witches beliefs or behaviour which might clearly separate them from their more learned brethren-in-magic? There is no shortage of potential evidence. Almost any community anywhere in Europe at any time during the Middle Ages and early-modern period could have produced a magician of one kind or another. Let us take three. Early in the fifteenth century in the region of Berne, Scavius ('Scabby') and Hoppo were believed to practise a wide range of harmful magic (*maleficia*). They knew how to steal someone's crops by preternatural means, raise hailstorms and destructive winds, push children into water without anyone knowing they had done it, make humans and animals sterile, hurt people and damage their goods, madden horses while they were being ridden or mounted, fly through the air, emit disgusting smells when they were in danger of being arrested, reveal things which were hidden, predict the future, see things which were in another place as though they were present in front of them and kill anyone they felt like by means of a bolt of lightning. (Nider: *Formicarius* 5.4) Second: Nikolaus Lachenmayer in Obergermaringen, arrested in 1609, foretold the future and helped his local community with blessings, roots, herbs and other means described as 'natural'. Third: in 1623, John Lambe was imprisoned 'for sorcery on Lord Windsor', and a rape (of which he was pardoned in 1624 on the grounds that the evidence against him was unsatisfactory). Then in 1625 it was noted that Lady Purbeck had visited him in prison 'to procure charms from him'. When charged with this, Lambe apparently tried to claim they were merely *praestigia*, in other words, that they were no more than conjuring-tricks; but he had used this excuse before and the authorities were very suspicious. It may be that Lady Purbeck was actually seeking *veneficia* from Lambe, ingredients such as powdered root, herb, bark, or mineral which would prove poisonous in their effect either naturally or through magic, because she herself was arrested in 1625 on the grounds that

> she is said to have worked on her husband with powders and potions, and to have tried the same on [the Duke of] Buckingham: this is confessed by one Lambe, a notorious rascal, condemned for a rape last summer, and before that arraigned for witchcraft.

That these powders and potions were regarded as more than simple poisons is indicated by a note on 12 March 1625 that she had been charged with sorcery.[3]

So here we have a wide range of magical activities done by men. Do they differ in any important way from those attributed to women, or from the aims and operations of a ritual magician? Scavius and Hoppo, according to Nider's evidence, concerned themselves principally with crops and the weather, horses and hunting (if we take it that their raising a bad smell is similar to the action of a hunted animal). Lachenmayer blessed and healed, while Lambe sought to facilitate poisoning. Now, Eva Labouvie has suggested that in the Sacer region of Germany most of these magical actions would have been seen as more strongly associated with men than with women who tended to concentrate on magic connected for good or evil with birth, death, procreation and love, and that women rather than men enjoyed easier access to spirits and demons.[4] It is an interesting proposition but does not seem to be altogether supported by evidence from elsewhere – Scotland, for example, where male and female witches performed much the same range of magic – and so the differences may reflect local conditions rather than universal roles. Ritual magicians, on the other hand, while being capable of performing many of these functions, tended to concentrate on the wonder-working aspects of natural magic and the evocation of spirits for the particular purpose of eliciting hidden knowledge, and it was certainly this last which might cause people to be very suspicious of them. Agrippa wrote:

> A good many people think that ritual magic (*theurgia*) is not illicit on the grounds that it is regulated by good angels and the presence of God. But actually it is most frequently involved in the wicked deceits of demons [masquerading] under the names of God and angels.
>
> (*De vanitate et incertitudine scientiarum*, chapter 46)

Moreover, in as much as a witch, charmer, cunning person or ritual magician had dealings, overt or covert, with non-human entities, they all laid themselves open more or less equally to a charge of idolatry, and this basic consideration, along with the attendant possibilities of murder or malicious damage to person or property, undoubtedly entered the minds of those who accused them of 'witchcraft' and of those who sat in judgement upon them. The fact of the matter is, the ritual magician did indeed have more in common with other magical practitioners than he may have realised or cared to acknowledge.

There were those who did their best to make a distinction. Elias Ashmole wrote:

> Howbeit, the ignorance and malice of some times and the common custom of ours has most falsely and abusively called necromancy and what other arts are raised from the doctrine of devils, magic; without affording that just and due distinction which ought to be made between them: and what greater injury to learning than without distinction to confound laudable knowledge with what is impious and devilish? For, if there be anything in what we call magic other than a searching into those hidden virtues which God has been pleased to bestow upon created things, (though closely locked up by the general curse) whereby we may aptly and naturally apply agents to patients; I say if in it there be anything else, they are only subtle falsehoods that shelter and shroud themselves under that title, and which would gladly be esteemed leaves of that plant, from whose root they never sprang. And therefore is it not less absurd than strange to see how some men (who would have the world account them learned, and whom I believe to be so learned, as to have read and found out what latitude is due to the word *magus*, how it is accepted by the judicious, and what a vast difference there is between the doctrine of a magician and the abuse of the word), will not forbear to rank true magicians with conjurors, necromancers, and witches (those grand imposters) who insolently intrude themselves into magic, as if swine should enter into a fair and delicate garden, and (being in league with the Devil) make use of his assistance in their works to counterfeit and corrupt the admirable wisdom of the *magi*, between whom there is as large a difference as between angels and devils.

> (*Theatrum Chemicum Britannicum*, 1652, p.443)

If we are prepared to allow that he has a point, then perhaps we can add that the one unmistakable major difference between a ritual magician and others is that he seems either to have been a priest or to have performed his magic after assuming a quasi-sacerdotal role. He was thus an inheritor and continuer of a tradition of clerical magic, which had been common since the early Byzantine period and continued without let throughout the Middle Ages and early-modern centuries; and while his interest in natural magic was gradually taken away by the natural philosopher and *his* reincarnation as a 'scientist' (in the modern sense of the word), and the *praestigiator* continued to flourish, becoming ever more ingenious in the production of his illusions, the ritual magician began to concentrate his energies more and more upon that aspect of his semi-priestly role which had been there from the start but was occasionally lost in the pursuit of working marvels – entry into the divine presence, or conversation with angels.

6

Enlightenment Magicians in Fact and Fiction

In 1770, an anonymous compiler presented to the general public *The Compleat Wizzard*, 'a collection of authentic and entertaining narratives of the real existence and appearance of ghosts, demons, and spectres'. The opening paragraph of his preface gives a very clear notion of the gentlemen's conspiracy of self-congratulation characteristic of the ambience in which many of the eighteenth-century educated and their admirers moved:

> It is the general persuasion that the moderns are arrived at a pitch of knowledge greatly superior to that of their forefathers; that, by the liberty we enjoy of treating all manner of subjects with the utmost freedom, our minds are greatly inlarged, and our views of things much more extensive than the narrowness of their education, or their prejudiced attachment to some old and unfashionable doctrines and principles, would permit them to entertain. They, good souls! Giving credit to the stories they read in the bible, imagined there were sufficient grounds to believe that there is an invisible world of spirits; that there is a devil the grand adversary of mankind, who is constantly employed in works of darkness and mischief against the peace and happiness of the human race; that there is likewise an hierarchy of angels and blessed

saints, some or other of whom never fail in their attendance on good and virtuous persons, in treating them with love and tenderness, and doing them all the good offices in their power. From the same anti-quated book they likewise imbibed strange notions of the real exis-tence of magicians, sorcerers, and witches; and that these ministers of satan were permitted to practise their diabolical acts, in subservience to some great and wise ends of providence. But whatever notions our grave ancestors entertained of these matters, we, their more enlight-ened children and successors, have more elegant and refined ideas: We will take nothing upon trust, nor believe any thing but what is brought home to our senses. We are not to be frightened by witches, spectres, ghosts, and such kind of idle romantic stuff, we leave them to old nurses to quiet their children with.

(iii–v)

But how far can this easy assumption of a break between past and present be taken seriously? If we look at much of what was actually going on in the eighteenth century, we are likely to modify our facile adoption of Whig criteria – 'every day, in every way, we are getting better and better' – and acknowledge that there is no simple and con-stant distinction between occult or demonological conceptions and 'science' to be had in this period. In 1728, for example, Johann Ludemann graduated from the University of Harderwijk on the basis of a thesis which related seven kinds of dropsy to the seven planets, and regularly used astrology and consultation with subterranean spir-its in diagnosing his patients' illnesses. Astrology, indeed, in one form or another continued to influence even the most apparently scientific of medical procedures. One of the most innovating scientists of the day, Franz Anton Mesmer, published a book in 1766, *De influxu plan-etarum in corpus humanum* ('Planetary Influx into the Human Body') which propounded a variant upon the theory of stellar rays, which had been commonplace since the early Middle Ages: namely, that an invisible fluid flows everywhere throughout creation and provides the vehicle whereby planets transmit their influences to human beings. This vital spirit, he said, can be captured in a suitable receiver which may be a person in whom the vital spirit is particularly strong, or a metal container in which the spirit can be concentrated with the help of magnetised water and iron filings. Metal rods emerging from Mesmer's box then conveyed the spirit to anyone who held on to them and thus transmitted a natural cure for any of their ailments. Mesmer delighted Vienna and Paris with a whole series of cures, some of which appeared to be almost miraculous, until his patron and patient, Court de Gébelin, died suddenly during a public consultation.

In Victorian times, the box was replaced by a person, the mesmeriser or magnetiser, who passed his or her hands over the patient and thereby occasioned extraordinary reactions – bizarre bodily contortions reminiscent of those seen in people possessed by demons, and speaking in tongues – which opponents of the practice quickly denounced either as the results of demonic forces or as fraudulent attempts to disprove the assertions of 'science'. Mesmer's box reminds us of an experiment by Joseph Priestley, best known as the discoverer of oxygen, who tried to exorcise a woman possessed by a demon with the help of an electrical machine, while by contrast, a French disciple of Mesmer, Jean Dupotet de Sennevoy, who published several books on mesmeric magnetism, actually taught in his *La magie dévoilée* (1852) that it is possible for a person to kill by magic just as she or he would by using electricity.

Priestley, however, was actually much more concerned with prophecy. Late eighteenth-century Dissenting millennialists such as Priestley and his friend Richard Price were convinced that God's eternal kingdom was at hand, and this conviction dictated not only their religious but also the rest of their intellectual outlook. Thus, Priestley interpreted the French revolution as a sign from God that the Second Coming was indeed at hand. It was an understanding of historical events and a sensitivity to portents and wonders entirely characteristic of the time. Richard Brothers, an ex-naval officer, had a series of visions which told him that God was about to destroy London, and published an account of them in 1794 to the immediate applause and support not only of the uneducated, but of doctors, chemists, mathematicians and Members of Parliament, many of whom rushed to prove, with the help of their various sciences, that Brothers was right and the millennium was on its way.

Such narratives spread quickly, aided by broadsheets and pamphlets, and provided the basis for people to interpret phenomena – be they dreams, comets, rains of blood, instances of witchcraft – in accordance with the social, political, and religious life of their community. Thus, for example, an immense display of lights in the sky above London in March 1716 was seen as a series of aerial battles not unconnected with the recent Jacobite uprisings and the execution of two of the leading Jacobite lords; while in 1719, William Whiston interpreted these and other celestial appearances as portents of the coming apocalypse. Even disputes about the nature of electricity were not necessarily conducted in purely 'scientific' terms, for they could easily be infused with the pervasive anti-clericalism, anti-Catholicism, and xenophobia of many sections of English society during this period. 'On my word, Cleonicus', says one of the characters in Benjamin Martin's *Young Gentleman and Lady's Philosophy* (1755), 'if you were to shew these [electrical] Experiments in some Countries with a black Rod in your hand and a three-corner'd Cap, and a rusty furred Gown on, they would certainly take you for a Conjurer and believe you had the Art of dealing with the Devil' (1.311) – a probable snipe at the French – while his *Panegyrick on the Newtonian Philosophy* (1749) poured scorn on 'the Wizards and Necromancers, the pseudo-Prophets, the Demoniacs, the wonder-working relicts and the group of omnipotent priests that formerly swarm'd in this Island' (pp.51-2). The idea that scientific discovery and experiment was taking place without the participants' being thoroughly imbued with their own and other people's prior belief is fantasy. The boundaries between the natural and the magical philosophies were more than a little blurred.

But we should also take into account another important point. The eighteenth century, which liked to think of itself as a period of renewal and enlightenment in contrast to the vulgarity, superstition, and ignorance which had preceded it and were still to be found in the peasantry and labouring classes, was actually in many ways a period of theatrical self-titillation in which the *bien pensants* and their noble imitators emoted as much as was fashionably possible, and preened themselves on their exquisite sensibility. Thus, in Jacques-François Blondel's novel of 1774, *L'homme du monde éclairé par les arts*, the jaded Comte de Saléran finds himself roused from the boredom of life by his experience of the arts:

> My spirit was lifted towards their brilliant sphere, contemplation gave birth to ardour, ardour aroused transports, the soul hurled itself to the place where enchantments dwell. What purity of light! What fields in which to make comparisons! What a source of pleasures! The heart which I had exhausted, the senses which I had lost – everything was restored to me, and my springtime, illuminated by the most pure fires, was a new dawn.

This blather seeps out of the period almost everywhere one looks. Not even the landscape was allowed to pass unscathed. Christian Hirschfeld, acknowledged as the great European authority on the garden, envisaged it as 'a place which has been re-formed by art in order to strengthen its natural effect' (*Theorie der Gartenkunst*, 1779-85, 4.26), and many of the carefully managed features found in pictur-esque gardens, such as broken pillars, subterranean caverns and spiral staircases in Gothic towers, were intentionally Masonic and occult points of reference for the initiated owner and visitor. In other words, the garden and the park provided a theatrical backdrop to the respon-siveness of the individual, their carefully orchestrated components intended both to appeal to a person's sensitivity and to mould it. But even nature in the raw was treated in much the same way, becoming a change of stage scenery in a constantly unfolding drama of personal emotionalism. We can see this, for example, in *La nouvelle Héloïse* by Jean-Jacques Rousseau, where the heroine Julie receives a letter from her lover Saint-Preux, describing his reactions to climbing in the Alps:

> After I had walked in the clouds, I came to a more serene place from where, at the right time, you see thunder and storm forming below

you, a too flattering image of the soul of the sage, the paradigm of which never existed, or exists only in the same places from which one has taken the sign. It was there, in the purity of the air in which I found myself, that I discerned and felt the true reason for my change of temperament, and for the return of that inner peace I had lost for such a long time. In fact, this is a general impression everyone experiences, although not everyone notices it – that on the high mountains where the air is pure and thin, you feel you breathe more easily, that your body is lighter, that your mind is more serene, pleasures are less ardent there, and the passions more under control. One's thoughts take on a grand, sublime character I cannot explain, in proportion to the objects which strike one's attention, and an indescribable calm voluptuousness which has nothing bitter or sensual about it. It seems that in raising yourself above the abode of men, you leave there all base feelings connected with earth, and the nearer you come to the ethereal regions the more your soul acquires something of their unchangeable purity.

(Part 1, letter 23)

This emotional play-acting may also be observed in the immense proliferation of Masonic and pseudo-Masonic orders and degrees invented during the same period. They preached the brotherhood of Man while promising exclusive access to hidden truths and superior insights, all by means of amateur dramatics a world removed from the original Freemasonry which had begun in Scotland at the end of the sixteenth century as a mean for workmen and gentlemen to acquire some of the elements of Hermetic philosophy. But the continuing discoveries of hidden faces and powers of nature (discoveries which were proceeding, it seemed, at an ever-increasing rate) gave substance to these hopes of occult secrets which would unlock further the treasure-house of creation. Ever more and more fascinating, this pursuit of detailed knowledge of nature, however, was deemed by many who tried to keep abreast of it to be rather like running after chimeras. 'True' knowledge, an intuitive as well as an intellectual understanding of the unchanging principles behind the apparent machine into which Science seemed to be turning the universe, became the grand desideratum, and Freemasonry and its offshoots and imitators held out some kind of promise that this was attainable.

Such a turbulent psychology, of course, laid itself open to exploitation, and the period is virtually awash with people seeking to forge a movement or a career from the abundance of willing credulity available. This sounds like a suggestion of duplicity, but here one has to be careful not to introduce a kind of sweeping Whig dismissiveness into the argument. People believed as they always had believed, with greater or lesser degrees of scepticism according to individual temperament and experience, and the prevailing social, religious, and political *mores* of their community. It was perhaps the approval of the intensity of personal feeling as a sign of inner virtue – a secularisation of the religious mystic's trance – that permitted those with an interest in turning this to their advantage to manipulate the desire for such an experience, and shape it to specific ends. 'Exploitation', though a word with negative connotations, need not necessarily imply fraud. Founders of mystical movements, for example, such as Louis-Claude de Saint-Martin, the so-called 'unknown philosopher' who taught that material reality is no more than a set of deceptive images and that Truth lies where we cannot see it; or Adam Weishaupt who founded the secret society of *Illuminati* in Bavaria in 1776 with the aim of bringing spiritual and intellectual enlightenment first to its members, then to the rest of society; or founders of magical movements, such as Martines de Pasqually who founded 'The Order of Knights-Masons, Elected Priests of the Universe', the first rite of which aimed to evoke the guardian angel of the initiate with the notion of uniting or re-integrating them, were certainly taking advantage of the spiritual and intellectual ambience of the eighteenth century; but neither kind of founder could, by any stretch of the imagination, be called a fraud or a charlatan.

Others, it is true, were more ambiguous. Giuseppe Balsamo, known as 'Cagliostro', a Sicilian born in Palermo in 1743, made a name for himself throughout Europe as a magician and healer and founder of one of the burgeoning Masonic orders, the Egyptian Rite. This last was an interesting invention. Freemasonry had been imported into

Italy by the French and the British, where it attracted condemnation from both Church and State, largely on the grounds that it operated in secret and therefore had something undesirable to conceal. Cagliostro, however, became a Freemason in London in April 1776, many members of his lodge being French or Italian. The Esperance Lodge was unusual in more than one way. It allowed a parallel women's lodge to operate alongside it – Cagliostro's wife Seraphina, for example, was initiated with him – and it belonged to the Strict Observance Rite, a version of Freemasonry founded in Germany in 1754 as a deliberate counter to what was increasingly perceived as the dry spiritual void being created by the French Enlightenment. Its fundamental myth involved the Knights Templar who were supposed to have gone underground in Scotland after their suppression by the French King Philippe V, where they preserved their magical secrets and occult power before re-appearing as Scottish Masons. Add to this the story of Christian Rosenkreutz, a Rosicrucian brother whose teaching of secret wisdom learned during his travels in Africa and the Middle East he then transmitted to Europe, a story relayed in a series of influential pamphlets published at the beginning of the seventeenth century, and we see the fertile soil out of which grew not only other, more elaborate Masonic orders, but also Cagliostro's Egyptian Rite.

Its particular origins seem to lie in a manuscript treatise on the supposed Egyptian roots of Freemasonry, written by one George Cofton about whom nothing is known for certain. The Rite Cagliostro developed after reading it required the initiate to leave home and live in complete isolation for forty days in a mountain-top pavilion whose measurements and construction are laid down in exact detail. During his or her isolation, the initiate meditates for six hours every day, and creates and consecrates magical instruments for another nine. On the thirtieth day, he or she is promised, angels will communicate a password and a seal. Physical ordeals involving fasting and purgation were added to this régime, and at certain times substances strongly reminiscent of the alchemical elixir of life were to be ingested in food or wine. All this will sound familiar. We have already come across these requirements, or instructions and practices very like them, in ancient ritual magic, and we shall meet them again in rites practised during the twentieth century.

Cagliostro, or 'The Great Copt' as he called himself in relation to this rite, also practised spirit-invocation and divination. In front of the Strict Observance Masons of Mitau in northern Germany, for example, he held a séance, using the young son of the Landmarschal Otto von Medem as his medium. Cagliostro smeared oil over the child's head and left palm, and asked the Landmarschal to whisper a question in such a way that the child could not hear. 'What are his mother and sister doing at this moment?' was the question. 'My sister is holding her hand to her heart and kissing my brother Charles', was the answer. The Landmarschal protested that this could not be true, as Charles, a soldier, was away on army exercises. When a deputation went over to the house to check the child's vision, however, they found it was perfectly true. Charles had been given unexpected leave, and the sister had been so excited, she had felt palpitations. Further séances were equally convincing to those present, particularly one occasion when the Archangel Michael appeared in visible form and kissed the child medium.

Apart from demonstrations such as these, Cagliostro also effected cures, partly by means of medicines which owed much to his skill in alchemy, partly through spirit-agencies alone. Again, records of almost miraculous recoveries from the most severe of illnesses are available from all over Europe, and indeed it was the importunate demands of the sick who valued his apparently extraordinary powers and pursued him almost without respite, which caused him to remove himself from one country to another more than the political or social difficulties into which his magical activities landed him. But Catherine the Great of Russia objected to his Masonic proselytising and forced him out of both Russia and Poland where he had made a great impression as an alchemist. In France he suffered the misfortune of being involved in the affair of Marie Antoinette's necklace. Cagliostro had produced, by alchemy, a diamond which was valued very highly by a jeweller working for Cardinal de Rohan. His name was thus linked with diamonds, and when the Comtesse de la Motte acquired a diamond necklace which the Cardinal wanted to offer the Queen, and the complex swindle the Comtesse had woven around this business fell apart, Cagliostro was arrested on charges of complicity in the affair. He was subsequently acquitted, but his reputation was ruined. He fled to London where he met only hostility; so after several further flights to Basel, Turin and Roveredo in Austria, pursued all the time by various authorities, he finally returned to Rome where, at the insistence of the Vatican which objected to his continuing attempts to establish Masonic lodges in the city, he underwent his final arrest and imprisonment, and died in close confinement in 1795.

Can he be taken seriously as a magician? That is to say, was he merely an intelligent and resourceful trickster, or was there more to him than simple *praestigia*? That there was an element of hucksterism in his career cannot be doubted or denied. But his predictions often turned out to be accurate, and his abilities as a healer were agreed by contemporaries to have been formidable. Nor was his foundation of his Egyptian Rite a cynical ploy to draw income from the pockets of well-heeled would-be initiates. The rigorous nature of the rite seems to have sprung from Cagliostro's genuine fascination with and attachment to the corpus of esoteric Egyptian wisdom as it was understood at the time. We can detect, therefore, in his character that mixture of intense seriousness and theatrical self-promotion typical of the eighteenth century, a combination modern psychology finds difficult to understand.

More comprehensible, perhaps, because less complex, is the other famous magician of eighteenth-century Europe, a contemporary of Cagliostro, the Comte de St Germain. He was born allegedly at some time near the beginning of the Middle Kingdom of ancient Egypt. A sceptic who told one of St Germain's servants that his master was a liar received the dignified reply that the servant knew it perfectly well. The Comte, he said, told everyone he was 4,000 years old, but he (the servant) had been in his employment for a hundred years, and when he first began his service, the Comte told him he was 3,000 years old. So where had the extra 900 disappeared to? The Prince of Hesse, however, wrote in his memoirs that St Germain told him he was eighty-eight when he came to Schleswig-Holstein in 1779, an age which is certainly more feasible than 4,000 or even 3,000, but one which is not necessarily accurate, since St Germain had always been mysterious not only anent his age but also his origins, and his talents, real and claimed, reflect the inextricable twining of fact and fiction which characterises his life and career. Thus, he moved easily in royal and diplomatic circles, dropping into his conversation reminiscences of his gossiping with the Queen of Sheba or his recollections of the marriage at Cana. He spoke and read eleven languages, painted very well, played both harpsichord and violin like a virtuoso, understood and practised alchemy and the art of dyeing, wrote music, invented the steamboat, effected remarkable cures with his medicines, was praised by Casanova as one of the finest conversationalists he had ever met, and rendered himself invisible at will.

These gifts, along with a handsome face and elegant manners, enabled him to be received most warmly at the Court of Louis XV and Madame de Pompadour, who were fascinated by, among other aspects of his behaviour, his refusing all food and drink, however tempting, with the explanation that he subsisted entirely upon a mysterious elixir he concocted for himself. From France he went to Britain and then to Russia where he enjoyed equal notoriety until finally he came to rest under the patronage of Prince Karl of Hesse-Cassel. His death in February 1784 did not, however, according to popular post-mortem legends, put an end to his travels, since it was said that he appeared to Madame du Barry as she was preparing to be guillotined after the French revolution, to the Comtesse d'Adhémar several times between 1793 and 1820, and in the early 1920s in a state visible only by clairvoyance to Charles Leadbeater who, along with Helena Blavatsky and Annie Besant, announced that St Germain was a great Adept and a Brother of the White Lodge which, in theosophical philosophy, guides the fortunes and destiny of the world.

Needless to say, two such figures as Cagliostro and St Germain provided irresistible copy for the satirists and novelists of the day. The English cartoonist Gillray mocked Cagliostro's attempt to introduce his Egyptian rite to London, while the Marquis de Luchet brought him and St Germain together in a scene which is entirely fictitious, but has been taken seriously by many who should have known better:

Comte Cagliostro asked him for a private audience so that he could prostrate himself before the god of the believers. St Germain appointed two o'clock in the morning. When the moment arrived, Cagliostro and his wife, wearing white garments with rose-coloured belts around the waist, presented themselves at the château. The drawbridge was lowered, and a man seven feet tall, clad in a long grey robe, led them into a dimly lit room. Once they were in the room, some folding doors opened suddenly, and they saw a temple illuminated by a thousand lights and the Comte de St Germain enthroned upon the altar. At his feet, two acolytes swung golden thuribles from which spread sweet, subtle odours. The 'god' wore on his breast a diamond pentagram whose radiance was almost intolerable; a majestic figure, at once white and diaphanous, was holding up, on the steps of the altar, a vessel on which was written 'elixir of immortality', a huge mirror was on the wall, above which was written, 'storehouse of wandering souls', and a regal figure walked up and down in front of it. A very deep silence prevailed in this sacred retreat.

But a voice, which scarcely seemed to be a voice, pronounced these words.'Who are you? From where have you come? What do you want?' The Comte and Comtesse prostrated themselves and then, after a long pause, the Comte replied, 'I come to invoke the god of the faithful, the son of nature, the father of truth. I come to demand from him one of the fourteen thousand, seven hundred secrets which are hidden in his breast. I come to proclaim myself his slave, his apostle, and his martyr'.

The god did not reply, but after a long silence the same voice asked, 'What is the intention of the partner of your long wanderings?' 'To obey and to serve', answered Lorenza.

The moment she spoke, the bright light was followed by profound darkness, the peace and quiet by clamour, trust by terror, hope by fear,

and a sharp, menacing voice shouted, 'Woe to those who cannot bear
the tests!'

> (*Mémoires authentiques pour servir à l'histoire du Comte de Cagliostro*,
> 2nd ed. Strasbourg 1786, 4-5)

This is the portentous language and over-blown description one associates with occult fiction during the eighteenth and nineteenth centuries. The pattern was set, however, in the seventeenth with the
publication of *Comte de Gabalis* in 1670. It was written by a priest, the
Abbé Montfaucon de Villars, and enjoyed an immediate success perhaps not surprising in a society which, by the end of the decade,
would be thrilled and scandalised by revelations that Louis XIV's mis-
tress, Madame de Montespan, had allegedly paid a priest, the Abbé
Guibourg, to celebrate three Satanic Masses over her naked body as
part of a magical process intended to make the King repudiate the
Queen and put Madame de Montespan in her place. It is divided into
five chapters called 'discourses' because they consist entirely of conversations between the narrator (the Abbé) and the Comte de Gabalis,
a mysterious figure who arrives out of the blue in the Abbé's study
while the Abbé is reading a letter.

> A very good-looking man came in and bowing gravely to me, said in
> French but with a foreign accent, 'Adore, oh my Son, adore the very
> good and the very great God of the Sages, and never allow yourself to
> become puffed up with pride because He sends one of the Children
> of Wisdom to initiate you into their Order, and to make you a sharer
> in the wonders of His Omnipotence'. The novelty of the salutation
> startled me, and for the first time in my life, I began to question whether
> people may not sometimes see apparitions; nevertheless, collecting
> myself as best I could, and looking at him as politely as my slight fear
> permitted, I said, 'Who ever you may be whose greeting is not of this
> world, your visit does me great honour; but, before I adore the God of
> the Sages, may it lease you to let me know to what Sages and to what
> God you refer, and if agreeable to you pray take this armchair and have
> the kindness to enlighten me as to this God, these Sages, this Order,

and, before or after all this, as to the manner of being to whom I have the honour of speaking'.

The elevated style of one age becomes the pomposity of another, and we must be careful not to misjudge the tone of this passage. Nevertheless, it is made clear that we are about to enter upon no ordinary exchange, and indeed the lofty tone adopted throughout enables de Villars to exaggerate on the one hand and undercut on the other when he wants to signal that his reader should not take altogether seriously some of the extravagance to which he is listening.

The Comte's aim in the following conversations is to persuade the Abbé to form an alliance (that is, enter into marriage) with one of the elemental forces as a mean whereby he can be initiated into Higher Knowledge, and he does not have an easy job. The Abbé is both nervous and suspicious from the start – 'As common sense has always made me suspect the existence of much claptrap in all the so-called occult sciences, I have never been tempted to waste time in perusing books which treat of them', he informs the reader before the Comte arrives – but the Comte's appearance and manner reassure him to some extent: 'I am sure... that this is a man of exalted rank', he says, '[and] that he has inherited a yearly income of £50,000. Can it be that he has lost his head over these occult follies?' Concern, however, that Gabalis may be a sorcerer still lingers, although the Abbé is puzzled how a sorcerer could be as devout as the Comte appears to be.

On their second meeting, the Comte discourses at length on the four elements under their forms as sylphs, nymphs, gnomes and salamanders. The Abbé is not impressed. 'Who would care to converse with such an ugly beast as a salamander, male or female?' he asks. 'You are mistaken' [replies Gabalis], 'that is merely the idea which ignorant painters and sculptors have of them. The salamander women are beautiful, more beautiful than any of the others, since they are of a purer element'. The Comte's suggestion that the Abbé unite with one of these, however, shocks the Abbé considerably, and he repudiates the suggestion with some force. But Gabalis gradually calms his trepidation – "'Thanks be to God, sir'", I answered, "I no longer have so much fear as this afternoon'" – and then goes on to explain that intercourse with an elemental will enable the spirit to enter Heaven and become immortal.

The third discourse is taken up with the Abbé's attempts to argue against what he has been told so far:

> I kept searching antiquity for some counter arguments which he would be unable to refute... [and] it crossed my mind that what he had said concerning the false gods, for whom he had substituted the sylphs and other elementary peoples, might be refuted by the pagan oracles whom Scripture everywhere calls devils, and not sylphs.

But the Comte proves more than equal to the argument and points out that divination of various kinds takes place in Paris every day, right under the Abbé's nose, a fact of which the Abbé seems to be completely unaware; and after overwhelming him with history both ancient and Patristic, the Comte returns to his original suggestion:

> I advise you not to postpone entering into communion with the Elementary Peoples. You will find them very sincere folk, learned, benevolent, and God-fearing. I am of the opinion that you should begin with the Salamanders, for you have Mars in mid-heaven in your horoscope, which signifies that there is a great deal of fire in all your actions. And as for marriage, I rather think that you should choose a Sylphid. You would be happier with her than with any of the others, for you have Jupiter in the ascendant with Venus in sextile.

The fourth discourse is devoted to explanations of how such alliances have happened in the past and that these precedents should persuade the Abbé to listen favourably to the Comte's urging, a line of argument which is interrupted by the arrival of a visitor. After the visitor leaves, however, the conversation continues with the fifth and final discourse in which the Comte explains that Satan has better things to do than waste his time on the kind of trivia alleged of him by conventional witchcraft narratives, and at last takes his leave of the Abbé with the observation,

> I do not doubt that you are now recovered from your panic terrors. Therefore I leave you that you may have leisure to meditate and to deliberate in the presence of God as to which species of elementary beings will be most appropriate to his glory and to your own, as a participant in your immortality.

Noel Argonne, writing in 1725, remarked that 'the world has never known whether [de Villars] merely wished to jest or whether he spoke in good faith', and critics from the early years of the twentieth century endeavoured to find in him a subverter, not of the occult sciences but of religion, their proposition being that the force of his argument and the effect of his phraseology equate the occult with superstition, and superstition with religion. This, however, is to push de Villars' careful ambiguities in one preferred direction. No such equivalences can be read into his work unless one is determined to find them there, and it is always possible to interpret him as a sincere, if hesitant supporter of the occult, as indeed a subsequent generation seems to have done. For in 1715 or 1720 there appeared a practical handbook on divination attributed to the Abbé's authorship, precisely the kind of work we have seen foisted upon earlier figures such as Albertus Magnus because they were believed to be magicians or, at the very least, authorities on the subject. If, therefore, de Villars was mocking his subject-matter, he was doing so in a subtle, elusive manner which was as liable to mislead as it was to enlighten.

No such finesse troubled the Abbé Laurent Bordelon, whose novel, *L'histoire des imaginations extravagantes de Monsieur Oufle*, appeared in 1710. The story, told at great length, concerns a credulous individual with plenty of money and a library well-stocked with works of demonology, magic and the other allied occult sciences who is led by his reading into a series of largely imaginary adventures. For example,

Monsieur Oufle had no doubt that it was entirely possible to be changed into different shapes. He believed, with the same certainty, that it was not at all difficult to bring about such a change in other people: that, for example, one could change a wine-merchant into a frog; that a woman could give one man the shape of a beaver and another that of an ass. He found no problem in these transformations because he had read they had been done.

(Chapter 3)

So it was not long before Oufle, emboldened one night by drink, dressed up in a bear costume in order to give his wife a fright (by way of a joke). Unable to interrupt her for the moment because her maid was with her, he retreated to his study and there picked up a copy of Jean Bodin's *Demon-mania of Male and Female Witches* which happened to fall open at the section dealing with werewolves. The combined effects of the wine and a good fire sent him to sleep, from which he was brusquely awoken by his wife's maid; and, forgetting he had put on a bear-costume, he immediately thought he had turned into a werewolf and, in accordance with what he conceived to be the proper behaviour of such an animal, decided to leave the house and roam the streets, howling dreadfully at passers-by – an impulse he followed at once with ridiculous effects which are described in the following chapters.

This gives a fair idea of the tone of the book. Monsieur Oufle survives his adventures as a werewolf only to become suspicious that his wife is being unfaithful to him. So he makes use of various magical practices to test her fidelity:

He had someone look for a frog and a pigeon, and removed the head of the former and the heart of the latter. Then he had these dried and reduced to powder, put this powder on his poor wife's stomach which she was asleep, and spent the whole night awake himself, the reason being, as he claimed, that his superstitious books had promised she would not fail to talk in her sleep and say everything she had done while she was awake. Alas! The worthy Madame Oufle slept so well that night, perhaps she had never had such a good night's sleep. It

163

seemed this powder was better for procuring a good sleep than for anything else. She snored, it's true, but she did not say anything.

(Chapter 7)

Oufle's brother, rather obviously called Noncrede ('non-believer') tries to disabuse him of what he regards as simple nonsense, but Oufle rejects his arguments and sticks to his credulity.

This leads on to a re-affirmation of his belief in phantoms, ghosts and other spirit-apparitions, giving Bordelon a chance to harangue his readers at length before returning to his plot and introducing a ruse by Oufle's younger daughter, Ruzine – a name which sounds a little like 'trickster' – and his valet, Mornand, whereby they can afford themselves both amusement and profit at his expense. Ruzine had noticed her father receiving a purse of 1,000 *louis*, which he had locked in a desk drawer in his room. Waiting until her father was out of the house, she used a skeleton-key to get into his study and attached threads to the bolts on the door so that they could be made to close noisily and, to all appearances, without human agency. Oufle, needless to say, begins to think his room is haunted, especially when he finds a large sheet of paper covered in magical characters and signs, which Ruzine has left there for him. In order to terrify her father even more, Ruzine also contrives to have the desk containing the money move by itself, so when, on the following day, Oufle finds magical papers everywhere, the windows open, and the purse of money gone, he has no hesitation in blaming the theft on mischievous spirits, much to the diversion of his daughter and valet.

Finally, Monsieur Oufle and his equally credulous son, the Abbé Doudou, are subjected by the author to a long tirade on judicial astrology – a subject Bordelon had treated twenty years previously in a condemnation under the title *De l'astrologie judiciaire* (1689) – and the novel ends with the celebration of Ruzine's marriage, a marriage to which Monsieur Oufle had originally been opposed because he was convinced the stars were against it.

Now, these two novels illustrate themes and approaches to magic and its allied sciences, which tend to be repeated in one way or another thereafter. On the one hand, we have the magician as a mysterious, somewhat overwhelming figure, immensely learned in a great range of abstruse subject-matter and almost hypnotically compelling in his effect on anyone he wishes to impress or convert. Thus, we find a similar though, unlike the Comte de Gabalis, quite unaristocratic character in Daniel Defoe's Dr Boreman who is described in *A System of Magick* (1726). Defoe tells us that:

> in discoursing many years upon this subject with a particular friend, a judicious and learned man, and one that was not easily imposed upon, I seemed to be doubtful of the reality of the thing in general, and whether there was indeed such a thing as that of men having intercourse with the world of spirits, and whether we might distinguish between that and witchcraft, insisting that I thought it was all witchcraft, sorcery, and the Devil.
>
> (Part 2, chapter 3)

His friend, however, demurs and tells him about a young man of his acquaintance, who had a problem and wanted to visit a 'cunning man', as he called him. The cunning man he had in mind was a Dr Boreman who lived not far from Maidstone in Kent, and the two of them decided to visit the Doctor together:

> He was a grave old man, with a long black velvet gown on, his beard long, and the upper lip of it trimm'd into a kind of muschato, a cap on his head with a border of hair within it.

Dr Boreman asks the young man to write an account of his problem, and while this is being done, he and the narrator retire to another room. Here they enter into a lengthy conversation about the nature of the Doctor's art and practices, during which Dr Boreman observes that his two visitors almost certainly had pre-conceived ideas about him when they came to visit:

You and your friend took me for a necromancer, a magician, one that deals with the Devil, can raise the Devil, converses with him, and by his help can resolve difficult questions, give answers in doubtful cases; and in short, that I am a conjurer.

Asked how he does what he is credited with doing, the Doctor ascertains that the narrator believes in the existence of a world of spirits, and then tells him he has actually 'conversed' – that is, seen, spoken to and heard – the spirits of the invisible world, for which he gives Biblical precedents. But nowadays, he explains, spirits have ceased general conversation with human beings because since the Flood humans have become too gross and too unworthy in their manners and morals to warrant such a privilege. Consequently, only those who 'render themselves acceptable and worthy by a life of earnest application to the study of divine science [theology], and who seek after the high illumination are likely to have that privilege restored. Unfortunately, however, although the spirits are still willing to enter into converse with suitable human beings,

the custom of the world has been, and still is, to be shy and afraid of them, take them to be evil spirits, and, as the world calls them, devils, so that a good spirit cannot now offer its assistance to Man, or go about to do any good to mankind, but they are frighted and terrify'd, and cry out *the Devil*, fly from it, and refuse to accept the benefit offer'd.

We discover the results of this fear when we are told what local people think of Dr Boreman. The landlord of the lodging-house where the narrator and his young friend are staying, for example, admits that the Doctor is a good and respectable man, but says he does many strange things which frighten ordinary folk, such as exorcising an evil spirit or laying a ghost, charming and casting spells, and drawing a circle to protect a young girl from a man's unwanted sexual attentions, which held the man fast until the Doctor came and released him. Despite these good reports, however, the narrator remains convinced that Dr Boreman must work magic in conjunction 'with such spirits or such beings as I should still call *devils*', as some of his alleged practices seem to suggest:

> Three young fellows being gotten into an orchard, which I suppose was under his particular care, he caus'd a large bell to hang to the heel of their shoes behind, like a heel-spur, by which they alarm'd the house and raised the people, who surrounding the orchard, took them all. When they were taken, the bells being to be pull'd off, could not be seen, and yet the sound of them was heard all the way they went to the justice of the peace, till he committed them, and then ceased.

The narrator's conclusion, therefore, is that Dr Boreman is not altogether to be trusted, but he has had to shake himself free both from the Doctor's personal charisma and the local acknowledgement of his power and effectiveness by the somewhat unhappy device of drawing a sudden comparison between Dr Boreman and Jakob Boehme 'who pretended [claimed] to see things invisible and hear things unutterable', and published works which are incomprehensible to the general reader. The grinding of *non sequiturs* as Defoe tries to tell us that this is justification enough for not taking Dr Boreman seriously is almost audible.

Making mockery of people's credulousness and undermining the effect of demonological learning, which is to some extent Defoe's aim and entirely that of the Abbé Bordelon, leads naturally to the subject of deliberate fraud, and Defoe includes in his *System of Magick* the story of a magician who elicits from a young woman a confession that she is pregnant by a youth called Thomas, and then uses his assistant George to play the part of a ghost in order to persuade Thomas that he is haunted, and that the only way he can be free of his troublesome spirit is to marry the girl he was prepared to abandon to her fate – a piece of knockabout fun, on a par with some of the episodes in *L'histoire des imaginations extravagantes*. Now, the magicians in each of these fictional pieces have certain things in common. They tend to be portrayed as learned, but they are not ritual magicians. Indeed, with the exception of the Comte de Gabalis, they are closer to cunning folk or witches, and their magic is treated either as a subject for caution or for laughter. It is trickery or flannel, and they themselves are figures of fun, or slightly dubious characters. The fictional legacy of the eighteenth century, therefore, tends to portray magic and its male practitioners – there is a different agenda when it comes to depicting female witches – as odd, neither fully integrated into everyday life nor yet entirely removed from it, and therefore either unsettling or increasingly irrelevant.

This, however, runs contrary to what was happening in real life beyond the charmed circle of some graduate scientists and middle-class novelists. A figure such as Francis Barrett was, for example, more common than the sceptics. Author of a highly influential collection of occult material, *The Magus, or Celestial Intelligencer* (1801) and perhaps also *The Lives of Alchemystical Philosophers* (1815), he describes himself on the title-page of the former as 'Professor of Chemistry, natural and occult Philosophy, the Cabala, etc. etc.' and as a Brother of the Rosy Cross, a claim referring to a secret society of philosophers, Kabbalists and alchemists dating from the announcement of the existence of such an organisation at the beginning of the seventeenth century. Barrett taught magic in London, and a number of later occultists maintained they had been his pupils, although it is possible they were merely elevating their own reputations by seeking a connection with the author of a particularly famous book. *The Magus* includes a mass of material derived from earlier grimoires and especially from the *De occulta philosophia* of Cornelius Agrippa. He also translated Pietro d'Abano's *Heptameron*, one of the most important of the Mediaeval grimoires, and included an essay on the Kabbalah, which reintroduced this Jewish mystical system to western occultists.

But Barrett also shows himself to be a man of his own time by including a section on magnetism, prefacing it with the remark that,

> however impudent in their assertions, and bigoted to their own false opinions some of our modern philosophers may be, yet we have seen two or three individuals, who, by dint of perseverance, have proved the truth and possibility of Magnetism, by repeated and public

experiments. Indeed, the ingenious invention of the Magnetic Tractors
prove at once that science should never be impeded by public slander
or misrepresentation of facts that have proved to be of general utility

– a clear reference to Franz Mesmer and his magnetic cures.

But if Barrett was influential, far more important was Alphonse
Louis Constant (1810-75), the son of a French cobbler, who was trained
as a priest in the somewhat unconventional seminary of Saint-Sulpice,
was created deacon, but then left to scratch a living on the fringes of
socialist-cum-royalist journalism. Between about 1839 and 1847 he
joined a number of secret societies derived from Freemasonry, studied a wide range of esoteric subjects ranging from Templar history to
alchemy, and listened to some of the odder characters to be found in
mid-nineteenth century Paris, such as the prophet Ganneau who used
to work himself into a rhetorical frenzy – literally foaming at the
mouth – as he theorised about the creation of the universe and the
Fall of humankind. More notable, perhaps, was a Polish sage, Josef
Maria Höne-Wronski, who taught a form of esoteric Messianism
mingled with Kabbalistic Martinism, and had invented a machine, the
'prognometer', intended to produce accurate predictions mechani-
cally. Fired by such people and teachings as these, and by his own
researches into the occult sciences, Constant (who published under
the name 'Eliphas Lévi' – an interesting indication of how deeply
Wronski's Jewish eclecticism had penetrated his consciousness) began
to put into print the results of his lucubrations. *Le dogme et rituel de la
haute magie* ('The Teaching and Ritual of High Magic') appeared in
1856.[1] It treats its various subject-matters in what can only be called a
cavalier fashion, lopping, distorting, inventing wherever necessary in
order to support Lévi's own particular theories. But the re-interpre-
tations are based on Lévi's own genuine belief that he had discovered
truths about human history and the human condition, which were
important to convey to others, so we must not attempt to dismiss him
as a mere fantasist or cynical Grub-Streeter.

The book also contains his personal account of a near-successful
evocation of the spirit of Apollonius of Tyana, a necromantic

experience which clearly left him shaken, for he was at basis a theo-
rist, not a practitioner of magic:

> In the spring of the year 1854 I had undertaken a journey to London,
> that I might escape from internal disquietude and devote myself, with-
> out interruption, to science. I had letters of introduction to persons of
> eminence who were anxious for revelations from the supernatural world.
> I made the acquaintance of several and discovered in them, amidst much
> that was courteous, a depth of indifference or trifling. They asked me
> forthwith to work wonders, as if I were a charlatan, and I was somewhat
> discouraged, for, to speak frankly, far from being inclined to initiate
> others into the mysteries of Ceremonial Magic, I had shrunk all along
> from its illusions and weariness... I buried myself therefore in the study
> of the transcendent Kabbalah, and troubled no further about English
> adepts, when, returning one day to my hotel, I found a note awaiting
> me. This note contained half of a card, divided transversely, on which I
> recognised at once the seal of Solomon. It was accompanied by a small
> sheet of paper, on which these words were pencilled: 'Tomorrow, at
> three o'clock, in front of Westminster Abbey, the second half of this card
> will be given you'. I kept this curious assignation.

He met a veiled woman who engaged him in conversation and, once
she had demonstrated her serious interest in magic, together they
decided that Lévi would perform a ritual of evocation at her house:

> The cabinet prepared for the evocation was situated in a turret; it con-
> tained four concave mirrors and a species of altar having a white marble
> top, encircled by a chain of magnetised iron. The Sign of the
> Pentagram... was graven and gilded on the white marble surface; it was
> inscribed also in various colours upon a new white lambskin stretched
> beneath the altar. In the middle of the marble table there was a small
> copper chafing-dish, containing charcoal of alder and laurel wood;
> another chafing-dish was set before me on a tripod. I was clothed in a
> white garment, very similar to the alb of our Catholic priests, but
> longer and wider, and I wore upon my head a crown of vervain leaves,

intertwined with a golden chain. I held a new sword in one hand, and in the other the ritual.

I kindled two fires with the requisite prepared substances, and began reading the evocations of the ritual in a voice at first low, but rising by degrees. The smoke spread, the flame caused the objects upon which it fell to waver, then it went out, the smoke still floating white and slow about the marble altar; I seemed to feel a quaking of the earth, my ears tingled, my heart beat quickly. I heaped more twigs and perfumes on the chafing-dishes, and as the flame again burst up, I beheld distinctly, before the altar, the figure of a man of more than normal size, which dissolved and vanished away. I recommenced the evocations and placed myself within a circle which I had drawn previously between the tripod and the altar. Thereupon the mirror which was behind the altar seemed to brighten in its depth, a wan form was outlined therein, which increased and seemed to approach by degrees. Three times, and with closed eyes, I invoked Apollonius. When I again looked forth there was a man in front of me, wrapped from head to foot in a species of shroud, which seemed more grey than white. He was lean, melancholy and beardless, and did not altogether correspond to my preconceived notion of Apollonius.

I experienced an abnormally cold sensation, and when I endeavoured to question the phantom I could not articulate a syllable. I therefore placed my hand upon the Sign of the Pentagram, and pointed the sword at the figure, commanding it mentally to obey and not alarm me, in virtue of the said sign. The form thereupon became vague, and suddenly disappeared. I directed it to return, and presently felt, as it were, a breath close by me; something touched my hand which was holding the sword, and the arm became immediately benumbed as far as the elbow. I divined that the sword displeased the spirit, and I therefore placed it point downwards, close by me, within the circle. The human figure reappeared immediately, but I experienced such an intense weakness in all my limbs, and a swooning sensation came so quickly over me, that I made two steps to sit down, whereupon I fell into a profound lethargy, accompanied by dreams, of which I had only a confused recollection when I came again to myself.

Lévi goes on to evaluate the experience:

> I am stating facts as they occurred, but I would impose faith on no one. The consequence of this experience on myself must be called inexplicable. I was no longer the same man; something of another world had passed into me; I was no longer either sad or cheerful, but I felt a singular attraction towards death, unaccompanied, however, by any suicidal tendency... Am I to conclude from all this that I really evoked, saw and touched the great Apollonius of Tyana? I am not so hallucinated as to affirm or so unserious as to believe it. The effect of the preparations, the perfumes, the mirrors, the pentacles, is an actual drunkenness of the imagination, which must act powerfully upon a person otherwise nervous and impressionable. I do not explain the physical laws by which I saw and touched; I affirm solely that I did see and that I did touch, that I saw clearly and distinctly, apart from dreaming, and this is sufficient to establish the real efficacy of magical ceremonies... There are evocations of intelligence, evocations of love and evocations of hate; but, once more, there is no proof whatsoever that spirits leave the higher spheres to communicate with us: the opposite, as a fact is more probable. We evoke the memories which they have left in the Astral Light, or common reservoir of universal magnetism.
>
> (*Transcendental Magic*, chapter 13)

Lévi's principal contribution to the development of magic in the nineteenth century is perhaps his interpretation of Mesmer's universal vital fluid, or animal magnetism, as this 'astral light'.

Q. What is man?

A. Man is an intelligent and corporeal being made in the image of God and of the world, one in essence, triple in substance, mortal and immortal.

Q. You say, 'triple in substance'. Has man, then, two souls or two bodies?

A. No; there is in him a spiritual soul, a material body, and a plastic medium.

Q. What is the substance of this medium?

A. Light, partially volatile, and partially fixed.

Q. What is the volatile part of this light?

A. Magnetic fluid.

Q. And the fixed part?

A. The fluidic or fragrant body...

Q. Give us some notions of this plastic medium.

A. It is formed of astral or terrestrial light, and transmits the double magnetisation of it to the human body. The soul, by acting on this light through its volitions, can dissolve it or coagulate it, project it or withdraw it. It is the mirror of the imagination and of dreams. It reacts upon the nervous system, and thus produces the movements of the body. This light can dilate indefinitely, and communicate its reflections at considerable distances; it magnetises the bodies submitted to the action of man, and can, by concentrating itself, again draw them to him. It can take all the forms evoked by thought, and, in the transitory coagulations of its radiant particles, appear to the eyes; it can even offer a sort of resistance to the touch. But these manifestations and uses of the plastic medium being abnormal, the luminous instrument of precision cannot produce them without being strained, and there is danger of either habitual hallucination, or of insanity.

Q. What is animal magnetism?

A. The action of one plastic medium upon another, in order to dissolve or coagulate it. By augmenting the elasticity of the vital light and its force of projection, one sends it forth as far as one will, and withdraws it completely loaded with images.

(*The Key of the Mysteries*, Part 2, second series)

Control of the astral light would give the magician almost boundless power, and therefore the various components of any magical ritual – incense, colours of clothing, impedimenta, words and gestures – are designed to assist him to focus his concentration and direct his will to achieve this end.

Dogme et Rituel is an excellent example of Lévi's talent for synthesis which also enabled him to blend various key elements of pseudo-history involving the legend of the earthly paradise before the Fall, the Egyptians, the Templars, Kabbalah, Tarot, Rosicrucianism and Freemasonry, and so produce a coherent but subversive history of Western culture which would transcend that offered by the secret societies of his day, and appeal to anyone who wished to explore spiritual life beyond the bounds of orthodox Christianity.

But if this made him influential, it did not make him unique. We need to remember that the nineteenth century was a period in which, for example, Spiritualism flourished, spirit photography was developed, astrology saw a resurgence in popularity and local cunning folk or wizards or witches or sorcerers were consulted over a great many pressing questions, just as they always had been. The 'disenchantment of the world' described by Max Weber was little more than a pious hope or fantasy of the intellectuals he was addressing. As Maureen Perkins puts it,

> there was no decline of magic... Joseph Powell, the astrologer... was consulted by clients who might easily be described as engaging in a process of 'recreation', seeking reassurance about important decisions at a time of rapid change. Like the sports and pastimes which, despite considerable attempts by reformers to ban them altogether, continued through the nineteenth century in altered form, the magical practices of astrology and fortune-telling are still with us today, having negotiated the Victorian labyrinth of disapproval, scorn, and legal control.[2]

In France, by contrast, *spiritisme* became politicised and turned into another rod with which to beat the Catholic Church, while ritual magic, too, increasingly took on a subversive, parallel form which mocked as it imitated – the distorted mirror-image of orthodoxy some late-Mediaeval and early-modern demonologists had feared could be found in witchcraft, but actually waited to materialise in the age of the train and the telegraph. At roughly speaking the same time, the Abbé Boullan founded his Society for the Reparation of Souls, which practised a curious blend of exorcism and demonic magic. Eugène Vintras, a factory-foreman from Tilly-sur-Seulles, had increasingly frequent visions which caused him to found the 'Church of Carmel' and celebrate Masses of his own devising. Boullan met him and was much impressed, and declared himself a convert to this new Church which he then attempted to direct after Vintras's death in 1875. In 1886, however, Boullan was made the object of magical warfare by an aristocrat, Stanislas de Guaita, himself about to be the founder of a new magical order, the 'Kabbalistic Order of the Rose Croix' (1888), in company with a novelist, Joseph Aimé Péladan, who soon disagreed with him about the basic philosophy of their order and left to found his own version in 1890.

Meanwhile, Britain was seeing the emergence of societies devoted to the exploration of non-material worlds. Ever since the end of the eighteenth century, the East had been associated in the western mind with occult wisdom and hidden masters, and this tendency found its best-known and longest-living expression in the foundation of the Theosophical Society in 1875 by Helena Blavatsky, Henry Olcott and William Judge. From New York, where it started, to Adyar near Madras in India in 1883, and thence to Britain in 1884 and the rest of Europe, theosophy spread rapidly, partly because the appeal of its principal aim was strong – 'to investigate the hidden mysteries of Nature and the physical powers latent in man' – and partly because of the apparently remarkable psychic powers of Blavatsky herself, although these had nothing to do with magic. In fact, Blavatsky was, if anything, hostile to the European magical tradition and forbade her followers to practise it. But she did pass on one very important legacy to much of the modern tradition, and that was the Eastern notion of reincarnation, the idea that there could be a kind of Darwinian evolution of the soul. It is an idea which can clearly be seen informing the magical endeavours of twentieth-century magicians, who often see themselves as trying, through their magical work, to ascend to higher levels in preparation for the next stage of human development.

In 1881, the Society for Psychical Research was founded with the aim of studying paranormal phenomena according to objective (by which they meant 'scientific', so not actually 'objective') criteria; and in 1884 there emerged, through a newspaper advertisement, notice of an order whose intention was to train its initiates in some of the arts of practical magic in the 'Hermetic Brotherhood of Luxor'. The arts upon which it concentrated were those of clairvoyance and clairaudience, because by means of these the initiate would be enabled to contact adepts and non-human entities belonging to the celestial hierarchies from whom she or he would receive further instruction and enlightenment. To assist them, initiates used mirrors or crystals, setting them up in a room dressed in violet and white, the scryer wearing a white surplice and addressing a prayer to God that he might allow the Archangel Michael to exercise his influence upon the mirror or crystal and thus permit the celestial spirit who was being evoked to assume an angelic form, appear therein, and answer the initiate's questions. It is a procedure of ritual magic reminiscent of the workings directed by John Dee and Edward Kelly. As well as mirrors or crystals, initiates could also use drugs to help them separate their astral doubles from their physical body, and so rise upon the planes. There was nothing unusual about this. Opium and hash were legal and easily obtainable at the time, and their expanding effects were thought to be legitimate, just as were those of LSD in the mid-twentieth century.

But it was in 1888 that there sprang into being what was to be in essence a magical university, the 'Hermetic Order of the Golden Dawn'. It was founded by William Woodman, Supreme Magus of the Societas Rosicruciana in Anglia. This was a society founded in 1865 or 1866 by Robert Little, a Freemason and student of the works of Eliphas Lévi, with the notion of providing an order devoted to the exploration of the Kabbalah, Hermetic texts and various aspects of ancient (that is, Classical) wisdom. Co-founders were William Wynn Westcott, secretary of the SRIA, and Samuel Liddell Mathers, a student of occult literature and a syncretiser of genius, far surpassing Eliphas Lévi in his ability to produce a coherent magical system from a multiplicity of western texts in both Hermetic and other magic. The history of the Golden Dawn (GD) is well known and is not here our immediate concern. What does need a little description, perhaps, is the system which Mathers created. The order was divided into three stages. The third existed only on a spiritual plane, so for practical purposes only the first two were significant. The first of these concentrated on four grades preceded by an initiatory grade in which the candidate was known as a 'neophyte'. This introduced him or her (for the GD, like Cagliostro's Egyptian rite, admitted women as well as men) in a ceremony heavily based on its Masonic equivalent, to the otherworld of the order in which the officers bore Greek names but represented Egyptian divinities, and the furniture and impedimenta of the temple related to the Kabbalistic Tree of Life. Thus psychologically prepared for the magical system he or she was about to encounter, the neophyte entered upon the four grades proper of the first stage. These concentrated their energies upon the four elements – earth, air, water, and fire – bore the names of the equivalent grades of the Societas Rosicruciana – Zelator, Theoricus, Practicus, and Philosophus – and were numbered in relation to the Kabbalistic Tree. So Zelator = grade 1 in the GD and also 10, 'Malkuth', the lowest *sephira* on the Tree, which relates specifically to earth. Theoricus is therefore 2 = 9, Practicus, 3 = 8, and so forth. Progress through these grades was not easy. The candidate was given lectures to read and absorb, and homework to do, and there were examinations to take and pass before she or he was permitted to pass to the next grade.

These initial grades trained the candidate in the theory of magic. Above all, perhaps, they made her or him intimately familiar with the Kabbalah, an indispensable system of mystical advancement intended to raise the practitioner beyond the material and into the angelic and divine worlds. Developed in various directions by Jewish mystics and scholars from about the seventh century onwards, the Kabbalah was spread into Europe from Spain after the expulsion of the Jews in 1492. Christian theologians and philosophers saw in it proof of monotheism, as well as a powerful mechanism for finding out the secret names of God and a myriad of his angels, and so of learning how to control the power inherent therein. The 'Tree' is, in effect, a diagram which illustrates how God, in creating the universe, sent out an emanation of himself into the void. This emanation then sent out further emanations until the total of ten was reached. These emanations are known as *sephiroth* and are connected to each other by twenty-two paths, each represented in the Kabbalistic system by one of the twenty-two letters of the Hebrew alphabet. Each *sephira* receives energy from the one before it along the appropriate path, and transmits an accumulation of energy – that which it has received, along with its own – to the *sephira* next in order. Kabbalists seek to use these twenty-two paths to ascend via each *sephira* to a state of reintegration with God.

The second stage of initiation took the candidate further up the Kabbalistic Tree into a set of grades based on the Rosicrucian legend of Christian Rosenkreutz. For these, an elaborate construction known as 'the Vault of the Adepts' was required and, as in the first stage, the candidate had to pass through a complex prefatory ritual called 'the Portal' which was intended to introduce her or him to the process of becoming a practical (as opposed to theoretical) magician via symbolic death and resurrection within the vault. Here followed in practice three adept grades during which the candidate learned an extraordinary amount of operative magic and other necessary or desirable disciplines, at the end of which he or she would have mastered, at very great personal effort, a remarkable amount of occult learning, and would have become a technically advanced magical operator. Examinations during this lengthy learning process involved the making and effective consecration of magical implements, spirit vision, astral projection, divination according to a variety of forms, and the Enochian system of magic based on the angelic revelations given to John Dee.

All this represents a quite extraordinary fusion of the various occult streams which went to make up the western tradition of magic, and it was the work of Samuel Liddell Mathers. Mathers was born in 1854, initiated into Freemasonry in 1877 and into the SRIA where he met Woodman and Westcott, his co-founders of the GD. He devoted himself early on to the study of the occult sciences, spending long hours in the reading-room of the British Museum where he read and translated much arcane material, such as the *Book of the Sacred Magic of Abra-Melin the Sage*, a manuscript perhaps dating to the end of the seventeenth century but claiming to be much older and of Jewish provenance. It was the long time devoted to such studies, allied to a remarkable imagination which could draw out elaborate ceremonies from the slightest of hints, which enabled him not only to fuse into a coherent whole the most disparate of materials, but also to make that syncretism work. W.B. Yeats, a leading member of the GD for many years, may have dismissed Mathers as a man of 'much learning but little scholarship', but scholarship was not required for the task he had in hand. Learning, however, was essential and that Mathers had in abundance.

Magical orders, particularly those which seek to impose strict discipline and a single vision on their members, tend to be fissiparous, and it is well known that the GD was unable to sustain itself as a unified organisation. Mathers's autocratic and increasingly uncertain temperament did not help. But the GD came into being as a great school of ritual magic and, however variant its offshoots, this is what it has remained. Anyone with any claim to work within the western magical tradition during the twentieth century owed something – and usually a great deal – in one way or another to the system and order which Mathers had created, and this is both his legacy and his legitimate claim to fame.

7

Twentieth-Century Magicians: The Children of Freud and the Therapists

Two quotations point the way to what was to become an acknowledged feature of the twentieth-century ritual magician, the focusing of the will. 'To affirm and will what ought to be is to create; to affirm and will what ought not to be is to destroy' (Eliphas Lévi: *The Key of the Mysteries*); and Nathaniel Hawthorne's fictional thumbnail sketch of a wizard, 'a small, grey, withered man, with fiendish ingenuity in devising evil, and superhuman power to execute it, but senseless as an idiot and feebler than a child to all better purposes' ('Anne Doane's Appeal', 1835). Perhaps the best-known magician to come out of the Golden Dawn personified this impulse to the will and the reputation for evil which often accompanied it more vividly than any other. Aleister Crowley (1875-1947) was born into a family of Plymouth Brethren and inherited a fortune which enabled him to live a life of ease and indulgence until he had spent it all, after which the rest of his life was dominated by poverty. A man of several talents – his mountaineering skills may have been underestimated but he himself overestimated his gift for poetry – the one great work into which he poured everything throughout most of his life – energy, money, thought – was magic. Already well versed in the subject by the time he became an initiate of the Golden Dawn in 1898, he was disappointed by the early grades of the order, regarding them as ludicrously simple, but much impressed by a GD member who undertook to be his tutor in magic, Allan Bennett. Bennett himself was a magician of no mean degree. We have already come across him in chapter two, blasting a sceptic with his glass staff, and he used this same staff to trace figures in the air which would be visible to others, standing out in a faint bluish light. He and Crowley lived together for a while, practising magic and taking drugs to 'open the gates of the World behind the Veil of Matter', as Bennett put it; but Bennett was more interested in Buddhism and yoga than practical magic (interests he passed on to Crowley, who accumulated no mean knowledge and understanding of them), and later became a Buddhist monk in Ceylon (Sri Lanka).

As Crowley advanced in knowledge and magical ability, he was able to see beyond material appearances and deal with the reality lying behind them. This, at any rate, is how we should interpret a number of anecdotes he tells of his magical experiences. For example:

Gerald Kelly showed considerable perturbation of mind and on being asked by Frater P [Crowley] what was exercising him, Gerald Kelly replied, 'Come and free Miss Q from the wiles of Mrs M'. Being asked who Mrs M was, Gerald Kelly answered that she was a vampire and a sorceress who was modelling a sphinx with the intention of one day endowing it with life so that it might carry out her evil wishes; and that her victim was Miss Q. [Crowley] wishing to ease his friend's mind asked Gerald Kelly to take him to Miss Q's address, at which Mrs M was then living. This Gerald Kelly did.

Miss Q, after an interview, asked [Crowley] to tea to meet Mrs M. After introduction, she left the room to make tea – the White Magick and the Black were left face to face.

On the mantelpiece stood a bronze head of Balzac, and [Crowley], taking it down, seated himself in a chair by the fire and looked at it.

Presently a strange dreamy feeling seemed to come over him, and something velvet-soft and soothing and withal lecherous moved across his hand. Suddenly looking up he saw that Mrs M had noiselessly quitted her seat and was bending over him; her hair was scattered in a mass of curls over her shoulders and the tips of her fingers were touching the back of his hand.

No longer was she the middle-aged woman, worn with strange lusts; but a young woman of bewitching beauty.

At once recognising the power of her sorcery, and knowing that if he even so much as contemplated her Gorgon head, all the power of his Magick would be petrified, and that he would become but a puppet in her hands, but a toy to be played with and when broken cast aside, he quietly rose as if nothing unusual had occurred; and placing the bust on the mantelpiece turned towards her and commenced with her a magical conversation; that is to say a conversation which outwardly had but the appearance of the politest small talk, but which inwardly lacerated her evil heart, and burnt into her black bowels as if each word had been a drop of some corrosive acid.

She writhed back from him, and then again approached him even more beautiful than she had been before. She was battling for her life now, and no longer for the blood of another victim. If she lost, hell yawned before her, the hell that every once-beautiful woman who is approaching middle age sees before her; the hell of lost beauty, of decrepitude, of wrinkles and fat. The odour of man seemed to fill her whole subtle form with a feline agility, with a beauty irresistible. One step nearer and then she sprang at [Crowley] and with an obscene word sought to press her scarlet lips to his.

As she did so [Crowley] caught her and holding her at arm's length smote the sorceress with her own current of evil, just as a would-be murderer is sometimes killed with the very weapon with which he has attacked his victim.

A blue-greenish light seemed to play round the head of the vampire, and then the flaxen hair turned the colour of muddy snow, and the fair skin wrinkled, and those eyes, that had turned so many happy lives to stone, dulled and became as pewter dappled with the dregs of wine. The girl of twenty had gone; before him stood a hag of sixty, bent, decrepit, debauched. With dribbling curses she hobbled from the room.

(*Confessions*, 335-6)

There is no point in trying to 'rationalise' this account. We do not actually know what took place on that occasion, nor Crowley's exact state of mind at the time. Any reinterpretation we may care to adduce, therefore, will merely set up our unsupported predilection in place of his, and will neither explain nor elucidate Crowley's narrative in any sustainable or satisfactory way. The same may be said of one of the key experiences of Crowley's magical life, the appearance of the spirit Aiwass. In March 1904 he and his wife, Rose Skerrett, were in Cairo and Crowley was trying to conjure up sylphs (elemental spirits of air). Rose seemed to enter some kind of trance and told Crowley that 'Horus' was waiting for him, a surprise to Crowley because Rose knew nothing about magic or, indeed, the Egyptian pantheon. So he tested her by asking detailed questions about the person she was seeing, and was astonished to be given detailed, accurate answers. Further ceremonies of invocation, however, revealed that the spirit was not actually Horus himself, but a messenger, named Aiwass, and, after an interval of two weeks, Aiwass began to dictate to Crowley a short book which Crowley called *The Book of the Law*, and which formed the basis of his magical philosophy thereafter. It announced the dawn of a new age for humanity, the Aeon of Horus, of which Crowley was to be the prophet. Everyone, said this new philosophy, in an echo of Nietzsche's prophecy of the coming of a more-than-human person who would transcend the slave values of Christianity, has the right to develop in accordance with his or her own will in harmony with the rest of creation, and one can see therein the stimulus for Crowley's definition of magic – 'the art and science of causing change to occur in conformity with Will'. 'Everything', he explained further, 'springs with absolute logic from the singular principle, "Do what thou wilt shall be the whole of the Law".' In 1920, conscious of his role as prophet of and model for the coming Aeon, he founded a small community in Cefalù, a small town about forty miles east of Palermo in Sicily, which he called *The Abbey of Thelema*, *thelema* being a Greek word for 'will'.

'My main idea', he wrote in his *Confessions*,

TWENTIETH-CENTURY MAGICIANS

had been to found a community on the principles of The Book of the Law, to form an archetype of a new society. The main ethical principle is that each human being has his own definite object in life. He has every right to fulfil this purpose, and none to do anything else. It is the business of the community to help each of its members to achieve this aim; in consequence all rules should be made, and all questions of policy decided, by the application of this principle to the circumstances. We have thus made a clean sweep of all the rough and ready codes of convention which have characterised past civilisations. Such codes, besides doing injustice to the individual, fail by being based on arbitrary assumptions which are not only false, but insult and damage the moral sense. Their authority rests on definitions of right and wrong which are untenable. As soon as Nietzsche and others demonstrated that fact, they lost their validity. The result has been that the new generation, demanding a reason for acting with ordinary decency, and refusing to be put off with fables and sophistries, has drifted into anarchy. Nothing can save the world but the universal acceptance of the Law of Thelema as the sole and sufficient basis of conduct. Its truth is self-evident. It is as susceptible of the strictest mathematical demonstration as any other theorem in biology. It admits that each member of the human race is unique, sovereign and responsible only to himself. In this way it is the logical climax of the idea of democracy. Yet at the same time it is the climax of aristocracy by asserting each individual equally to be the centre of the universe.

(pp.848-9)

This will to power, then, quite evidently had the most profound influence on Crowley, and there is little doubt to whom he owed the notion. 'To redeem the past and to transform every "it was" into an "I wanted it thus" – that alone I call redemption', wrote Nietzsche in *Thus Spoke Zarathustra*; and one can see therein the stimulus for Crowley's definition of magic – 'the art and science of causing change to occur in conformity with Will'. Crowley bolstered and encouraged his will by means of sex and drugs. Magical workings in the Abbey of Thelema often saw him using both, as in his so-called Cephaloedium ritual which involved Crowley himself, Cecil Russell, an American initiate of Crowley's magical order, the *Argentinum Astrum* which he had founded in 1907, and another American, Leah Hirsig, one of his 'Scarlet Women' who he used as sexual magic partners. After the usual cleansing of the temple by banishings intended to remove any unwanted non-human entities from the space of ritual working, and the purifications and consecrations customary on such occasions, Russell was given ether and buggered Crowley, who then had intercourse with Leah. But the ritual was deemed a failure for reasons perhaps best left unexplained.

Crowley had used sex for magical purposes before. Indeed, for a period of six weeks in 1914 he had carried out twenty-four such rituals with his principal acolyte and disciple of the time, Victor Neuberg, not always with great success; and we have already come across his terrifying rituals in Algeria in 1909 also performed with Neuberg. Together they made the Enochian calls or 'aethyrs' originally transmitted to Edward Kelly in the angelic tongue and recorded by John Dee. As each call proceeded, Crowley says, he experienced a stream of visions, each of which initiated him further as a magical adept, until, on 28 November, Crowley 'heard a command' to build a circle and rough altar from stones in their immediate neighbourhood, and on top of the altar he and Neuberg had sex, dedicating the act to the Greek god Pan, deity of extreme fear. It was with this act that Crowley believed he had become more than human, and it was during the ritual which followed that Neuberg experienced the dreadful struggle with Choronzon, 'the first and deadliest of all the powers of evil', which we noted before.

Sexual magic was, of course, nothing new. Knowledge of Tantric practices had been imported into Europe from India and China during the nineteenth century, and they were discussed in learned tomes such as Hargrave Jennings's *Phallicism, Celestial and Terrestrial* (1884), although the man who did more than almost anyone else to publicise sexual magic in the English language was Edward Sellon, a soldier and pornographer who wrote about the external practices of Indian Tantra in *Annotations upon the Sacred Writings of the Hindus* (1865), but without much apparent understanding of the philosophy which lay beneath them. In Germany, Karl Kellner founded a magical order in December 1902 generally known as the *Ordo Templi Orientis* ('The Order of the Temple of the East') whose last two degrees (VIII and IX) taught masturbatory and heterosexual magic. Crowley, who met the then head of the order, Albert Reuss, in 1912 and later took over the British part of the organisation himself, added another degree, XI – X being merely an administrative grade – so that homosexual magic could be included in the system.

Crowley's experiments with sex magic were more than sufficient to make him notorious, of course, but although they form quite a large part of his magical experiences, they play no part in his immensely influential books on ritual magic, *Magick in Theory and Practice* (1929) and *Magick Without Tears*, a collection of letters originally entitled *Aleister Explains Everything*, which was eventually published after his death, in 1954. Indeed, what was perhaps the most significant magical perform-ance of his life did not involve sex. It took place in Boleskine, a big late eighteenth-century lodge on the north side of Loch Ness, which he bought in November 1899 with a view to performing the Abramelin ritual. This had not long been translated by Mathers, and was designed to enable the practitioner to evoke and enter into converse with his own guardian angel. Like all such operations, it required long and rig-orous preparation by the candidate, including a six-month retreat from the outside world and a daily régime of prayer, purification and med-itation. To Crowley, Boleskine in its isolated situation seemed perfect for the attempt. In February 1900 he began by taking an oath of per-severance, but almost at once he sensed that malevolent forces were marshalling to interrupt him. A man he had invited to help him in this magical endeavour ran away after only a day or two; a replacement also fled precipitately; his teetotal lodge-keeper suddenly took to drink and tried to kill his wife and children; his housekeeper did a moonlight flit; and a workman went mad without warning and made a murderous assault on Crowley himself.

News of fracas in the Golden Dawn down in London then reached Crowley, and he decided to break off the ritual in order to enter the fray on Mathers's side – almost certainly a grave magical mistake, for apart from the fact that he thereby broke his oath of perseverance, there is every chance that, in his haste to be away, he forgot to close down the Boleskine working properly so as to ensure that none of the spirit-forms or elementals which may have been alerted by what he was doing remained trapped between worlds and therefore inclined to panic and be aggressive. His *Confessions* record the unfortunate aftermath of his departure:

> During my absence, the reputation of the house had become more formidable than ever before. Have little doubt that the Abra-Melin devils, whatever they are, used the place as convenient headquarters and put in some of their spare time in terrifying the natives. No one would pass the house after dark. Folk got into the habit of going round through Strath Errick, a detour of several miles. There were a great many definite legends; but I made rather a point of refraining from making a collection. I was completely committed to rationalism and the occurrence of miracles was a nuisance. I should have liked to deny the reality of the whole Abra-Melin business, but the phenomena were just as patent as the stones of the house.
>
> (p.359)

What are we to think of Crowley as a magician? The opportunities to dismiss him as a lunatic, a drug addict, a fraud, or any combination of the three are, of course, plentiful, and the fact that he embellished many of the details of episodes in his life does not help in any assessment. But too many hostile accounts of him have a tendency to confuse the man, whom they dislike, with the magician, whom they do not understand or refuse to take seriously. Somerset Maugham painted one of the most notorious portraits of him in his novel *The Magician* (1908) when Crowley had not yet caught journalists' (and therefore public) imagination. Maugham portrays him as Oliver Haddo, a hypnotic and evil magician who takes over, Svengali-fashion, a young woman, Margaret Dauncey, in order to spite her plodding, resolutely rationalist lover, Arthur Burdon, who made the mistake of insulting

Haddo to his face. Haddo's first appearance, in a restaurant, is shot through with interesting ambiguities. The reader is meant to be simultaneously repelled by a self-publicist and alarmed by his sinister charisma:

> Having succeeded in capturing the attention of everyone in the room, Oliver Haddo proceeded to eat these dishes in the order he had named. Margaret and Burdon watched him with scornful eyes, but Susie, who was not revolted by the vanity which sought to attract notice, looked at him curiously. He was clearly not old, though his corpulence added to his apparent age. His features were good, his ears small, and his nose delicately shaped. He had big teeth, but they were white and even. His mouth was large, with heavy moist lips. He had the neck of a bullock. His dark, curling hair had retreated from the forehead and temples in such a way as to give his clean-shaven face a disconcerting nudity. The baldness of his crown was vaguely like a tonsure. He had the look of a very wicked, sensual priest. Margaret, stealing a glance at him as he ate, of a sudden violently shuddered; he affected her with an uncontrollable dislike. He lifted his eyes slowly, and she looked away, blushing as though she had been taken in some indiscretion. These eyes were the most curious thing about him. They were not large, but an exceedingly pale blue, and they looked at you in a way that was singularly embarrassing. At first Susie could not discover in what precisely their peculiarity lay, but in a moment she found out: the eyes of most persons converge when they look at you, but Oliver Haddo's, naturally or by a habit he had acquired for effect, remained parallel. It gave the impression that he looked straight through you and saw the wall beyond. It was uncanny. But another strange thing about him was the impossibility of telling whether he was serious. There was a mockery in that queer glance, a sardonic smile upon the mouth, which made you hesitate how to take his outrageous utterances. It was irritating to be uncertain whether, while you were laughing at him, he was not really enjoying an elaborate joke at your expense. His presence cast an unusual chill upon the party.
>
> (pp.25-6)

Haddo is very learned in a number of abstruse occult subjects, but shows a special interest in that aspect of alchemy which maintained that it is possible to create a living being, a homunculus, in the laboratory. He exercises power over Margaret partly by his hypnotic presence, and partly by what appear to be *praestigia*. Thus, on one occasion he uses alchemically-produced material which seems to contradict the ordinary laws of nature:

> On the stove was a small bowl of polished brass in which water was kept in order to give a certain moisture to the air. Oliver Haddo put his hand in his pocket and drew out a little silver box. He tapped it with a smile, as a man taps a snuff-box, and it opened. He took an infinitesimal quantity of a blue powder that it contained and threw it on the water in the brass bowl. Immediately a bright flame sprang up, and Margaret gave a cry of alarm. Oliver looked at her quickly and motioned her to remain still. She saw that the water was on fire. It was burning as brilliantly, as hotly, as if it were common gas; and it burned with the same dry, hoarse roar. Suddenly it was extinguished. She leaned forward and saw that the bowl was empty. The water had been consumed, as though it were straw, and not a drop remained.
>
> (p.91)

It is reminiscent of a *praestigium* used for a serious purpose in the neophyte grade of the Golden Dawn. When the candidate has almost completed the ceremony, he or she is asked to pour drops of an apparently transparent liquid on to a plate. He or she is told that within this liquid lie hidden elements which look like blood. Then the officer known as the Kerux pours another liquid on top of the first, and the combination of the two immediately produces red. There is no attempt to suggest that this is magic, and it is perhaps typical of the nineteenth century that it should use a chemical reaction to make a moral point. Haddo, however, is a fictional character and so his motives and actions can afford to be ambiguous. After disturbing Margaret with his display of burning water, he adds dried and powdered leaves to the dish and the resulting fume induces extraordinary visions which both repel

and fascinate her. No wonder, then, that his reputation in the immediate neighbourhood of his isolated house called 'Skene' is baleful:

> Oliver was the local magnate, and his wealth would have made him an
> easy topic of conversation even without his eccentricity. The landlady
> roundly called him insane, and as an instance of his queerness told
> Arthur, to his great dismay, that Haddo would have no servants to sleep
> in the house; after dinner everyone was sent away to the various cot-
> tages in the park, and he remained alone with his wife [Margaret]. It
> was an awful thought that Margaret might be in the hands of a raving
> madman, with not a soul to protect her. But if he learnt no more than
> this of solid fact, Arthur heard much that was significant. To his amaze-
> ment the old fear of the wizard had grown up again in that lonely
> place, and the garrulous woman gravely told him of Haddo's evil influ-
> ence on the crops and cattle of farmers who had aroused his anger. He
> had had an altercation with his bailiff, and the man had died within a
> year. A small freeholder in the neighbourhood had refused to sell the
> land which would have rounded off the estate of Skene, and a disease
> had attacked every animal on his farm so that he was ruined. Arthur
> was impressed because, though she reported these rumours with mock
> scepticism as the stories of ignorant yokels and women, the innkeeper
> had evidently a terrified belief in their truth. No one could deny that
> Haddo had got possession of the land he wanted, for, when it was put
> up to auction, no one would bid against him, and he bought it for a
> song.

(pp. 160-1)

Clearly this fictional portrait is something of a travesty. It is interesting that although Maugham parodies the atmosphere of Boleskine,
the magical malevolence he attributes to Haddo is that of a witch, not
a ritual magician. The real Crowley was not particularly interested in
alchemy, nor did he go in for chemical *praestigia*, and the purpose of
his life and art was far removed from the dreadful mockery of God
which Haddo's experiments suggest. Still, Maugham did catch something of Crowley's manner, especially his somewhat theatrical mode

of talking, and when the two men met in 1909 Maugham acknowledged he had not only borrowed a good many phrases and sentiments
uttered by Crowley during an earlier conversation they had had, but
had quoted wholesale from several books on occult subjects, which
Crowley had recommended to him. Haddo, however, is a parody of a
surface. Crowley was much more elevated in his ideals and intentions
and much more seriously inclined than Maugham either allowed or
lets his readers guess.

Fiction, as we have seen already, has a way of distorting the figure
of the magical operator to make him or her fit what the author conceives to be the most readily accessible representation of someone
who, in real life, would be regarded either as eccentric or mad or dangerous. Bulwer-Lytton's stage villain Arbaces in *The Last Days of
Pompeii* (1834) is described as 'the wise Magian, the Hermes of the
Burning Belt, the last of the royalty of Egypt', a man who

> imagined that Nature not only worked miracles in her ordinary course,
> but that she might, by the cabala of some master soul, be diverted from
> that course itself. Thus he pursued Science, across her appointed bound-
> aries, into the land of perplexity and shadow. From the truths of astron-
> omy, he wandered into astrologic fallacy. From the secrets of chemistry
> he passed into the spectral labyrinth of magic; and he who could be
> sceptical as to the power of the gods, was credulously superstitious as
> to the power of man.
>
> (Book 2, chapter 8)

Yet, when it comes to the actual working of magic in the novel,
Arbaces turns to a female witch for a poisonous philtre wherewith he
can remove a rival in love, just as though he were no more than a
layman in the art. The reason for this blatant inconsistency probably
lies in the preconceptions of Bulwer-Lytton's readership which was
familiar with the convention that witches had to be old women, and
that poisoning, whether by magic or not, was a woman's weapon, not
a man's. The immensely colourful portrait of Arbaces as a master-
magician therefore turns out to be nothing more than flannel. He is

a cardboard cut-out in a Pollock theatre, and performs not a single wonder throughout the novel.

Modern popular notions that the laws of nature are fixed and cannot be suspended or altered underlie the figure of Gandalf in Tolkien's *Lord of the Rings* and J.K. Rowling's *Harry Potter* series. There is an echo of theosophy and the Golden Dawn in Tolkien's mission of five wizards, led by Gandalf and Saruman to Middle Earth, to contest the power of evil, for Helena Blavatsky maintained that she was instructed by secret masters who lived in the Himalayas and guided the destinies of humankind, while the Golden Dawn was supposed to be governed by hidden chiefs who existed on the non-human plane but directed the affairs of GD initiates through the order's elemental and adept grades. Harry Potter is, for once, not a fully-blown magical adept but a pupil, a status which presupposes that magic consists of a series of techniques capable of being taught. This is reminiscent of the Azande of southern Sudan who seem to distinguish between witchcraft as a physical trait or an inborn and inheritable disposition and sorcery as a set of methods which can be learned. Potter and his friends, according to this definition, are thus sorcerers who apply their lessons to the suspension of natural law, although Rowling's distinction between magical families and Muggles appears to suggest that there is something about magic which is innate and transmittable. If so, then Harry Potter and the rest would be witches in Azande eyes. But these distinctions are not important to the stories. The *Harry Potter* books are, in many ways, exercises in nostalgia, and their magic is all of the wonder-working kind, applied to utilitarian purposes, *praestigia* which really work, like the magic of Dr Schrepfer in Gustav Meyrink's 1916 novel, *Meister Leonhard*; and the pith of the novels consists of the self-development of the principal characters as they battle with evil in their quest for good and use magic as children imagine it – 'I wish things to be so, therefore they are' – an interesting variant upon Crowley's Nietzschean impulse of the Will.

But none of these fictional characters is actually a ritual magician. Whatever expectations their authors may have given their readership, of course, there is a grey area in the definition of such a figure, and we have seen how popular understanding of what a ritual magician is tends to shift among those aspects of the magical tradition it recognises, from witch to wonder-worker to fraud and so forth. The genuine ritual magician, too, is not fixed. His or her aims and practices are capable of change and development, and we have seen certain figures, such as Agrippa or Lévi, who have made significant contributions to this slowly mutating tradition – and Crowley's name should also be added to the list.

For Crowley was a great innovator. Societies such as the Societas Rosicruciana in Anglia or the Golden Dawn rest heavily upon Masonic and Rosicrucian foundations. Crowley, with a well-developed, knowledgeable and practical interest in yoga – the first part of *Magick in Theory and Practice*, for example, is entirely devoted to the subject – made use of some of its techniques, especially those concerned with breathing, to advance methods of meditation for his pupils and followers; and his reading and understanding of Hindu and Buddhist texts, along with his ability to syncretise large amounts of disparate material drawn from them into something comprehensible and useful to the west, were far in advance of his time. The practice of using magic every day as a constant feature of one's life was something he had learned from the Golden Dawn; but the practice of keeping a magical record, now routine for those who regularly work in almost any field of magic, was something he himself advocated as a way of gauging the success or failure of any given ritual or set of rituals, almost as though the magician were a scientist conducting experiments. His emphasis on magic as a means to self-development and self-exaltation was well in advance of the cult of solipsism characteristic of the west in the second half of the twentieth century. His use of drugs and sex was also innovative in the west, especially perhaps the former, which anticipated the 1960s' conscious employment of psychedelic substances to alter states of mind, although his pupil and secretary, Israel Regardie, while not disapproving of drugs in general, thought they had a very limited usefulness in magic, in as much as when their effects faded, so did the 'enlightenment' they were supposed to have produced, and therefore it was important to combine their use with rigorous magical training so that the practitioner could remember the advances he or she had made in spiritual condition, and return to that state *at will*.

The Golden Dawn which had been so influential on Crowley's early experiences in magic produced a number of other magicians, of course. First among these should be counted A.E. Waite, (almost always referred to thus by his initials), who was initiated into the order on 21 November 1899. As is well known, the Golden Dawn flew apart under internal strains, partly because of tensions aroused by Mathers's autocratic manner, partly because various members wanted to practise magic or other occult disciplines outwith the control of the rulers of the order. Waite himself tried to take over the order as a means whereby he could launch a somewhat different order of his own devising; and while he did not succeed in this aim, he did begin his *Independent and Rectified Rite* in 1903 at the same time as another GD member, R.W. Felkin, founded his version of the Golden Dawn, the *Stella Matutina* ('morning star'). The principal difference between the two was that Waite tried to encourage mysticism within his rite by excising magic, whereas Felkin wanted to preserve as much magic as possible. He also emphasised the astral projection and travel which had been taught in the Golden Dawn, but which was not there afforded particular prominence. Waite's main achievement, however, was his creation of yet another order, the Fellowship of the Rosy Cross, in 1915. In this, while the grade structure is still that of the GD, all magic has gone and the symbolism of the grades is entirely Christian and Rosicrucian. So for any to whom mysticism rather than magic appealed, Waite provided an ideal vehicle for their aspirations, despite his being cruelly dismissed by Israel Regardie as a librarian of the most dogmatic kind.

All these orders admitted women as well as men and were keen thus to balance the polarities. Best-known of all the female magicians belonging at one time or another to the GD was Violet Firth who changed her name to Dion Fortune, a contraction of her magical motto *Deo, non fortuna* ('by God, not luck'). Alan Richardson has said of her that she 'was never less than one of the most extraordinary women of our century, who brought a clarity, depth, excitement, and sheer power to the Magical revival which has never been equalled'. (*Twentieth-Century Magic*, xi) She was initiated into the Golden Dawn in 1919, but quickly became dissatisfied with what she felt was its lack of ritual power, and transferred to a temple under the rule of Mathers's wife, Moina. By 1922 she felt she was ready to form her own magical group, and in 1924 she was expelled from the GD by Moina Mathers who believed Dion was betraying the order's secrets to outsiders. There followed a series of hostile magical assaults which Dion described as follows:

> My first intimation of it was a sense of uneasiness and restlessness. Next came a feeling as if the barriers between the Seen and the Unseen were full of rifts and I kept on getting glimpses of the astral mingling with my waking consciousness. This, for me, is unaccustomed, for I am not naturally psychic, and in the technique in which I was trained we are taught to keep the different levels of consciousness strictly separate and to use a specific method for opening and closing the gates. Consequently one seldom gets spontaneous psychism. One's vision resembles the use of a microscope in which one examines prepared material...
>
> Very soon some curious things began to happen. We became most desperately afflicted with black cats. They were not hallucinatory, for our neighbours shared in the affliction, and we exchanged commiserations with the caretaker next door who was engaged in pushing bunches of black cats off doorstep and window-sill with a broom, and declared he had never in his life seen so many, or such dreadful specimens. The whole house was filled with the horrible stench of the brutes. Two members of our community at that time went out to business every day, and at their offices, in different parts of London, they found the same penetrating reek of the tom-cat.
>
> At first we attributed this persecution to natural causes, and concluded that we were near neighbours of some fascinating feline female, but incidents succeeded each other which made us feel that things were not quite in the ordinary course of nature. We were getting near to the Vernal Equinox, which is always a difficult time for occultists;

there was a sense of strain and tension in the atmosphere, and we were all feeling decidedly uncomfortable. Coming upstairs after breakfast one morning, I suddenly saw, coming down the stairs towards me, a gigantic tabby cat, twice the size of a tiger. It appeared absolutely solid and tangible. I stared at it petrified for a second, and then it vanished. I instantly realised that it was a simulacrum, or thought-form that was being projected by someone with occult powers. Not that the realisation was any too comforting, but it was better than an actual tiger. Feeling decidedly uncomfortable, I asked one of my household to join me, and as we sat in my room meditating we heard the cry of a cat from without. It was answered by another, and another. We looked out of the window, and the street as far as we could see was dotted with black cats and they were wailing and howling in broad daylight as they do on the roofs at night.

I rose up, gathered together my paraphernalia, and did an exorcism then and there. At the end we looked out of the window again. The visitation was at an end. Only our normal population of local mousers remained to us.

The Vernal Equinox was now upon us. I must explain that this is the most important season of the year for occultists. Great power-tides are flowing on the Inner Planes, and these are very difficult to handle. If there is going to be astral trouble, it usually blows up for a storm at this season. There are also certain meetings which take place on the Astral Plane, and many occultists attend them out of the body. In order to do this, one has to throw oneself into a trance and then the mind is free to travel. It is usual to get someone who understands these methods of work to watch beside the body while it is vacated to see that it comes to no harm.

In the ordinary way, when an occult attack is afoot, one clings to waking consciousness at all costs, sleeping by day and keeping awake and meditating while the sun is below the horizon. As ill-luck would have it, however, I was obliged to make one of these astral journeys at this season. My attacker knew this as well as I did. I therefore made my preparations with all the precautions I could think of; gathered together a carefully chosen group to form the watching circle, and sealed up the place of operation with the usual ceremonial. I had not much faith in this operation under the circumstances, for my attacker was of a much higher grade than I was, and could come through any seals I might set. However, it afforded protection against minor unpleasantness...

My enemy's task was therefore not a difficult one; for she knew about the time I must make this journey and the symbol I must use in order to get out of the body. I was therefore prepared for opposition, though I did not know what form it would take.

These astral journeys are really lucid dreams in which one retains all one's faculties of choice, will-power and judgement. Mine always begin with a curtain of the symbolic colour through whose folds I pass. No sooner was I through the curtain on this occasion than I saw my enemy waiting for me, or, if another terminology is preferred, I began to dream about her. She appeared to me in the full robes of her grade, which were very magnificent, and barred my entry, telling me that by virtue of her authority she forbade me to make use of these astral pathways. I replied that I did not admit her right to close the astral paths to me because she was personally offended, and that I appealed to the Inner Chiefs, to whom both she and I were responsible. Then ensued a battle of wills in which I experienced the sensation of being whirled through the air and falling from a great height and found myself back in my body. But my body was not where I had left it, but in a heap in the far corner of the room, which looked as if it had been bombed. By means of the well-known phenomenon of repercussion the astral struggle had apparently communicated itself to the body, which had somersaulted round the room while an agitated group had rescued the furniture from its path.

I was somewhat shaken by this experience which had not been a pleasant one. I recognised that I had had the worst of it and had been effectually ejected from the astral paths; but I also realised that if I accepted this defeat my occult career was at an end. Just as a child who has been thrown by his pony must immediately get up and remount if he is ever to ride again, so I knew that at all costs I must make that astral journey if I were to retain my powers. So I told my group to pull themselves together and re-form the circle because we must make another attempt; I invoked the Inner Chiefs, and went out once more. This time there was a short sharp struggle, and I was through. I had the Vision of the Inner Chiefs, and returned. The fight was over. I have never had any trouble since.

But when I took off my clothes in order to go to bed my back felt very sore, and taking a hand-glass I examined it in the mirror, and I found that from neck to waist I was scored with scratches as if I had been clawed by a gigantic cat.

(*Psychic Self-Defence*, 1930, 144-8)

The group she founded, the Society of the Inner Light, was and is a conscious continuation of the western magical tradition which is integrated, in no matter how unorthodox a fashion, into Christian concepts of creation and redemption. The modern practical side of this tradition lays great stress on certain techniques such as meditation and visualisation which enable the practitioner to attract, absorb and transmit energies, messages or symbols from other, non-human beings on other, non-human planes of existence. For example, Dion Fortune has her fictional magician, Dr Taverner, 'go subconscious' every so often in order to find out what may be happening elsewhere by picking up vibrations radiating from ritual performances. 'When I was subconscious just now', he says in one story, 'I heard one of the rituals of my own Order being worked, but worked as no Lodge I have ever sat in would perform it'; and it is by such means that Taverner, an occult detective who is also a doctor running a nursing-home, manages to uncover the various cases of vampirism, demonic magic, trapped elementals, and other unwanted non-human phenomena with which he is called to deal.

But ritual in such an occult context is still important, in as much as it assists and eases the participants into the right frame of mind for such communications, and opens the requisite channels through which they can be made. Essentially, however, stress is laid upon the interiority of such workings which marks the practice as peculiarly modern – post-Freudian, in fact. Hence one of the most common modes of contemporary magical working is the guided meditation known as a 'pathworking'. After whatever preliminaries may be considered necessary or desirable, the person acting as guide gives directions to a scene on the astral plane, which the participants must visualise so intensely as to become aware of their real presence within the scene, thereby substituting, as it were, astral for physical reality. Thus, let us say, the guide says that the participants are standing outwith the gates of an Egyptian temple This is described in greater or lesser detail, but the participants must be able to visualise it in such a way as to be able to feel the stone beneath their fingers and the heat reflected from its surface on their skin. The temple gates open and the participants are led through four courtyards, each of which is representative of a different element – one full of breezes, with fluttering yellow flags; one cool, with fountains splashing into deep blue fishponds: one with beds of earth newly turned by the spade: and one extremely hot, built of fiery red bricks which trap and throw back the heat. Next, the participants move into a long dark corridor within the temple, which leads to a small chamber containing a statue of Horus (or Isis or Ra or any other appropriate Egyptian deity), and the participants pause there to worship and contemplate and listen for the voice of the deity who may be pleased to communicate with them. Then the participants reverse their journey, stage by stage, until they are once more outwith the temple gates. There they are recalled to physical reality by the guide who grounds them and lets them meditate on the experience they have just shared and yet which has been individual to each of them.

This kind of interiority, while modern in its application, is actually very old. St Ignatius of Loyola's *Spiritual Exercises*, for example, are just such guided visualisations intended to provide jumping-off points for extended meditation, and to the extent that path workings are done properly and are not simply opportunities for emotional self-indulgence where feeling is mistaken for spiritual experience, they are highly effective in creating conditions in which a genuine spiritual experience may happen.

Perhaps aware of the pitfalls which may await the untrained venturer into this type of activity, another magician brought up in the

Golden Dawn tradition, Israel Regardie, was keen that candidates for the GD should have been through some form of intensive psychotherapy before attempting to embark on GD work so that she or he could be 'willing and able to face all components of his own personality, without either ignoring them, repressing them, or denying them'. The danger inherent in this approach is, of course, that magic becomes a rather superior branch of psychiatry, a set of methods which

> reveal our secret selves more directly, and unlock the vast store of wisdom and power within our souls, showing us how to control them in ways that neither psychoanalysis nor modern science has succeeded.
>
> (*Art and Meaning in Magic*, 26)

The subtitle of one of Regardie's other books, *A Co-Relation of the Principles of Analytical Psychology and the Elementary Techiques of Magic*, indicates how far he was willing to identify the energies, communications, symbols, angels and spirits of the magical otherworld with aspects of the individual's unconscious, and the aim of magic as that of integrating the human personality. It is a long way from Mediaeval and early-modern understanding of magic, which maintained the independent and real existence of all these things.

Nevertheless, there are still those who are willing to undertake the lengthy, dangerous Abramelin ritual which caused Crowley so much grief, and may have given rise to all kinds of unwanted effects in his neighbourhood. In autumn 1972, William Bloom, a young novelist and publisher, made his way to an old hunting-lodge in the High Atlas mountains of Morocco and there spent six months in preparation for and performance of this magical operation. Interestingly enough, he had had an intensive course of Freudian psychoanalysis before he thought of starting this attempt to evoke and enter into converse with his guardian angel, although it should be said that his reasons for doing so were mixed and personal. What the analysis did, however, was to reassure him that his interest in mysticism and the occult sciences was not merely escapism from personal problems, but soundly based in a relatively stable personality. Bloom was accompanied to and in Morocco by his lover, and together she and he found the hunting-lodge where he built the necessary chapel or oratory and altar, and prepared the other necessary magical paraphernalia, while she made his magical robes, undertook the practical running of the lodge during those times when Bloom was occupied with ritual or meditation or prayer, and practised non-Abramelin magic herself.

Bloom's progress is contained in the diary he kept. It began on the spring equinox of 1973. Everything went fairly well during March, and on the thirtieth of the month he had his first vision, although he does not say what it was. Attacks by malevolent entities began in mid-April – he describes one such as a feeling of suffocation and smothering, which reminds one of similar experiences, sometimes referred to as the Old or Night Hag, complained of in early-modern witchcraft accusations – and by May he was starting to feel physical effects from the intensity of his application, although the low periods were balanced by others of calm or spiritual excitement. At this point in his diary, he uses the word 'battle' quite frequently, but also notes that he is aware of being helped on the inner planes by a teacher who made himself known visibly by images from the western magical tradition, Gnostic Christianity and the Templar and Rosicrucian orders.

The next two months continued the battle with malevolent entities amid alternating days of tranquillity and disorientation. Physical pain and a sense of shame and weakness plagued him throughout most of June, but at the end of the month he had a feeling of respite, the effects of which he tends to express in the language of Buddhism, using such words as *karma* and *maya* ('illusion'). July saw a combination of opposites – complete bliss one day, exhausting fights with a fiend on another – with Bloom now near complete exhaustion, mental and physical, until at the end of the month he thought he had emerged from this particularly tortuous period. On 7 August, he writes that a great surge of spiritual energy had begun a week previously and that it is impossible to describe, although someone who has used LSD might have an inkling of what it was like. The rest of the month and the first half of September were occupied in his trying to gain control over the effects of this experience; then on 21 September he began the seven days of consecration, convocation and conjuration demanded by the Abramelin ritual.

The climax actually arrived on 23 and 24 September, when he first experienced a feeling of complete emptiness and abandonment, followed after a few hours by a sensible presence of his guardian angel who spoke to him, communicating love and a promise never to leave him alone again. Three more days completed the ritual and the experience, and left him both spiritually and personally transformed to the extent that, as he says at the end of his account, 'the angelic realms are a living and relevant reality to me'.

Bloom thus reaches across the centuries to join hands with those ritual magicians who have attempted to raise themselves into the presence of God and to have conversation with the angels and spirits who inhabit the non-material worlds of his creation; and his testimony provides moving evidence that neither his nor their efforts were undertaken in vain. If the wizards are the 'wise men' of the magical spectrum, they are wise in a particular way. In the words of St Paul,

> because that which may be known of God is manifest in them; for God hath shewed it unto them. For the invisible things of him from the creation of the world are clearly seen, being understood by the things that are made, even his eternal power and Godhead.
>
> (*Romans* 1.19-20)

Notes

CHAPTER 1: THE RITUAL MAGICIAN AND HIS WORK

1. See St Isidore of Seville, *De rerum natura*.
2. See, for example, *Leiden Papyrus*, col. 1 and Apuleius, *Apologia* 42. Cf. the sixteenth- or seventeenth-century Jewish text *Cod. Gaster* 315 in Daiches, *Ancient Jewish Oil-Magic*, 14-16.
3. See further the names of the angels presiding over the planets, the names of the angels presiding over the houses of the zodiac, and the names of the twenty-eight angels ruling in the twenty-eight mansions of the moon, all of which are recorded in the early seventeenth-century *Treatise on Angel Magic*, 41-2. Cf. the seven heavens and the names of their presiding angels as described by a Jewish magician of the third or fourth century AD in *Sefer ha-Razim*, 'The Book of Secrets'.
4. 'Woman' because *superstition* is a feminine noun in French.
5. 'Farting as a defence against unspeakable dread', *Journal of Analytical Psychology* 41 (1996), 176.
6. *Culture, Thought, and Social Action*, 60. Cf. Catherine Bell, 'Ritualisation is generally a way of engaging in some wide consensus that those acting are doing so as a type of natural response to a world conceived and interpreted as affected by forces that transcend it... Ritualisation tends to posit the existence of a type of authoritative reality that is seen to dictate to the immediate situation'. *Ritual*, 169

CHAPTER 2: EVOCATION AND ECSTACY IN THE ANCIENT WORLD

1. Another well-known female, Sosipatra, sometimes referred to as a magician,

may have been a real person, although the details of her life contain much that is exotic. We are told that when she was five years old her father entrusted her to two elderly strangers, perhaps magicians, perhaps *daimones*, who returned her five years later transformed into a clairvoyant. But it is notable that, in spite of her extraordinary prophetic gifts, when she needed to be rescued magically from a passion for her cousin Philometor, she turned to a man, Maximus, to work the necessary magic. (Eunapius: *Vitae sophistarum* 6.6-7, 9-10)

2. 'Théorie poétique et esthétique' in *Oeuvres* 2 vols. (Gallimard, Paris 1957), 1.1333-34

3. It is interesting to note that when Jesus cured a deaf mute, he uttered a long-voiced breath or wailing noise (*estenaxe*), almost certainly reminiscent to at least some of his hearers of the inarticulate sounds made by ritual magicians, Mark 7.34.

4. *Chaldaean Oracles*, fragments 146-48. One is reminded of Exodus 3.2 in which an angel appears to Moses in a fiery flame in the middle of a bush.

5. See further Lesses, *Ritual Practices to Gain Power*, 59, 63, 70-71, 90-91, 254-60.

6. See further Philo Judaeus who associates a respectable form of magic with rulers, and another, disreputable version with wandering beggars, charlatans, loose women, and slaves, *De specialibus legibus* 3.100.

7. Emperor from AD 96-98. Apollonius had been supporting his candidacy as Emperor to replace Domitian.

8. See further D.D. Hughes, *Human Sacrifice in Ancient Greece* (Routledge, London 1991), 115-30.

9. Eusebius: *Historia Ecclesiae* 4.11.4. St Jerome, *Epistulae* 133.4. Meletios Homologetes, *Alphabetalphabetos*, (p.611).

10. Ralph of Coggeshall, *Chronicon Anglicanum*, folios 90b-91. Her flight is overtly compared with that of Simon Magus.

11. A man might be accounted a possessor of extraordinary magical powers without necessarily being regarded as divine or semi-divine as well, of course. The third-century AD philosopher Plotinos was credited with defensive magical abilities when a rival philosopher tried to paralyse him magically, and at the request of an Egyptian priest evoked his own familiar spirit in the Temple of Isis in Rome. Nevertheless, when his biographer, Porphyry, calls him 'an extraordinary man', although the adjective might also mean 'heaven-sent' or 'divine', the noun he chooses to use specifically refers to a human being as opposed to a god. Consequently, we are presented with a portrait which deliberately stays this side of deification. (*Vita Plotini* 10.23)

CHAPTER 3: THE PATTERN AND AIMS OF A RITUAL MAGICIAN

1. Note the entirely different tradition (of a very much earlier source) which says that heavenly entities, the Watchers, coupled with human women and taught their subsequent offspring magical arts. This magic, however, was immediately

practical rather than ritual – how to bind and loose, the properties of herbs, divination from heavenly bodies. (1 *Enoch* 7.1; 8.3)

2. i.e. he can interpret the meaning of phenomena, such as comets or monstrous births.

3. *De medico Hebraeo enarratio apologetica*, 1588, chapter 11.

4. The whole of Part II is given over to similar, more detailed instructions.

5. The exaggerated numbers are given in Iamblichus: *De mysteriis* 8.1.260-61. Clement of Alexandria in *c.*AD 00 claimed to know of forty, *Stromata* 6.4.

6. i.e. almost in the manner of ventriloquists. Ventriloquism was a skill well known to the ancients. It was employed for religious or magical purposes, not for entertainment and so the context is the right one for the suggestiveness of 'projecting'.

7. Seventeenth-century, but derived from a sixteenth-century chronicle.

8. *Heavenly Necromancers*, 27-9.

9. *De vita triplici* Book 3, chapter 1.

10. Hernandez, *Le procès inquisitorial de Gilles de Rais*, 78.

11. Hernandez, *op. cit.* 97-8, 68-9, 73.

12. Memory of stage-demons or fairies will not account for all reports by accused witches or their prosecutors, of course. But the banalisation of the demonic especially, which one sees in legal material, may on occasion owe something to this process.

13. There were a few sessions later than this, and Dee had been engaged in contacting angels and spirits from some time in the late 1560s. The 1580s sessions, however, were intensive and more or less continuous.

14. The black obsidian mirror in the British Museum is not one of these shewstones, and its association with Dee rests entirely upon the 1748 catalogue of Horace Walpole's collection of curiosities.

15. *Signifi.* This is meaningless in Latin, but appears so in the manuscript. It may be short for *significa*, or it may be contemporary spelling of the English word 'signify'. Either way, I have translated it as an imperative.

16. J.P. Kildahl: *The Psychology of Speaking in Tongues* (Hodder & Stoughton, London 1972), 40.

17. With or without mediation.

18. He was arrested in England for coining money, and almost certainly tricked Dee via fraudulent 'angelic' messages into a bout of wife-swapping. He was probably an English spy, too, during his stay at the Imperial Court in Prague and elsewhere on the Continent, for which he was eventually arrested. His natal horoscope, drawn by Dee, indicated a highly intelligent man destined for both fame and disaster, while the positive aspects of his character were undermined by the influence of Mars which rendered him boastful, deranged and treacherous.

CHAPTER 4: NATURAL MAGIC AND THE BLURRED BORDERS OF DECEPTION

1. *Conformité du langage français avec le grec* (Paris 1562), 27.
2. *Paradiso*, Canto 2.136–38.
3. C. Wright, *The Maze and the Warrior* (Harvard University Press 2001), 50, 162, 192.
4. i.e. of a long orbit, as opposed to those with a short orbit.
5. And is therefore silent.
6. Synesius, *De insomniis*, chapter 3. Agrippa was familiar with Synesius's work.
7. *De occulta philosophia* Book 2, chapter 22. The names of the Intelligence and the Demon both add up to 325.
8. *De incertitudine et vanitate scientiarum* (1537). This is a work in which he repudiates much of the magic he had supported and advanced in *De occulta philosophia*.
9. *Journal de Voyage en Italie*, ed. C. Dédéyan (Paris 1946), 244–45.
10. *Sagassimi*, which primarily means 'people with a very keen sense of smell'. Agrippa is picking up the hunting metaphor he used in his passage on natural magic.
11. See further S. Clark, 'The reformation of the eyes', *Journal of Religious History* 27 (2003), 143–60, to whom I owe these last two references
12. 'Ancient automata and mechanical explanation', *Phronesis* 48 (2003), 347.

CHAPTER 5: WIZARD OR WITCH? A PROBLEM FOR THE AUTHORITIES

1. For De Bar, see Veenstra, *Magic and Divination at the Courts of Burgundy and France*, 67–69, 343–55.
2. See further D. Gentilcore, *Healers and Healing in Early Modern Italy* (Manchester University Press 1998), 168–73.
3. *Calendar of State Papers, Domestic*, October 123 to March 1625. The reference to Lachenmayer comes from Behringer, *Shaman of Oberstdorf*, 87.
4. 'Men in witchcraft trials', 52–56.

CHAPTER 6: ENLIGHTENMENT MAGICIANS IN FACT AND FICTION

1. Translated by A.E. Waite as *Transcendental Magic*. 'Teaching' and 'Ritual' were originally published separately.
2. 'The trial of Joseph Powell', 28.

List of Illustrations

All illustrations courtesy of the author unless otherwise specified

Select Bibliography

Antionetti, P., 'C'est li mireors perilleus: images et miroirs dans Le Roman de la Rose', in J.R. Scheidegger, S. Girardet, E. Hicks (eds), *Le Moyen Age dans la modernité* (Paris 1996), 33-47.

Apps, L. and Gow, A., *Male Witches in Early Modern Europe* (Manchester University Press 2003).

d'Arch Smith, T., *The Books of the Beast: Essays on Aleister Crowley, Montague Summers, Francis Barrett, and Others* (Crucible, Wellingborough 1987).

Ashton, M., 'Iconoclasm in England: official and clandestine', in P. Marshall (ed.), *The Impact of the English Reformation, 1500-1640* (Arnold, London 1997), 167-92.

Barrett, F., *The Magus, or Celestial Intelligencer* (London 1801, reprinted Aquarian Press, Wellingborough 1989).

Bates, D., 'The mystery of truth: Louis-Claude de Saint-Martin's enlightened mysticism', *Journal of the History of Ideas* 61 (2000), 635-55.

Becker, M., 'Die Magie – Problematik der Antike: Genügt ein sozialwissenschaftliche Erfassung?' *Zeitschrift für Religions und Geistesgeschichte* 54 (2002), 22.

Béhar, P., *Les langues occultes de la Renaissance*, (Editions Desjonquères 1996).

Behringer, W., *Shaman of Oberstdorf: Chonrad Stoeckhlin and the Phantoms of the Night*, English trans. (University of Virginia 1998).

Bell, C., *Ritual, Perspectives and Dimensions* (Oxford University Press 1997).

Berger, K., 'Prospero's art', *Shakespeare Studies* 10 (1977), 211-39.

Bevir, M., 'Annie Besant's quest for truth: Christianity, secularism, and New Age thought', *Journal of Ecclesiastical History* 50 (1999), 62-93.

Bila, C., *La croyance à la magie au xviiie siècle en France* (Paris 1925).

Bloom, W., *The Sacred Magician: A Ceremonial Diary* (Gothic Image Publications, Glastonbury 1992).

Booth, M., *A Magick Life: A Biography of Aleister Crowley* (Hodder & Stoughton, London 2000).

Bremmer, J.N., 'The birth of the term "magic"', *Zeitschrift für Papyrologie und Epigraphik* 126 (1999), 1–12.

Butler, E.M., *Ritual Magic* (1969, reprinted Sutton, Stroud 1998).

Calder, I.R.F., 'A note on magic squares in the philosophy of Agrippa of Nettesheim', *Journal of the Warburg and Courtauld Institutes* 12 (1949), 196–99.

Campbell, L.B., *Scenes and Machines on the English Stage during the Renaissance* (Cambridge University Press 1923).

Ciraolo, L. and Seidel, J., (eds), *Magic and Divination in the Ancient World* (Leiden, Brill-Styx 2002).

Clark, S., 'Demons, natural magic, and the virtually real', in G.S. Williams and C.D. Gunnoe (eds), *Paracelsian Moments: Science, Medicine, and Astrology in Early Modern Europe* (Truman State University Press 2002), 223–45.

—, 'The reformation of the eyes: apparitions and optics in sixteenth- and seventeenth-century Europe', *Journal of Religious History* 27 (2003), 143–60.

Clerc, J.B., *Homines Magici: étude sur la sorcellerie et la magie dans la société romaine impériale* (Lang, Berlin 1995).

Clulee, N.H., *John Dee's Natural Philosophy: Between Science and Religion*, (New York 1988).

Crowley, A., *Magick* (Guild Publishing, London 1988).

—, *The Confessions: An Autohagiography* (Arkana, London 1989).

Davenport-Hines, R., *Gothic: Four Hundred Years of Excess, Horror, Evil and Ruin* (North Point Press, New York 1998).

Davies, O., 'Newspapers and the popular belief in witchcraft and magic in the modern period', *Journal of British Studies* 37 (1998), 139–65.

—, *A People Bewitched: Witchcraft and Magic in Nineteenth-Century Somerset* (Bruton 1999).

—, *Witchcraft, Magic, and Culture 1736-1951* (Manchester University Press 1999).

—, *Cunning Folk: Popular Magic in English History*, (Hambledon & London, London 2003).

Dee, J., *Heptarchia Mystica*, ed. R. Turner, (Aquarian Press, Wellingborough 1986).

Devlin, J., *The Superstitious Mind: French Peasants and the Supernatural in the Nineteenth Century* (Yale University Press 1987).

Drury, N., *Don Juan, Mescalito, and Modern Magic* (Arkana, London 1978).

Durrani, O., 'The character and qualities of Mephistopheles', in P. Bishop (ed.), *A Companion to Goethe's Faust Parts I and II* (Camden House, Woodbridge 2001), 76–94.

Eamon, W., *Science and the Secrets of Nature: Books of Secrets in Medieval and Early Modern Culture* (Princeton University Press 1994).

Eco, U., *The Search for the Perfect Language*, English trans. (Blackwell, Oxford 1995).

—, *Serendipities: Language and Lunacy*, (Weidenfeld & Nicolson, London 1999).

Fanger. C., (ed.), *Conjuring Spirits: Texts and Traditions of Medieval Ritual Magic* (Sutton, Stroud 1998).

Faivre, A., *Access to Western Esotericism* (State University of New York Press 1994).

—, *The Eternal Hermes: From Greek God to Alchemical Magus*, English trans. (Phanes Press, Michigan 1995).

Ferreiro, A., 'Simon Magus: the Patristic – Mediaeval traditions and historiography', *Apocrypha* 7 (1996), 147-65.

—, 'Simon Magus, Nicolas of Antioch, and Muhammad', *Church History* 72 (2003), 53-70.

Forbes, C., 'Pauline demonology and/or cosmology? Principalities, powers, and the elements of the world in their Hellenistic context', *Journal for the Study of the New Testament* 85 (March 2002), 51-73.

Fortune, D., The *Secrets of Dr Taverner*, 3rd revised ed. (Llewellyn Publications, Minnesota 1979).

Fowden, G., *The Egyptian Hermes: An Historical Approach to the Late Pagan Mind*, (Princeton University Press 1986).

Frankfurter, D., 'Ritual expertise in Roman Egypt and the problem of the category "magician"', in Schäfer and Kippenberg, *Envisioning Magic* q.v. 115-35.

Freyburger, G., 'Prière silencieuse et prière murmurée dans la religion romaine', *Revue des études latines* 79 (2001), 26-36.

Fruchtman, J., *The Apocalyptic Politics of Richard Price and Joseph Priestley: A Study in Late Eighteenth-Century English Republican Millennialism* (American Philosophical Society, Philadelphia 1983).

Fuller, J.O., *The Comte de Saint-Germain*, (East-West Publications, London 1988).

—— *The Magical Dilemma of Victor Neuberg*, revised ed. (Mandrake, Oxford 1990).

Gager, J., *Moses in Graeco-Roman Paganism* (Nashville, Abingdon Press 1972).

Gallagher, E.V., *Divine Man or Magician? Celsus and Origen on Jesus* (Scholars Press, Chico, California 1982).

Garrett, S.R., 'Light on a dark subject and vice versa: magic and magicians in the New Testament', in Neusner etc. *Religion, Science, and Magic* q.v. 142-65.

Gervaso, R., *Cagliostro*, English trans. (Gollancz, London 1974).

Gibbons, B.J., *Spirituality and the Occult from the Renaissance to the Modern Age* (Routledge, London & New York 2001).

Gilbert, R.A., *A.E. Waite: Magician of Many Parts*, (Crucible, Wellingborough 1987).

—, *Revelation of the Golden Dawn: The Rise and Fall of a Magical Order* (Quantum, Slough 1997).

Godwin, J., *Harmonies of Heaven and Earth: The Spiritual Dimension of Music from Antiquity to the Avant-Garde* (Thames & Hudson, London 1987).

Godwin, J., Chanel, C., Deveney, J.P., *The Hermetic Brotherhood of Luxor: Initiatic and Historical Documents of an Order of Practical Occultism* (Samuel Weiser, Maine 1995).

Gouk, P., *Music, Science, and Natural Magic in Seventeenth-Century England* (Yale University Press 1999).

Granada, M.A., *Giordano Bruno: Universo Infinito, Unión con Dios, Perfección de Hombre* (Herder, Barcelona 2002).

Greene, T.M., 'Language, signs, and magic', in Schäfer and Kippenberg, *Envisioning Magic* q.v. 255-72.

Greenwood, S., *Magic, Witchcraft, and the Otherworld: An Anthropology* (Berg, Oxford 2000).

Haar, S., *Simon Magus, the First Gnostic?* (De Gruyter, Berlin-New York 2003).

Hammerstein, R., *Macht und Klang, Tönende Automaten als Realität und Fiktion in der alten und mittelalterlichen Welt* (Berlin 1986).

Harkness, D., 'Shows in the showstone: a theatre of alchemy and apocalypse in the angel conversations of John Dee (1527-1608/9)' *Renaissance Quarterly* 49 (1996), 707-37.

—, *John Dee's Conversations with Angels: Cabala, Alchemy, and the End of Nature* (Cambridge University Press 1999).

Harrison, P., 'Curiosity, forbidden knowledge, and the reformation of natural philosophy in early modern England', *Isis* 92 (2001), 265-90.

Heim, F., 'Le dieu et sa statue: des traces d'Hermétisme chez les apologistes latins', *Revue des sciences religieuses* 77 (2003), 31-42.

Heintz, F., *Simon le magicien: Actes 8.5-25 et l'accusation de magie contre les prophètes thaumaturges dans l'antiquité* (Paris, Gabalda 1997).

Hernandez, L., *Le procès inquisitorial de Gilles de Rais* (Paris 1921).

Howe, E., *The Magicians of the Golden Dawn: A Documentary History of a Magical Order, 1887-1923* (Aquarian Press, Wellingborough 1985).

Hutton, R., *The Triumph of the Moon: A History of Modern Pagan Witchcraft* (Oxford University Press 1999).

Hyatt, C.S. (ed.), *An Interview with Israel Regardie* (Falcon Press, Phoenix 1985).

Idel, M., 'Jewish magic from the Renaissance period to early Hasidism', in Neusner etc., *Religion, Science, and Magic* q.v. 82-117.

—, 'On Judaism, Jewish mysticism, and magic', in Schäfer and Kippenberg, *Envisioning Magic* q.v. 195-214.

Jankovic, V., 'The politics of sky battles in early Hanoverian Britain', *Journal of British Studies* 41 (2002), 429-59.

Johnston, S.I., 'Rising to the occasion: theurgic ascent in its cultural milieu, in Schäfer and Kippenberg, *Envisioning Magic* q.v. 165-94.

Kaplan, A., *Meditation and Kabbalah* (Samuel Weiser, Maine 1982).

Kaczynski, R., *Perdurabo: The Life of Aleister Crowley* (New Falcon Publications, Tempe 2002).

Keefer, M.H., 'Agrippa's dilemma: Hermetic "rebirth" and the ambivalences of De vanitate and De occulta philosophia', *Renaissance Quarterly* 41 (1988), 614-53.

—, *The Key of Solomon the King (Clavicula Salomonis)*, ed. S. Liddell MacGregor Mathers, (1888, Routledge & Kegan Paul 1981).

King, F.X., *The Flying Sorcerer* (Oxford, Mandrake 1992).

Kirsch. I., 'Demonology and science during the scientific revolution', *Journal of the History of the Behavioural Sciences* 16 (1980), 359-68.

Knox, K.C., 'Lunatick visions: prophecy, signs, and scientific knowledge in 1790s London', *History of Science* 37 (1999), 427-58.

Labouvie, E., 'Men in witchcraft trials: towards a social anthropology of "male" understandings of magic and witchcraft' in U. Rublack (ed.), *Gender in Early Modern German History* (Cambridge University Press 2002), 49-68.

Laycock, D.C., *The Complete Enochian Dictionary* (Askin Publishers, London 1978).

The Lemegeton: A Medieval Manual of Solomonic Magic, ed. K. Wilby (Hermetic Research Series, Felindenys, Silian 1985).

Levenda, P., *Unholy Alliance: A History of Nazi Involvement with the Occult* 2nd ed. (Continuum, London 2002).

Lévi, E., *The History of Magic* (1860, English trans. Rider, London 1913).

—, *The Key of the Mysteries* (1861, English trans. Rider, London 1959).

—, *La science des esprits: révélation du dogme secret des Kabbalistes*, (Paris 1865).

—, *Transcendental Magic* (1896, English trans. Rider, London 1984).

Lewy, H., *Chaldaean Oracles and Theurgy: Mysticism, Magic, and Platonism in the Later Roman Empire* (Paris 1978).

Llorente, J.A., *Historia critica de la Inquisición de España* (Madrid 1822).

Luhrmann. T., *Persuasions of the Witch's Craft* (Blackwell, Oxford 1989).

Maggi, A., *Satan's Rhetoric, A Study of Renaissance Demonology* (University of Chicago 2001).

Mandrou, R. (ed.), *Possession et sorcellerie au xviie siècle* (Fayard, Paris 1979).

Margalioth, M. (ed.), *Sefer ha-Razim* (Jerusalem 1966).

Marquis, J.C., *Loups, sorciers, criminels: fait divers en Seine-Intérieure au xixe siècle* (Editions Bertout, Luneray 1993).

Marshall, P., 'The rod of Boxley, the blood of Hailes, and the defence of the Henrician church', *Journal of Ecclesiastical History* 46 (1995), 689-96.

Mathiesen, R., 'A thirteenth-century ritual to attain the beatific vision from the Sworn Book of Honorius', in Fanger, *Conjuring Spirits* q.v. 143-62.

McCalman, *The Seven Ordeals of Count Cagliostro* (Century, London 2003).

McIntosh, C., *Eliphas Lévi and the French Occult Revival* (Rider, London 1972).

—, *The Devil's Bookshelf* (Aquarian Press, Wellingborough 1985).

McLean, A., 'Interpreting a magical diagram', *Hermetic Journal* 2 (1978), 20-3.

Melchior-Bonnet, S., *The Mirror: A History*, English trans. (Routledge, London 2001).

Mendoza, R.G., *The Acentric Labyrinth: Giordano Bruno's Prelude to Contemporary Cosmology*, (Element Books, Dorset 1995).

Meyer, M. and Mirecki, P., (eds), *Ancient Magic and Ritual Power*, (Leiden, Brill 1995).

The Miscellany of the Spalding Club Vol. 1 (Aberdeen 1841).

Molland, A.G., 'Cornelius Agrippa's mathematical magic', in C. Hay (ed.), *Mathematics from Manuscript to Print, 1300-1600* (Oxford 1988), 209-19.

Monro, J.W., 'Cartes de visite from the other world: spiritism and the discourse of laïcisme in the early Third Republic', *French Historical Studies* 26 (2003), 119-53.

Mowat, B.A., 'Prospero's book', *Shakespeare Quarterly* 52 (2001), 1-33.

Moyer, I., 'The initiation of the magician: transition and power in Graeco-Egyptian ritual', in D.B. Dodd and C.A. Faraone (eds), *Initiation in Greek Ritual and Narratives*, (Routledge, London 2003).

Nelson, M., 'Narcissus: myth and magic', *Classical Journal* 95 (2000), 363-89.

Neusner, J., Frerichs, E.S., McCracken Flesher, P.V. (eds), *Religion, Science, and Magic: In Concert and in Conflict* (Oxford University Press 1989).

Neusner, J., 'Science and magic, miracle and magic in formative Judaism: the system and the difference', in Neusner etc., *Religion, Science, and Magic.* q.v. 61-81.

Olausson, M., 'Freemasonry, occultism, and the picturesque garden towards the end of the eighteenth century', *Art History* 8 (December 1985), 413-33.

Palmer, P.M. and More, R.P., *The Sources of the Faust Tradition from Simon Magus to Lessing* (Oxford University Press 1936).

Perkins, M., 'The trial of Joseph Powell, fortune-teller: public and private in early nineteenth-century magic', *Journal of Victorian Culture* 6 (2001), 27-45.

Peuckert, W.E., 'Das Sechste und Siebente Buch Mosis', *Zeitschrift für Deutsche Philologie* 76 (1957), 163-87.

Picatrix, ed. D. Pingree, (The Warburg Institute, London 1986).

Porter, R., 'Witchcraft and magic in Enlightenment, Romantic, and liberal thought', in B. Ankarloo and S. Clark (eds), *The Athlone History of Witchcraft and Magic in Europe*: Vol. 5 *The Eighteenth and Nineteenth Centuries* (Athlone Press, London 1999), 193-282.

Quinn, D.M., *Early Mormonism and the Magic World View*, revised ed. (Signature Books, Salt Lake City 1998).

Reed, R., *The Occult on the Tudor and Stuart Stage* (Christopher Publishing House, Boston 1965).

Regardie, I., *The Art and Meaning of Magic* (Helios, Toddington 1964).

—, *Ceremonial Magic: A Guide to the Mechanisms of Ritual* (Aquarian Press,

Wellingborough 1980).

—, *The Complete Golden Dawn System of Magic* (Falcon Press, Arizona 1984).

—, *The Middle Pillar* (1938, reprinted Llewellyn Publications, Minnesota 1991).

Richardson, A., *Twentieth-Century Magic and the Old Religion: Dion Fortune, Christine Hartley, Charles Seymour* (Llewellyn Publications, Minnesota 1991).

Riskin, J., *Science in the Age of Sensibility: The Sentimental Empiricists of the French Enlightenment* (University of Chicago 2002).

Ritner, R.K., 'Necromancy in ancient Egypt', in Ciraolo and Seidel (eds), *Magic and Divination in the Ancient World* q.v. 89-96.

Rossi, P., *The Birth of Modern Science* (Blackwell, Oxford 2001).

Round, N.G., 'Five magicians, or the uses of literacy', *Modern Language Review* 64 (1969), 793-805.

Schäfer, P. and Kippenberg, H.G. (eds), *Envisioning Magic* (Brill, Leiden 1997).

Scotti, P., 'Necromancy and Monsignor Benson', *The Downside Review* 423 (April 2003), 135-49.

Smith, M., *Jesus the Magician* (London, Victor Gollancz 1978).

Tambiah, S.J., *Culture, Thought, and Social Action* (Harvard University Press 1985).

—, 'Form and meaning of magical acts', in M. Lambek (ed.), *A Reader in the Anthropology of Religion* (Blackwell 2002), 340-57.

Thibodeau, P., 'Optical illusions in ancient Greece', in G.W. Bakewell and J.P. Sickinger (eds), *Gestures* (Oxbow Books, Oxford 2003), 136-51.

Thompson, R.C., *Semitic Magic, its Origins and Development* (London 1908).

Thurschwell, P., *Literature, Technology, and Magical Thinking, 1880-1920* (Cambridge University Press 2001).

Tolstoy, N., *The Quest for Merlin* (Hamish Hamilton, London 1985).

Tomlinson, G., *Music in Renaissance Magic: Towards a Historiography of Others* (University of Chicago 1993).

Torijano, P.A., *Solomon the Esoteric King: From King to Magus, Development of a Tradition* (Leiden, Brill 2002).

Torres-Alcalá, A., *Don Enrique de Villena: un mago al dintel del Renacimiento* (Madrid 1989).

Traister, B.H., *Heavenly Necromancers: The Magician in English Renaissance Drama* (University of Missouri, Columbia 1984).

A Treatise on Angel Magic, ed. A. McLean (Phanes Press, Michigan 1990).

Vakaloudi, A.D., 'Demonic-mantic practices – the implication of the theurgists and their power of submission in the early Byzantine Empire', *Byzantinoslavica* 60 (1999), 87-113.

Veenstra, J. R., (ed.), *Magic and Divination at the Courts of Burgundy and France* (Brill, Leiden 1998).

de Waardt, H., 'From cunning man to natural healer', in H. Binneveld and R.

Dekker (eds), *Curing and Insuring* (Hilversum, Verloren 1993), 33–41.

Washington, P., *Madame Blavatsky's Baboon: Theosophy and the Emergence of the Western Guru* (Secker & Warburg, London 1993).

Waxman, S.M., 'Chapters on magic in Spanish literature', *Revue hispanique* 38 (1916), 325–463.

Whited, L.A. (ed.), *The Ivory Tower and Harry Potter: Perspectives on a Literary Phenomenon* (University of Missouri 2002).

Wilding, M., *Raising Spirits, Making Gold, and Swapping Wives* (Shoestring Press, Beeston 1999).

Williams, S.J., 'Roger Bacon and the Secret of Secrets', in J. Hackett (ed.), *Roger Bacon and the Sciences: Commemorative Essays* (Brill, Leiden 1997), 365–93.

Wood, R.C., *The Gospel According to Tolkien: Visions of the Kingdom in Middle Earth* (Westminster John Knox Press, Louisville 2003).

Woolley, B., *The Queen's Conjuror: The Science and Magic of Dr Dee* (Harper Collins, London 2001).

Index

priest 11, 13-15 passim, 19, 22-5 passim,
27, 29, 46, 47, 51, 69, 84, 86, 88, 94,
98, 116, 120, 128, 130, 132-4 passim,
137, 138, 145, 150, 159, 169, 170, 189
Priestley, Joseph 149
Prospero 72, 81-2

Regardie, Israel 11, 194, 195, 201
Rémond, Florimond de 15, 22
Reuchlin, Johannes 20
rhabdos, see wand
ring, magical 66, 67, 93, 120, 129, 130
ritual 11, 13, 14, 18, 22, 25-7 passim,
35-40, 41-3, 45, 46, 48, 49, 77-8, 86-9
passim, 128, 131, 171, 178, 186, 187,
199, 201-3
Rosicrucian 154, 168, 178, 202
Rousseau, Jean-Jacques 151-2

sacrifice 9, 35, 40, 53, 60, 61, 109, 129,
130
Saint Germain, Comte de 156-9
Saint-Martin, Louis-Claude 153
Saul, Barnabas 90-1, 99
Scotland 143, 152, 154
seven 16, 36, 38, 69, 102, 107, 115, 116,
124, 148, 158
sex 133, 186-7
Shakespeare, William 24, 72
sigils 11, 17, 73, 94
Solomon 65-8 passim, 93, 170
Somnium Scipionis 108
sound 37-40, 45-6, 108
spirits 7-9, 10, 11, 16, 17, 19, 21, 24, 36,

37, 46-9 passim, 51, 58, 60, 61, 65, 68-
73 passim, 75, 78, 84, 86, 89-91 passim, 94-5, 96, 98, 110, 116, 117, 128,
130, 132, 135-9 passim, 143, 147, 148,
155, 164-6 passim, 172, 184, 201, 203
(of the dead) 26, 35, 40, 41
staff, see wand
Stoecklin, Conrad 138, 140, 141
sympathy 11, 77, 117, 119

table, magical 73-4, 88, 93
Taverner, Dr 23-4, 199
Tetragrammaton 20, 45, 66
theurgy 48-9, 72, 143
three 15, 17, 69, 87, 102, 106, 171, 172,
176, 178
Torralva, Eugene 135-7, 141
triangle 18, 23, 74

Valéry Paul 38-9
Villena, Marqués de 83
vision 7, 19, 44, 47, 82, 95, 97, 99, 100,
112, 186, 190, 199

Waite, A.E. 195
wand 15, 33, 34, 36, 61, 64, 65, 94, 115,
116, 182
witch 15, 127, 132, 139, 140, 141, 144,
148, 168, 174, 191, 192
wizard 10-11, 125, 127, 147, 150, 174,
181, 191, 203
words of power 37, 47

Zoroaster 40, 59, 60, 62

DARK HISTORIES

A series of books exploring the darker recesses
of human history

SERIES EDITOR
William Naphy, Senior Lecturer and Head of History at
the University of Aberdeen

PUBLISHED
P.G. Maxwell-Stuart, *Witchcraft: A History*
'Combines scholarly rigour with literary flair'
The Independent on Sunday

P.G. Maxwell-Stuart, *Wizards: A History*

William Naphy & Andrew Spicer, *Plague*
'A chilling warning from history' *The Sunday Telegraph*

William Naphy, *Sex Crimes*
'A model mix of pin-sharp scholarship and deep empathy'
The Guardian

Further titles are in preparation

If you are interested in purchasing
other books published by Tempus, or in case you have
difficulty finding any Tempus books in your local
bookshop, you can also place orders directly through
our website

www.tempus-publishing.com